SOCIAL SECURITY LEGISLATION
SUPPLEMENT 2004/2005

General Editor
David Bonner, LL.B., LL.M.

Commentary by
David Bonner, LL.B., LL.M.
Professor of Law, University of Leicester
Formerly Member, Social Security Appeal Tribunals

Ian Hooker, LL.B.
Lecturer in Law, University of Nottingham
Formerly Member, Social Security Appeal Tribunals

Richard Poynter B.C.L., M.A. (Oxon)
Solicitor, District Chairman,
Appeals Service, Deputy Social Security Commissioner

Mark Rowland, LL.B.
Social Security Commissioner

Robin White, M.A., LL.M.
Professor of Law, University of Leicester,
Deputy Social Security Commissioner

Nick Wikeley, M.A.
Barrister, Professor of Law, University of Southampton,
Deputy Social Security Commissioner, Deputy District Chairman, Appeals Service

David Williams, LL.M., Ph.D., C.T.A.
Solicitor, Social Security and Child Support Commissioner, Deputy Special Commissioner of Income Tax and part-time Chairman of VAT and Duties Tribunal

Penny Wood, LL.B., M.Sc.
Solicitor, District Chairman
Appeals Service

Consultant to Vol. II
John Mesher, B.A., B.C.L., LL.M.
Barrister, Professor Associate of Law,
University of Sheffield,
Social Security and Child Support Commissioner

Consultant Editor
Child Poverty Action Group

LONDON
THOMSON
———✴———™
SWEET & MAXWELL
2005

GW00542742

Published in 2005 by
Sweet & Maxwell Limited of
100 Avenue Road, Swiss Cottage,
London NW3 3PF
(http://www.sweetandmaxwell.co.uk)
Typeset by Interactive Sciences Ltd, Gloucester
Printed in England by
MPG Books Ltd, Bodmin, Cornwall

No natural forests were destroyed to make this product.
Only farmed timber was used and re-planted.

A catalogue record for this book is
available from the British Library

ISBN 0 421 905 603

All rights reserved. Crown Copyright Legislation is reproduced under
the terms of Crown Copyright Policy Guidance issued by HMSO.

No part of this publication may be reproduced or transmitted,
in any form or by any means, or stored in any retrieval system
of any nature without prior written permission, except for
permitted fair dealing under the Copyright, Designs and
Patents Act 1988, or in accordance with the terms of a licence
issued by the Copyright Licensing Agency in respect of
photocopying and/or reprographic reproduction.
Application for permission for other use of copyright material
including permission to reproduce extracts in other published
works shall be mae to the publishers. Full acknowledgement
of author, publisher and source must be given.
Application for permission for other use of copyright material
controlled by the publisher shall be made to the publishers.
Material is contained in this publication for which publishing
permission has been sought, and for which copyright is
acknowledged. Permission to reproduce such material
cannot be granted by the publishers and application
must be made to the copyright holder.

Commentators have asserted their moral rights under
the Copyright, Designs and Patents Act 1988 to be identified
as the authors of the commentary in this Volume.

©

THOMSON

SWEET & MAXWELL
2005

CHILD POVERTY ACTION GROUP

The Child Poverty Action Group (CPAG) is a charity, founded in 1965, which campaigns for the relief of poverty in the UK. It has a particular reputation in the field of welfare benefits law derived from its legal work, publications, training and parliamentary and policy work, and is widely recognised as the leading organisation for taking test cases on social security law.

CPAG is therefore ideally placed to act as Consultant Editor to this 4-volume work—**Social Security Legislation 2004 and Supplement 2004/2005**. CPAG is not responsible for the detail of what is contained in each volume, and the authors' views are not necessarily those of the CPAG. The Consultant Editor's role is to act in an advisory capacity on the overall structure, focus and direction of the work.

For more information about CPAG, its rights and policy publications or training courses, its address is 94 White Lion Street, London N1 9PF (telephone: 020 7837 7979—website: *www.cpag.org.uk*).

PREFACE

This is the combined Supplement to the 2004 edition of the four-volume work, *Social Security Legislation*, which was published in September 2004.

Part I of the Supplement contains new legislation (Acts and Regulations), presented in the same format as the main volumes. This will enable readers to note very quickly new sets of legislation.

Parts II, III, IV and V contain the updating material—a separate Part for each volume of the main work—which amends the legislative text and key aspects of the commentary so as to be up to date as at November 30, 2004. Part VI, the final section of the Supplement, gives some notice of changes forthcoming between that date and the date to which the main work (2004 edition) will be up to date (mid-April), and some indication of the April 2005 benefit rates, and takes account of changes known to us as at January 31, 2005.

As always we welcome comments from those who use this Supplement. Please address these to the General Editor, David Bonner, at the Faculty of Law, The University, Leicester LE1 7RH.

David Bonner
Ian Hooker
John Mesher
Richard Poynter
Mark Rowland
Robin White
Nick Wikeley
David Williams
Penny Wood
February 7, 2005

CONTENTS

USING THE UPDATING MATERIAL IN THIS SUPPLEMENT

The amendments and updating contained in Parts II–V of this Supplement are keyed in to the page numbers of the relevant main volume of *Social Security Legislation 2004*. Where there have been a significant number of changes to a provision, the whole section, subsection, paragraph or regulation, as amended, will tend to be reproduced. Other changes may be noted by an instruction to insert or substitute new material or to delete part of the existing text. The date the change takes effect is also noted. Where explanation is needed of the change, or there is updating to do to existing annotations but no change to the legislation, you will also find commentary in this Supplement. The updating material explains new statutory material, takes on board Commissioners' or court decisions, or gives prominence to points which now seem to warrant more detailed attention.

This Supplement amends the text of the main volumes of *Social Security Legislation 2004* to be up to date as at November 30, 2004.

David Bonner
General Editor

PAGES OF MAIN VOLUMES AFFECTED
BY MATERIAL IN THIS SUPPLEMENT

VOLUME II

VOLUME III

VOLUME IV

TABLE OF ABBREVIATIONS USED IN THIS SERIES

Adjudication Regulations	Social Security (Adjudication) Regulations 1986
All E.R.	All England Law Reports (Butterworths)
AO	Adjudication Officer
AOG	HMSO, *Adjudication Officers Guide*
Attendance Allowance Regulations	Social Security (Attendance Allowance) Regulations 1991
Blue Books	HMSO, *The Law Relating to Social Security*, Vols 1–11
CBA 1975	Child Benefit Act 1975
CAO	Chief Adjudication Officer
CPAG	Child Poverty Action Group
CSO	Child Support Officer
Claims and Payments Regulations 1979	Social Security (Claims and Payments) Regulations 1979
Claims and Payments Regulations 1987	Social Security (Claims and Payments) Regulations 1987
C.M.L.R.	Common Market Law Reports
Commissioners Procedure Regulations	Social Security Commissioners (Procedure) Regulations 1999
Computation of Earnings Regulations 1978	Social Security Benefit (Computation of Earnings) Regulations 1978
Computation of Earnings Regulations 1996	Social Security Benefit (Computation of Earnings) Regulations 1996
DAT	Disability Appeals Tribunal
Decisions and Appeals Regulations 1999	Social Security and Child Support (Decisions and Appeals) Regulations 1999
Dependency Regulations	Social Security Benefit (Dependency) Regulations 1977
DLA	Disability Living Allowance
DMA	Decision-making and Appeals
DMG	HMSO, *Decision-Makers Guide*
Disability Working Allowance Regulations	Disability Working Allowance (General) Regulations 1991
DPTC	Disabled Person's Tax Credit
DWA	Disability Working Allowance
E.C.R.	European Court Reports

Table of Abbreviations used in this Series

EHRR	European Human Rights Reports
Eur. L. Rev.	European Law Review
Family Credit Regulations	Family Credit (General) Regulations 1987
General Benefit Regulations	Social Security (General Benefit) Regulations 1982
HASSASSAA 1983	Health and Social Services and Social Security Adjudication Act 1983
Hospital In-Patients Regulations	Social Security (Hospital In-Patients) Regulations 1975
Income Support Regulations	Income Support (General) Regulations 1987
IB Regulations	Social Security (Incapacity Benefit) Regulations 1994
I.L.J.	Industrial Law Journal
IWA	Social Security (Incapacity for Work) Act 1994
IW (General) Regulations	Social Security (Incapacity for Work) (General) Regulations 1995
IW (Transitional) Regulations	Social Security (Incapacity for Work) (Transitional) Regulations 1995
Invalid Care Allowance Regulations	Social Security (Invalid Care Allowance) Regulations 1976
JSA Regulations	Jobseeker's Allowance Regulations 1996
JSA (Transitional) Regulations	Jobseeker's Allowance (Transitional) Regulations 1996
J.S.W.L.	Journal of Social Welfare Law
JSWFL	Journal of Social Welfare and Family Law
JSSL	Journal of Social Security Law
MAT	Medical Appeal Tribunal
Maternity Benefit Regulations	Social Security (Maternity Benefit) Regulations 1975
Medical Evidence Regulations	Social Security (Medical Evidence) Regulations 1976
Ogus, Barendt and Wikeley	A. Ogus, E. Barendt and N. Wikeley, The Law of Social Security (4th ed., Butterworths, 1995)
Overlapping Benefits Regulations	Social Security (Overlapping Benefits) Regulations 1979
Overpayments Regulations	Social Security (Payments on account, Overpayments and Recovery) Regulations 1988
Persons Abroad Regulations	Social Security Benefit (Persons Abroad) Regulations 1975
Persons Residing Together Regulations	Social Security Benefit (Persons Residing Together) Regulations 1977

Prescribed Diseases Regulations	Social Security (Industrial Injuries) (Prescribed Diseases) Regulations 1985
Recovery of Benefits Act	Social Security (Recovery of Benefits) Act 1997
Recovery of Benefits Regulations	Social Security (Recovery of Benefits) Regulations 1997
RMO	Regional Medical Officer
SDA	Severe Disablement Allowance
Severe Disablement Allowance Regulations	Social Security (Severe Disablement Allowance) Regulations 1984
SMP	Statutory Maternity Pay
SSA 1975	Social Security Act 1975
SSA 1980	Social Security Act 1980
SSA 1985	Social Security Act 1985
SSA 1986	Social Security Act 1986
SSA 1988	Social Security Act 1988
SSA 1989	Social Security Act 1989
SSA 1998	Social Security Act 1998
SS (No. 2) A 1980	Social Security (No. 2) Act 1980
SSAT	Social Security Appeal Tribunal
SSHBA	Social Security and Housing Benefits Act 1982
SS (MP) A 1977	Social Security (Miscellaneous Provisions) Act 1977
SSP	Statutory Sick Pay
SSPA 1975	Social Security Pensions Act 1975
SSCBA 1992	Social Security Contributions and Benefits Act 1992★
SSAA 1992	Social Security Administration Act 1992★
SSCPA 1992	Social Security Consequential Provisions Act 1992
USI Regulations	Social Security (Unemployment, Sickness and Invalidity Benefit) Regulations 1983
WFTC	Working Families' Tax Credit
White Paper	Jobseeker's Allowance, Cm. 2687 (October, 1994)
Widow's Benefit and Retirement Pensions Regulations	Social Security (Widow's Benefit and Retirement Pensions) Regulations 1979
Wikeley, Annotations	N. Wikeley, *Annotations to Jobseekers Act 1995 (c.18), Currnet Law Statutes Annotated* (1995)
W.L.R.	Weekly Law Reports

★ Where the context makes it seem more appropriate, these could also be referred to as Contributions and Benefits Act 1992, Administration Act 1992.

TABLE OF CASES

TABLE OF SOCIAL SECURITY COMMISSIONER'S DECISIONS

Table of Social Security Commissioner's Decisions

TABLE OF EUROPEAN MATERIALS

TABLE OF STATUTES

TABLE OF STATUTORY INSTRUMENTS

PART I

NEW LEGISLATION

NEW STATUTES

Age-Related Payments Act 2004

(2000 c.10)

Payments for 2004

1. "Qualifying individual" and "relevant week".   1.001
2. Entitlement: basic cases.
3. Entitlement: special cases.
4. Disqualifications.
5. Procedure.
6. Payment to be disregarded for tax and social security.

Future payments

7. Power to provide for payments.

General

8. Interpretation.
9. Money.
10. Extent.
11. Citation.

GENERAL NOTE

The Age-Related Payments Act 2004 came into force on July 8, 2004 and   1.002
provides for a one-off payment—to be made during the Winter of 2004—to
"qualifying individuals" (see s.1) who were aged 70 or over on September 26,
2004 and were ordinarily resident in Great Britain for at least one day in the
preceding week ("the qualifying week"). The rules for the one-off payment are
similar, but not identical, to those for winter fuel payments from the social fund
(see pp.1264–1269 of the main volume). The payment is, in the most usual
cases, £100 for each household which contains a qualifying individual but the
rate of payment, and the identity of the payee, can vary according to the rules set
out in ss.2 and 3. There is no entitlement if the qualifying individual has been a
hospital in-patient for 52 continuous weeks ending with the qualifying week or
was in custody or subject to immigration control throughout that week (s.4). As

with winter fuel payments, the Secretary of State may make an age-related payment without receiving a claim. However, anyone who is entitled but who has not received the payment by December 31, 2004 must make a claim for it by March 31, 2005 or lose entitlement (s.5). The normal rules for revision, supersession and appeal to an appeal tribunal apply.

The Act also includes a general power for the Secretary of State to make "regulations providing for the making of payments by him to persons who have attained the age of 60 years". This power, which is not limited by any specification of the purposes for which the payment is to be made, is to be contrasted with the more limited power to make payments "to meet expenses for heating, which appear likely to the Secretary of State to have been or likely to be incurred in cold weather" in s.138(2) of SSCBA 1992 which is used to make cold weather payments and winter fuel payments.

Payments for 2004

"Qualifying individual" and "relevant week"

1.003   **1.**—(1) In this Act "qualifying individual" means an individual who—

(a) is ordinarily resident in Great Britain on at least one day in the relevant week, and

(b) attains the age of 70 years on or before the last day of the relevant week.

(2) In this Act "the relevant week" means the week beginning with Monday 20th September 2004 and ending with Sunday 26th September 2004.

Entitlement: basic cases

1.004   **2.**—(1) A qualifying individual shall be entitled to a payment of £100 if at any time in the relevant week—

(a) he is single, and

(b) either—

(i) he is not living with another qualifying individual, or

(ii) he is in receipt of state pension credit.

(2) A qualifying individual shall be entitled to a payment of £50 if at any time in the relevant week—

(a) he is single,

(b) he is not in receipt of state pension credit, and

(c) he is living with another qualifying individual.

(3) A qualifying individual shall be entitled to a payment of £100 if at any time in the relevant week he is part of a couple and—

(a) the other member of the couple is not a qualifying individual, or

(b) either member of the couple is in receipt of—

(i) state pension credit,

(ii) an income-based jobseeker's allowance, or

(iii) income support.

(4) A qualifying individual shall be entitled to a payment of £50 if at any time in the relevant week he is part of a couple and—

(a) the other member of the couple is a qualifying individual, and

4

(b) neither member of the couple is in receipt of state pension credit.

(5) This section is subject to section 3.

Entitlement: special cases

3.—(1) Where—

(a) two or more couples live together, and

(b) two or more individuals, each of whom is part of one of the couples, would (but for this subsection) be entitled to a payment under section 2(3)(a) (and not under section 2(3)(b)),

then each of those individuals shall instead be entitled to a payment of £50.

(2) Where each member of a couple would (but for this subsection) be entitled to a payment under section 2(3)(b)—

(a) the member who is to receive a payment in 2004 under the Social Fund Winter Fuel Payment Regulations 2000 (S.I. 2000/729) shall be entitled to the payment under section 2(3)(b), and

(b) the other member shall not be entitled to a payment under section 2(3)(b).

(3) Where—

(a) only one member of a couple is a qualifying individual,

(b) he would (but for this subsection) be entitled to a payment under section 2(3),

(c) the other member of the couple is to receive a payment in 2004 under the Social Fund Winter Fuel Payment Regulations 2000, and

(d) the qualifying individual is not to receive a payment in 2004 under those regulations,

then—

(i) that other member of the couple shall be entitled to a payment of £100, and

(ii) the qualifying individual shall not be entitled to a payment under section 2(3).

(4) Subsection (5) applies to a qualifying individual if—

(a) on the last day of the relevant week he is living in a care home, and

(b) throughout the period of 13 weeks ending with the relevant week his ordinary place of residence was a care home.

(5) Where this subsection applies to a qualifying individual—

(a) if he is not in receipt of state pension credit at any time in the relevant week, he shall be entitled to a payment of £50 (and he shall not be entitled to a payment under section 2), and

(b) if at any time in the relevant week he is in receipt of state pension credit, he shall not be entitled to a payment under section 2 or this section.

(6) Where a person to whom subsection (5) applies is part of a couple, in the application of section 2(3) and (4) to the other member of the couple the person to whom subsection (5) applies shall be treated as a non-qualifying individual.

5

Disqualifications

1.006   **4.**—(1) A qualifying individual who would (but for this section) be entitled to a payment under section 2 or 3 shall not be entitled to the payment if—

    (a) he is in receipt of free in-patient treatment throughout the period of 52 weeks ending with the relevant week,

    (b) he is in custody throughout the relevant week, or

    (c) he is subject to immigration control throughout the relevant week.

(2) For the purposes of subsection (1)—

    (a) the reference to receipt of free in-patient treatment shall be construed in accordance with regulation 2(2) and (2A) of the Social Security (Hospital In-patients) Regulations 1975 (S.I. 1975/555),

    (b) a person is in custody if he is detained in custody under a sentence imposed by a court, and

    (c) the reference to being subject to immigration control shall be construed in accordance with section 115(9) of the Immigration and Asylum Act 1999 (c. 33).

(3) Where a person to whom this section applies is part of a couple, in the application of section 2(3) and (4) to the other member of the couple the person to whom this section applies shall be treated as a non-qualifying individual.

Procedure

1.007   **5.**—(1) Where before 31st December 2004 the Secretary of State thinks that a person is entitled to a payment under section 2 or 3, the Secretary of State shall make the payment before that date (without a claim being required).

(2) A person who is entitled to a payment under section 2 or 3 and who does not receive it before 31st December 2004, may claim the payment.

(3) A claim under subsection (2) must—

    (a) be in writing to the Secretary of State,

    (b) be received by the Secretary of State before 31st March 2005, and

    (c) specify—

        (i) the claimant's name, address, date of birth and national insurance number (if he has one), and

        (ii) the date on which the claim is sent to the Secretary of State, and

    (d) include a declaration that the claimant was ordinarily resident in Great Britain on at least one day in the relevant week.

(4) If the Secretary of State thinks that a person making a claim under subsection (2) is entitled to a payment under section 2 or 3, the Secretary of State shall make the payment.

(5) The provisions of Chapter II of Part I of the Social Security Act 1998 (c. 14) (revision, appeal, &c.) shall apply to a decision of the Secretary of State about a person's entitlement to a payment under

section 2 or 3 (whether or not following a claim) as they apply to a decision of the Secretary of State under section 8 of that Act.

Payment to be disregarded for tax and social security

6. No account shall be taken of entitlement to a payment under section 2 or 3 in considering a person's— 1.008
(a) liability to tax,
(b) entitlement to benefit under an enactment relating to social security (irrespective of the name or nature of the benefit), or
(c) entitlement to a tax credit.

Future payments

Power to provide for payments

7.—(1) The Secretary of State may make regulations providing for the making of payments by him to persons who have attained the age of 60 years. 1.009

(2) Regulations under subsection (1) may provide for payments to be made—
(a) to persons in a specified class (which may be defined by reference to age or otherwise);
(b) in specified circumstances.

(3) Regulations under subsection (1) may, in particular—
(a) provide for payments to be made only once, at specified times or over a specified period,
(b) provide for exceptions,
(c) apply (with or without modifications) an enactment relating to social security (including, in particular, an enactment relating to claims, payments, evidence, revision of decisions, appeals or recovery of payment in error), and
(d) make different provision for different cases or circumstances.

(4) Regulations under this section—
(a) shall be made by statutory instrument, and
(b) may not be made unless a draft has been laid before and approved by resolution of each House of Parliament.

(5) *[Omitted]*

General

Interpretation

8.—(1) In this Act— 1.010
"care home"—
      (a) in relation to England and Wales, has the same meaning as that given by section 3 of the Care Standards Act 2000 (c. 14), and

(b) in relation to Scotland, means accommodation provided by a care home service within the meaning of section 2(3) of the Regulation of Care (Scotland) Act 2001,

"couple" means a man and a woman who share a household and who are, or who live as, husband and wife,

"income-based jobseeker's allowance" has the meaning given by section 1(1) and (4) of the Jobseekers Act 1995 (c. 18),

"income support" means income support under section 124 of the Social Security Contributions and Benefits Act 1992 (c. 4),

"qualifying individual" has the meaning given by section 1,

"the relevant week" has the meaning given by section 1,

"single", in relation to an individual, means not part of a couple, and

"state pension credit" has the meaning given by section 1(1) of the State Pension Credit Act 2002 (c. 16).

(2) The provisions of this Act shall apply, with any necessary modifications, to the parties to a polygamous marriage as if they together formed one couple.

Money

1.011   **9.** Expenditure of the Secretary of State under or by virtue of this Act shall be paid out of money provided by Parliament.

Extent

1.012   **10.** This Act shall extend only to—
(a) England and Wales, and
(b) Scotland.

Citation

1.013   **11.** This Act may be cited as the Age-Related Payments Act 2004.

NEW REGULATIONS

Social Security (Back to Work Bonus and Lone Parent Run-on) (Amendment and Revocation) Regulations 2003

(S.I. 2003 No. 1589)

Made by the Secretary of State under sections 123(1)(a), (d) and (e), 130(4), 131(10), 135(1), 136(3) and (5)(b), 137(1) and (2)(d), 175(1) and (3) to (5) of the Social Security Contributions and Benefits Act 1992, sections 26, 35(1) and (3) and 36(2) to (5) of the Jobseekers Act 1995 and sections 1(1), 5(1)(a) and (b), 6(1)(a) and (b), 78(2), 128A(1), 189(1), (4) and (5) and 191 of the Social Security Administration Act 1992.

In force   *25th October 2004*

Transitional Provisions

10.—(1) [¹ Subject to the amendments made by paragraphs (2) and (3)], the Back to Work Bonus Regulations shall continue to have effect as if regulation 8 of these Regulations had not been made, in relation to a person who—   1.014

  (a) satisfies the requirements of regulation 6 (waiting period) of the Back to Work Bonus Regulations on 24th October 2004; and either

  (b) satisfies regulation 7 (requirements for a bonus) or regulation 17 (persons attaining pensionable age) of the Back to Work Bonus Regulations on 24th October 2004 but whose claim for a bonus had not been determined on or before that date; or

  (c) satisfies the conditions contained in regulation 7 or regulation 17 of the Back to Work Bonus Regulations on any day during the period from 25th October 2004 to 28th January 2005; or

  (d) satisfies the conditions contained in regulation 7 or 17 on or before 28th January 2005 other than the requirement to make a claim within—

    (i) for a person who satisfies the conditions in regulation 7(2), the period specified in regulation 7(2)(c);

    (ii) for a person who satisfies the conditions in regulation 7(3), the period specified in regulation 7(3)(d);

    (iii) for a person who satisfies the conditions in regulation 7(4), the period specified in regulation 7(4)(c);

    (iv) for a person who satisfies the conditions in regulation 7(5), the period specified in regulation 7(5)(e); and

    (v) for a person who satisfies the conditions in regulation 17, the period specified in regulation 17(5)

but who satisfies the requirements set out in regulation 23(6) of the Back to Work Bonus Regulations [¹, or who makes a claim for a bonus after 28th January 2005 within the appropriate specified period].

(2) For the purposes of paragraph (1), in regulation 1 (citation, commencement and interpretation) of the Back to Work Bonus Regulations—

    (a) for the definition of "bonus period" substitute—

    " "bonus period" means a period beginning on the first day of entitlement to a qualifying benefit (provided that that day is not after 24th October 2004) in a period of entitlement to a qualifying benefit which falls after the waiting period and which ends on the last day of that period of entitlement or on 24th October 2004 whichever of these two dates is the earlier,";

    (b) for the definition of "waiting period" substitute—

    " "waiting period" means the period of 91 consecutive days to which regulation 6 refers, provided that none of those days falls after 24th October 2004;"

(3) For paragraph (3) in regulation 17 substitute—

"(3) In the case of a person who is entitled to a bonus in accordance with paragraph (1)—

    (a) the bonus period and the period of entitlement to a qualifying benefit shall end on the date he attained the age of 60, or as the case may be, pensionable age, whichever is the later, provided that that date is not after 24th October 2004;

    (b) where that date would be after 24th October 2004 the bonus period and period of entitlement to a qualifying benefit shall be treated as ending on 24th October 2004."

AMENDMENT

1.015   1. Back to Work Bonus (Amendment) Regulations 2004 (SI 2004/1655), reg.2 (October 25, 2004).

GENERAL NOTE

1.016   Regulation 8 of these Regulations revokes the Social Security (Back to Work Bonus) (No.2) Regulations 1996 (see pp.731–759 in Vol.II of the 2004 edition) with effect from October 25, 2004. However, reg.10 continues the 1996 Regulations in force (as modified by the amendments in paras (2) and (3)) in order to enable claimants to claim the bonus during a further period.

Regulation 10(1) provides that a person will be entitled to a back-to-work bonus if he has served the 13-week waiting period on October 24, 2004 (note in addition that the effect of the amended definition of "bonus period" in para.(2)(a) is that no further bonus can build up after October 24, 2004) and satisfies the conditions for a bonus to become payable:

    (i) on October 24, 2004 but his claim has not been decided by that date; or

(ii) on any day during the period from October 25, 2004 to January 28, 2005; or

(iii) on or before January 28, 2005, other than the need to make a claim within 12 weeks of the relevant triggering event (*i.e.* his ceasing to be entitled to income support or JSA, his training ending or his separation from his partner—see reg.7(2) to (5) of the Back to Work Bonus Regulations—or his reaching the age of 60 if he has ceased to be entitled to income support or pensionable age if he has ceased to be entitled to JSA—see reg.17(5) of the Back to Work Bonus Regulations) but who either shows continuous good cause for the delay in claiming (in which case the time for claiming can be extended to up to twelve months (see reg.23(6) of the Back to Work Bonus Regulations)), or who makes a claim after January 28, 2005 within the relevant specified time limit. Presumably this means the specified time limit as extended under reg.23(6) if appropriate, although this is not spelt out.

Thus the net effect of these somewhat convoluted provisions would seem to be that claimants who have served the 13-week waiting period on October 24, 2004 will be able to claim the bonus if they satisfy the conditions of entitlement for a bonus (including making a claim) during the period October 25, 2004 to January 28, 2005 or if they satisfy the other conditions of entitlement during that transitional period and make a claim after January 28, 2005 within the relevant time limit. But they will not be able to build up any further bonus after October 24, 2004.

The Social Security (Quarterly Work-focused Interviews for Certain Lone Parents) Regulations 2004

(S.I. 2004 No. 2244)

ARRANGEMENT OF REGULATIONS

GENERAL NOTE

1.018   These regulations provide for certain lone parents living in the Extended Schools Childcare Pilot areas to attend mandatory work-focused interviews on a quarterly basis. The purpose of the childcare schemes is said to be to provide high quality affordable childcare. The regulations apply to lone parents in the designated areas who have been in receipt of income support for 12 months, who are aged between 18 and 60 and whose youngest child is at least 12 years old. The regulations essentially come into force on September 30, 2004 but detailed commencement provisions are to be found in reg.1.

There are some stylistic differences in drafting these regulations compared with other regulations on work-focused interviews, but these appear not to be intended to give rise to any difference of treatment or approach. Some of the changes are clearly for the avoidance of doubt. An example is the provisions on deferment which make clear that there must be a determination of a future date on which liability to take part in an interview will arise. As with other regulations on work-focused interviews, there is an appeal against any decision that a person has failed to attend an interview without good cause for that failure.

The Secretary of State for Work and Pensions, in exercise of the powers conferred upon him by sections 2A(1)(b), (3)(b) to (f), (4)(b), (5)(a) and (b), (6) and (8), 2B(6) to (8), 189(4) to (6) and (7A) and 191 of the Social Security Administration Act 1992 and of all other powers enabling him in that behalf, after consultation with the Council on Tribunals in accordance with section 8(1) of the Tribunals and Inquiries Act 1992 and after agreement by the Social Security Advisory Committee that proposals in respect of these Regulations should not be referred to it, hereby makes the following Regulations:

Citation, commencement and interpretation

1.—(1) These Regulations may be cited as the Social Security (Quarterly Work-focused Interviews for Certain Lone Parents) Regulations 2004.   1.019

(2) These Regulations shall come into force—

(a) in respect of a lone parent—

    (i) who resides in an education authority area or a local education authority area identified in the Schedule to these Regulations;

    (ii) who has been entitled to a specified benefit for not less than 12 months immediately prior to 30th September 2004; and

    (iii) whose youngest child, for whom the lone parent is responsible and who is a member of the lone parent's household, is at least 12 years old on 30th September 2004;

on 30th September 2004;

(b) in respect of a lone parent—

    (i) who resides in an education authority area or a local education authority area identified in that Schedule;

    (ii) who after 30th September 2004 reaches the first anniversary of his entitlement to a specified benefit; and

    (iii) whose youngest child, for whom the lone parent is responsible and who is a member of the lone parent's household, reaches the age of 12 years after 30th September 2004,

on the date of that first anniversary or the date that child reaches the age of 12 years, whichever is the later.

(3) In these Regulations—

"benefit recipient" means a person who—

    (a) has not attained the age of 60; and

    (b) is entitled to a specified benefit at a higher rate referable to his partner;

"benefit week" means any period of seven days corresponding to the week in respect of which income support is due to be paid;

"education authority" means an education authority described in section 135(1) of the Education (Scotland) Act 1980 and "education authority area" shall be construed in accordance with the provisions of that section;

"interview" means a work-focused interview with a relevant person conducted for any or all of the following purposes—

    (a) assessing that person's prospects for existing or future employment (whether paid or voluntary);

    (b) assisting or encouraging that person to enhance his prospects of such employment;

    (c) identifying activities which that person may undertake to strengthen his existing or future prospects of employment;

    (d) identifying current or future employment or training opportunities suitable to that person's needs; and

    (e) identifying educational opportunities connected with the existing or future employment prospects or needs of that person;

"local education authority" means a local education authority described in section 12 of the Education Act 1996 (local education authorities and their areas) and "local education authority area" shall be construed in accordance with the provisions of that section;

"lone parent" means a person who has no partner and who is responsible for, and a member of the same household as, a child;

"officer" means a person who is an officer of, or who is providing services to or exercising functions of, the Secretary of State;

"partner" means a person who is a member of the same couple as a benefit recipient, or, in a case where a benefit recipient has more than one partner, a person who is a partner of the benefit recipient by reason of a polygamous marriage;

"polygamous marriage" means any marriage during the subsistence of which a party to it is married to more than one person and the ceremony of marriage took place under the law of a country which permits polygamy;

"relevant person" means a person—

    (a) to whom paragraph (2)(a) or (b) applies; and(b) who has attained the age of 18 but not attained the age of 60;

"specified benefit" means income support other than income support which is awarded where—

    (a) paragraph 7 of Schedule 1B to the Income Support (General) Regulations 1987 (prescribed categories of person —persons incapable of work) applies;

    (b) paragraph 24 or 25 of Schedule 1B to the Income Support (General) Regulations 1987 (prescribed categories of person—persons appealing against a decision which embodies a determination that they are not incapable of work) applies.

Requirement for a relevant person to take part in an interview

1.020   **2.**—(1) Subject to regulations 3 and 4, a relevant person shall be required to take part in an interview as a condition of that person continuing to be entitled to the full amount of a specified benefit which is payable apart from these Regulations.

(2) A relevant person shall first be required to take part in an interview under paragraph (1) as soon as is reasonably practicable after the date these Regulations come into force in respect of that person.

(3) Subject to regulations 3 and 4, a requirement under paragraph (1) shall arise at intervals of not less than 13 weeks beginning with—

    (a) the day on which the relevant person last took part in an interview in accordance with this regulation;

  (b) the day he was treated under regulation 3 as having complied with such a requirement; or
  (c) the day a relevant decision was made in accordance with regulation 6(3),

whichever is the later, as a condition of his continuing to be entitled to the full amount of a specified benefit which is payable apart from these Regulations.

Waiver of requirement to take part in an interview

3.—(1) A requirement imposed by these Regulations to take part in   1.021
an interview shall not apply where an officer determines that an interview would not be—

  (a) of assistance to the relevant person; or
  (b) appropriate in the circumstances.

  (2) A relevant person in relation to whom a requirement to take part in an interview has been waived under paragraph (1) above shall be treated for the purposes of regulation 2 as having complied with that requirement in respect of that interview.

Deferment of requirement to take part in an interview

4.—(1) An officer may determine, in the case of a relevant person,   1.022
that the requirement under regulation 2 to take part in an interview shall be deferred at the time the requirement to take part in an interview arises or applies because an interview would not at that time be—

  (a) of assistance to that relevant person; or
  (b) appropriate in the circumstances.

  (2) Where an officer determines in accordance with paragraph (1) that the requirement to take part in an interview shall be deferred, he shall also determine when that determination is made, the time when the requirement to take part in an interview is to apply in the relevant person's case.

  (3) Where a requirement to take part in an interview has been deferred in accordance with paragraph (1) then until—

  (a) a determination is made under regulation 3(1);
  (b) the relevant person takes part in an interview; or
  (c) a relevant decision has been made in relation to that relevant person in accordance with regulation 6(3),

that relevant person shall be treated for the purposes of his continuing to be entitled to the full amount of a specified benefit which is payable apart from these Regulations as having complied with that requirement.

The interview

5.—(1) An officer shall inform the relevant person who is required to   1.023
take part in an interview of the date, time and place of the interview.

  (2) An officer may determine that an interview is to take place in the relevant person's home where it would, in the officer's opinion, be unreasonable to expect that relevant person to attend elsewhere because

that person's personal circumstances are such that attending elsewhere would cause him undue inconvenience or endanger his health.

(3) An officer shall conduct the interview.

Taking part in an interview

1.024

6.—(1) An officer shall determine whether a relevant person has taken part in an interview.

(2) A relevant person shall be regarded as having taken part in an interview for the purposes of these Regulations if—

(a) he attends for the interview at the time and place notified to him by the officer;

(b) he provides answers (where asked) to questions and appropriate information about—

(i) the level to which he has pursued any educational qualifications;

(ii) his employment history;

(iii) any vocational training he has undertaken;

(iv) any skills he has acquired which fit him for employment;

(v) any paid or unpaid employment he is engaged in;

(vi) any medical condition which in his opinion puts him at a disadvantage in obtaining employment; and

(vii) any caring or childcare responsibilities he has.

(3) Where an officer determines that a relevant person has failed to take part in an interview and good cause has not been shown by the relevant person for that failure within five working days of the day on which the interview was to take place, a relevant decision shall be made for the purposes of section 2B of the Social Security Administration Act 1992 and the relevant person shall be notified accordingly.

Failure to take part in an interview

1.025

7.—(1) Where a relevant decision has been made in accordance with regulation 6(3), subject to paragraphs (2) and (7), the specified benefit payable to the relevant person shall be reduced as from the first day of the next benefit week following the day a relevant decision was made, by a sum equal to 20 per cent. of the amount applicable on the date the first reduction commences in respect of a single claimant for income support aged not less than 25.

(2) The specified benefit reduced in accordance with paragraph (1) shall not be reduced below ten pence per week.

(3) Where the rate of the specified benefit payable to a relevant person changes, the reduction described in paragraph (1) shall be applied to the new rates and any adjustments to the specified benefit against which the reduction is made shall take effect from the beginning of the first benefit week to commence for that relevant person following the change.

(4) Paragraph (1) shall apply to a relevant person each time a relevant decision is made in accordance with regulation 6(3) in respect of the relevant person.

(5) Where a relevant person whose specified benefit has been reduced in accordance with paragraph (1) subsequently takes part in an inter-

view, the whole of the reduction shall cease to have effect on the first day of the benefit week in which the requirement to take part in an interview was met.

(6) Where paragraph (4) applies, for the purposes of determining the amount of the specified benefit payable a relevant person shall be treated as receiving the amount of the specified benefit which would have been payable but for a reduction made in accordance with paragraph (1).

(7) The specified benefit shall not be reduced in accordance with paragraph (1) where the relevant person brings new facts to the notice of the Secretary of State within one month of the date on which a relevant decision was notified to him and—

(a) those facts could not reasonably have been brought to the Secretary of State's notice within five working days of the day on which the interview was to take place; and

(b) those facts show that the relevant person had good cause for his failure to take part in the interview.

(8) Where a reduction of specified benefit has been made in accordance with paragraph (1) the whole of that reduction shall cease to have effect on the date when the relevant person—

(a) is no longer required to take part in an interview as a condition for continuing to be entitled to the full amount of the specified benefit which is payable to the relevant person apart from these Regulations; or

(b) attains the age of 60.

Good cause

8. Matters to be taken into account in determining whether a relevant person has shown good cause for the relevant person's failure to take part in an interview include— 1.026

(a) that the relevant person misunderstood the requirement to take part in the interview due to any learning, language or literacy difficulties of the relevant person or any misleading information given to him by an officer;

(b) that the relevant person was attending a medical or dental appointment, or accompanying a person for whom the relevant person has caring responsibilities to such an appointment, and that it would have been unreasonable in the circumstances to rearrange the appointment;

(c) that the relevant person had difficulties with his normal mode of transport and that no reasonable alternative was available;

(d) that the established customs and practices of the religion to which the relevant person belongs prevented him from attending on the day or at the time or place fixed for the interview;

(e) that the relevant person was attending an interview with an employer with a view to obtaining employment;

(f) that the relevant person was pursuing employment opportunities as a self-employed earner;

(g) that the relevant person or a dependant or a person for whom the relevant person provides care suffered an accident, sudden illness or relapse of a physical or mental health condition;

(h) that the relevant person was attending the funeral of a close relative or close friend on the day fixed for the interview;

(i) that a disability of the relevant person made it impracticable for him to attend at the time fixed for the interview.

Appeals

1.027   **9.**—(1) This regulation applies to any relevant decision under regulation 6(3) or any decision made under section 10 of the Social Security Act 1998 (decisions superseding earlier decisions) superseding such a relevant decision.

(2) This regulation applies whether the decision is as originally made or as revised under section 9 of the Social Security Act 1998 (revision of decisions).

(3) In the case of a decision to which this regulation applies, the relevant person in respect of whom the decision was made shall have a right of appeal under section 12 of the Social Security Act 1998 (appeal to appeal tribunal) to an appeal tribunal.

SCHEDULE

1.028   1. For the purposes of regulation 1(2)—

    (a) the local education authority areas are Bradford, Greenwich, Haringey, Leicester, Leicestershire, Lewisham, Sandwell and Torfaen;

    (b) the education authority areas are Aberdeenshire and Fife.

The Social Security (Working Neighbourhoods) Regulations 2004

(S.I. 2004 No. 959)

In force 26th April 2004

ARRANGEMENT OF REGULATIONS

GENERAL NOTE

These regulations continue the development of work-focused interviews as a   1.030
means of getting people into work where that is an appropriate course of action.
The title to the regulations uses the term "working neighbourhoods" but the
term is not used anywhere else in the regulations. There are four other work-

focused interview schemes: the Work-Focused Interviews for Lone Parents Regulations 2000 (at 2.740 of Vol.III); the Jobcentre Plus Interviews Regulations 2002 (at 2.588 of Vol.III); the Jobcentre Plus Interviews for Partners Regulations 2003 (at 2.607 of Vol.III), and the Incapacity benefit Work-focused Interviews Regulations 2003 (at 2.572 of Vol.III). Anyone covered by the scheme in these Regulations is exempted from the requirements of the three earlier regulations. There is a further new set of work-focused interview regulations set out below: The Social Security (Quarterly Work-focused Interviews for Certain Lone Parents Regulations 2004.

The Schedule lists two types of area. Those areas listed in Pt I of the Schedule are straightforward work-focused interviews similar to those operating under other regulations requiring participation in interviews. Those who are not claiming on the basis of unemployment are put in broadly the same position as those who are so claiming. They are required to take part in a work-focused interview. Those areas listed in Pt 2 of the Schedule combine the interview process with a more intensive job search. The areas listed in Pt 2 are designated as employment zones; the job search in these areas will be supervised by personal advisors working for private contractors. The requirements of the regulations will operate after three months of unemployment.

Regulation 15 provides for a right of appeal against a decision that a claimant failed to attend an interview without good cause.

1.031   The Secretary of State for Work and Pensions, in exercise of the powers conferred upon him by sections 2A(1), (3) to (6) and (8), 2AA(1) and (4) to (7), 2B(6), 189(1), (4), (5) and (7A) and 191 of the Social Security Administration Act 1992, sections 60(1) to (4) and (9) and 83(4) and (6) of the Welfare Reform and Pensions Act 1999 and section 19(10) of the Jobseekers Act 1995, and of all other powers enabling him in that behalf, after consultation with the Council on Tribunals in accordance with section 8(1) of the Tribunals and Inquiries Act 1992, and after agreement by the Social Security Advisory Committee that proposals in respect of these Regulations need not be referred to it, hereby makes the following Regulations:

Citation and commencement

1.032   **1.** These Regulations may be cited as the Social Security (Working Neighbourhoods) Regulations 2004 and shall come into force on 26th April 2004.

Interpretation and application

1.033   **2.**—(1) In these Regulations—

"the 1998 Act" means the Social Security Act 1998;

"benefit week" means any period of seven days corresponding to the week in respect of which the relevant specified benefit is due to be paid;

"benefit recipient" means a person who—

    (a) has attained the age of 18 but has not attained the age of 60; and

    (b) is receiving any of the specified benefits at a higher rate referable to a partner;

"direction" means a direction to participate in an employment zone programme;

"employment zone" means the areas within Great Britain listed within Part 2 of the Schedule which are subject to the designation in regulation 16 for the purposes of these Regulations by the Secretary of State pursuant to section 60 of the Welfare Reform and Pensions Act 1999 as areas wherein employment zone programmes subject to these Regulations are established;

"employment zone programme" means a programme which is designed to assist jobseekers to obtain sustainable employment and which is established by the Secretary of State pursuant to section 60 of the Welfare Reform and Pensions Act 1999 for an employment zone;

"incapacity-based income support" means income support where paragraph 7 (persons incapable of work) of Schedule 1B to the Income Support (General) Regulations 1987 applies;

"interview" means a work-focused interview with a relevant person which is conducted for any or all of the following purposes—

(a) assessing that relevant person's prospects for existing or future employment (whether paid or voluntary);

(b) assisting or encouraging that relevant person to enhance his prospects of such employment;

(c) identifying activities which that relevant person may undertake to strengthen his existing or future prospects of employment;

(d) identifying current or future employment, training or, if appropriate, rehabilitation opportunities suitable to that relevant person's needs;

(e) identifying educational opportunities connected with the existing or future employment prospects or needs of that relevant person;

(f) identifying financial incentives that may be available to support the existing or future employment prospects of that relevant person;

"jobseeker" means a person claiming a jobseeker's allowance;

"officer" means—

(a) a person who is an officer of the Secretary of State; or

(b) for the purposes of regulations 3 to 15, a person who is providing services to or exercising functions of the Secretary of State; or

(c) for the purposes of regulations 16 to 21, such other person as may be designated as an employment officer for the purposes of sections 8 or 19 of the Jobseekers Act 1995 by an order made by the Secretary of State;

"partner" means a person who is a member of the same couple as a benefit recipient, or, in a case where a benefit recipient has more than one partner, a person who is a partner of the benefit recipient by reason of a polygamous marriage;

21

"personal capability assessment" means the assessment defined in Part III of the Social Security (Incapacity for Work) (General) Regulations 1995 (personal capability assessment);

"polygamous marriage" means any marriage during the subsistence of which a party to it is married to more than one person and the ceremony of marriage took place under the law of a country which permits polygamy;

"relevant person" means a person to whom regulations 3 to 15 apply by virtue of paragraph (3);

"specified benefit" means—

    (a) income support;

    (b) incapacity benefit;

    (c) severe disablement allowance; or

    (d) in relation to a requirement to take part in an interview for a partner only, an income-based jobseeker's allowance other than a joint-claim jobseeker's allowance.

(2) For the purposes of section 60 of the Welfare Reform and Pensions Act 1999 "employment" means employment whether under a contract of service or a contract of apprenticeship, or a contract for services, or otherwise than under a contract, and includes in particular self-employment and the holding of an office.

(3) Regulations 3 to 15 apply to a person who—

    (a) ordinarily resides in an area identified in either Part 1 or Part 2 of the Schedule;

    (b) has attained the age of 18 but has not attained the age of 60; and

    (c) either—

        (i) makes a claim for income support or incapacity benefit on or after 26th April 2004, or

        (ii) has been continuously entitled to income support (apart from incapacity-based income support) from a date before 26th April 2004, or

        (iii) is a partner.

(4) Subject to regulation 21, regulations 17 to 20 apply to a jobseeker who—

    (a) ordinarily resides in an area identified in Part 2 of the Schedule; and

    (b) has attained the age of 18.

Requirement for a relevant person claiming certain benefits to take part in an interview

1.034   **3.** Subject to regulations 6 and 7, a relevant person who makes a claim for income support or incapacity benefit is required to take part in an interview as a condition of the claim for that benefit.

DEFINITIONS

1.035   "relevant person": reg.2(1) and (3)
        "interview": reg.2(1)

GENERAL NOTE

The regulations apply to those who are ordinarily resident in an area identified   **1.036** in the Schedule who are between the ages of 18 and 60 and fall within one of the following groups:

(1) those claiming income support or incapacity benefit for the first time after April 26, 2004; or

(2) those who have been continuously in receipt of income support from any date before April 26, 2004 except those receiving incapacity-based income support as defined in reg.2; or

(3) a partner (again as defined in reg.2) of such a person.

Continuing entitlement to payment of full amount of a specified benefit dependent upon an interview

4.—(1) Subject to paragraphs (3) and (4) and regulations 6 to 9, a   **1.037** relevant person is required to take part in an interview—

(a) at the intervals prescribed in paragraph (2), and

(b) when any of the circumstances specified in paragraph (5) apply,

as a condition of that person, or, where the relevant person is a partner, the benefit recipient continuing to be paid the full amount of a specified benefit which is payable apart from these Regulations.

(2) A requirement under paragraph (1) shall arise at intervals of 13 weeks commencing with the day on which a relevant person attends an interview, with the first such requirement arising—

(a) 13 weeks from the day on which a relevant person attends an interview as a result of a requirement arising under regulation 3; or

(b) where a relevant person does not make a claim for income support or incapacity benefit and a requirement does not arise under regulation 3, on the day that the relevant person becomes subject to these Regulations by virtue of regulation 2(3).

(3) A relevant person shall not be required to attend more than—

(a) five interviews by virtue of paragraph (2) in relation to any one claim by the relevant person for incapacity benefit or incapacity-based income support; or

(b) eight interviews under this regulation in relation to any other claim for or award of income support or where the relevant person is a partner.

(4) Where a relevant person—

(a) has attended five interviews by virtue of paragraph (2) in relation to any one claim for incapacity benefit or incapacity-based income support, or

(b) is treated as incapable of work in accordance with the provisions of regulation 10 of the Social Security (Incapacity for Work) (General) Regulations 1995 (certain persons with a severe condition to be treated as incapable of work) and is subject to the exemption in regulation 8(1),

a requirement under paragraph (1) shall arise when any of the circumstances specified in paragraph (5) apply.

(5) The circumstances specified for the purpose of paragraph (4) are those where—

(a) it is determined in accordance with a personal capability assessment that the relevant person is incapable of work and therefore continues to be entitled to a specified benefit;

(b) the relevant person's entitlement (if any) to a carer's allowance ceases whilst his entitlement to a specified benefit continues;

(c) the relevant person becomes engaged or ceases to be engaged in part-time work; or

(d) the relevant person has been undergoing education or training, or has been participating in a rehabilitation programme or a programme provided in pursuance of arrangements made under section 2 of the Employment and Training Act 1973 (functions of the Secretary of State) or under section 2 of the Enterprise and New Towns (Scotland) Act 1990 (functions in relation to training for employment etc.), which has been arranged by an officer and that education, training or programme comes to an end or the relevant person leaves it before completing it.

DEFINITIONS

1.038   "relevant person": reg.2(1) and (3)
"interview": reg.2(1)
"partner": reg.2(1)
"benefit recipient": reg.2(1)
"specified benefit": reg.2(1)

Time when interview is to take place

1.039   **5.** An officer shall arrange for an interview to take place as soon as reasonably practicable after—

(a) a requirement under regulation 3 or regulation 4(1) arises; or,

(b) in a case where regulation 7(1) applies, the time when that requirement is to apply by virtue of regulation 7(2).

Waiver of requirement to take part in an interview

1.040   **6.**—(1) A requirement under these Regulations to take part in an interview shall not apply where an officer determines that an interview would not—

(a) be of assistance to the relevant person concerned; or

(b) be appropriate in the circumstances.

(2) A relevant person in relation to whom a requirement to take part in an interview has been waived under paragraph (1) shall be treated for the purposes of regulation 3 or 4 as having complied with that requirement in respect of that interview.

Deferment of requirement to take part in an interview

1.041   **7.**—(1) The requirement for a relevant person to take part in an interview shall be deferred, in the case of a requirement under regulation 3, at the time the relevant person makes his claim, or, in the case of a requirement under regulation 4, at the time the requirement to take part in an interview arises or applies until a time determined by an officer, if the officer determines that an interview would not until that time—

    (a) be of assistance to that relevant person; or

    (b) be appropriate in the circumstances.

(2) The officer shall determine the time when the requirement to take part in an interview is to apply to the relevant person at the time when the requirement to take part in an interview is deferred in accordance with paragraph (1) above.

(3) Where a requirement to take part in an interview has been deferred in accordance with paragraph (1), then until—

    (a) a determination is made under regulation 6(1);

    (b) the relevant person takes part in an interview; or

    (c) a relevant decision has been made in relation to that relevant person in accordance with regulation 11(4),

that relevant person shall be treated for the purposes of regulation 3 or 4 as having complied with that requirement, and no further requirements to take part in interviews shall arise under regulation 4.

Exemptions

8.—(1) A relevant person, who on the day on which a requirement to   **1.042** take part in an interview arises or applies under regulation 4(1) or 7(2) is treated as incapable of work in accordance with the provisions of regulation 10 of the Social Security (Incapacity for Work) (General) Regulations 1995 (certain persons with a severe condition to be treated as incapable of work), shall be exempt from that and any further requirement to take part in an interview under regulation 4(1) unless one of the circumstances specified in regulation 4(5) applies.

(2) A partner who, on the day on which a requirement to take part in an interview arises or applies under regulation 4(1) or 7(2), is in receipt of a specified benefit as a claimant in his own right shall be exempt from any requirement to take part in an interview under regulation 4(1) by virtue of being a partner.

Claims for two or more specified benefits

9.—(1) Subject to paragraph (2), a relevant person who would other-   **1.043** wise be required under regulation 4(1) to take part in interviews relating to more than one specified benefit—

    (a) is only required to take part in interviews in connection with one specified benefit during any period when the relevant person or, where the relevant person is a partner, the benefit recipient is in receipt of two or more specified benefits concurrently; and

    (b) those interviews shall count for the purposes of each of those benefits.

(2) Where a relevant person who is in receipt of at least one specified benefit makes a claim for income support or incapacity benefit then—

    (a) he is required to take part in an interview under regulation 3, and

(b) the next requirement to take part in an interview shall arise under regulation 4(1) in accordance with paragraph (2)(a) of that regulation.

The interview

1.044   **10.**—(1) An officer shall inform a relevant person who is required to take part in an interview of the date, place and time of the interview.

(2) The officer may determine that an interview is to take place in the relevant person's home where it would, in the officer's opinion, be unreasonable to expect that relevant person to attend elsewhere because that relevant person's personal circumstances are such that attending elsewhere would cause him undue inconvenience or endanger his health.

(3) An officer shall conduct the interview.

Taking part in an interview

1.045   **11.**—(1) The officer shall determine whether a relevant person has taken part in an interview.

(2) A relevant person shall be regarded as having taken part in the first interview which he attends under these Regulations, whether as a result of a requirement arising under regulation 3 or 4, if—

(a) he attends for the interview at the place and time notified to him by the officer;

(b) he participates in discussions with the officer in relation to the relevant person's employability, including any action the relevant person and the officer agree is reasonable and they are willing to take in order to help the relevant person enhance his employment prospects;

(c) he provides answers (where asked) to questions and appropriate information about—

(i) details of and the level to which he has pursued any educational qualifications;

(ii) his employment history;

(iii) his aspirations for future employment;

(iv) any vocational training he has undertaken;

(v) any skills he has acquired which fit him for employment;

(vi) any vocational training or skills which he wishes to undertake or acquire;

(vii) any paid or unpaid employment he is engaged in;

(viii) the extent to which any medical condition, in his opinion, restricts his ability to undertake or puts him at a disadvantage in undertaking employment;

(ix) his work related abilities;

(x) any caring or childcare responsibilities he has; and

(xi) his financial position and how this may be improved should he obtain or enhance his employment; and

(d) he assists the officer in the completion of an action plan which records the matters discussed in relation to sub-paragraph (b).

(3) A relevant person shall be regarded as having taken part in any subsequent interview which he attends as a result of requirements arising under either regulation 3 or 4 if—

(a) he attends for the interview at the place and time notified to him by the officer;

(b) he participates in discussions with the officer—

    (i) in relation to the relevant person's employability or any progress he might have made towards obtaining or enhancing his employment;

    (ii) about any action the relevant person or the officer might have taken as a result of the matters discussed in relation to paragraph (2)(b);

    (iii) about his current aspirations towards employment;

    (iv) about how, if at all, the action plan referred to in paragraph (2)(d) should be amended;

    (v) in order to review any of the programmes and support available to help the relevant person obtain or enhance his employment; and

    (vi) in order to review his financial position and how this may be improved should he obtain or enhance his employment;

(c) in the case of a relevant person in receipt of incapacity benefit or incapacity-based income support, he provides answers (where asked) to questions and appropriate information about—

    (i) the content of any report made following a personal capability assessment, insofar as that report relates to the relevant person's capabilities and employability; and

    (ii) his opinion as to the extent to which his medical condition restricts his ability to undertake or enhance his employment; and

(d) he assists the officer in the completion of any amendment of the action plan referred to in paragraph (2)(d) in the light of the matters discussed in relation to sub-paragraph (b) and, where relevant, the information provided in relation to sub-paragraph (c).

(4) Where an officer determines that a relevant person has failed to take part in an interview and good cause has not been shown by the relevant person or, where the relevant person is a partner, by either the relevant person or the benefit recipient for that failure within five working days of the day on which the interview was to take place, a relevant decision shall be made for the purposes of section 2B of the Social Security Administration Act 1992, and the relevant person and, where the relevant person is a partner, the benefit recipient shall be notified accordingly.

GENERAL NOTE

Note that the rules on what constitutes taking part in an interview are tough, **1.046** paralleling quite closely the requirements under the Incapacity Benefit Work-focused Interview Regulations. They involve the preparation of an action plan whose progress is monitored, though there is no sanction for failure to take any action specified. Interviews under the regime in these regulations can include questions about the claimant's financial position and how it might be improved by finding work. There is an obligation under para.(3)(b) to participate in discussions on such matters.

Failure to take part in an interview

1.047   **12.**—(1) Where a relevant decision has been made in accordance with regulation 11(4), a relevant person or, where the relevant person is a partner, the benefit recipient shall, subject to paragraph (13), suffer the consequences set out below.

(2) Those consequences are—

(a) where the requirement to take part in an interview arose under regulation 3 in connection with a claim for income support or incapacity benefit, that the relevant person to whom the claim relates is, subject to sub-paragraph (b), to be regarded as not having made that claim for that benefit;

(b) where the requirement to take part in an interview which arose under regulation 3 in connection with a claim for income support or incapacity benefit was deferred and that benefit became payable by virtue of regulation 7(3), that the relevant person's entitlement to that benefit shall terminate from the first day of the next benefit week following the date on which the relevant decision was made;

(c) where the relevant person or, where the relevant person is a partner, the benefit recipient has an award of a specified benefit and the requirement to take part in an interview arose under regulation 4, the specified benefit payable in respect of which the requirement to take part in an interview arose shall be reduced.

(3) The reduction made to benefit in accordance with paragraph (2)(c) shall (subject to paragraphs (4) and (5)) be by a sum equal to 20 per cent. of the amount applicable on the date the reduction commences in respect of a single claimant for income support aged not less than 25 and shall take effect either as from the first day of the next benefit week following the day on which the relevant decision was made, or, if the relevant person is a partner and if that date arises five days or less after the day on which the relevant decision was made, as from the first day of the second benefit week following the date of the relevant decision.

(4) Benefit reduced in accordance with paragraph (2)(c) shall not be reduced below ten pence per week.

(5) Where two or more specified benefits are in payment to a relevant person, or, where the relevant person is a partner, to the benefit recipient, a reduction made in accordance with this regulation shall be applied, except in a case to which paragraph (6) applies, to the specified benefits in the following order of priority—

(a) an income-based jobseeker's allowance;

(b) income support;

(c) incapacity benefit;

(d) severe disablement allowance.

(6) Where the amount of the reduction is greater than some (but not all) of the specified benefits listed in paragraph (5), the reduction shall be made against the first benefit in that list which is the same as, or greater than, the amount of the reduction.

(7) For the purpose of determining whether a specified benefit is the same as, or greater than, the amount of the reduction for the purposes of paragraph (6), ten pence shall be added to the amount of the reduction.

(8) In a case where the whole of the reduction cannot be applied against any one specified benefit because the amount of no one benefit is the same as, or greater than, the amount of the reduction, the reduction shall be applied against the first benefit in payment in the list of priorities at paragraph (5) and so on against each benefit in turn until the whole of the reduction is exhausted or, if this is not possible, the whole of the specified benefits are exhausted, subject in each case to ten pence remaining in payment.

(9) Where the rate of any specified benefit payable to a relevant person, or, where a relevant person is a partner, to a benefit recipient changes, the rules set out above for a reduction in the benefit payable shall be applied to the new rates, and any adjustments to the benefits against which the reductions are made shall take effect from the beginning of the first benefit week to commence for that relevant person or benefit recipient following the change.

(10) For the avoidance of doubt, paragraph (2)(c) shall apply each time a relevant decision is made in accordance with regulation 11(4) arising from a requirement to take part in an interview under regulation 4 in respect of a relevant person.

(11) For the avoidance of doubt, a relevant person who is regarded as not having made a claim for income support or incapacity benefit because he failed to take part in an interview as a result of a requirement arising under regulation 3 shall be required to make a new claim in order to establish entitlement to that benefit.

(12) For the purposes of determining the amount of any benefit payable, a relevant person, or where a relevant person is a partner, a benefit recipient shall be treated as receiving the amount of any specified benefit which would have been payable but for a reduction made in accordance with this regulation.

(13) Benefit shall not be reduced in accordance with this regulation where a relevant person or, where the relevant person is a partner, the relevant person or the benefit recipient, brings new facts to the notice of the Secretary of State within one month of the date on which the decision that the relevant person failed without good cause to take part in an interview was notified to him and—

(a) those facts could not reasonably have been brought to the Secretary of State's notice within five working days of the day on which the interview was to take place; and

(b) those facts show that the relevant person had good cause for his failure to take part in the interview.

29

Circumstances where regulation 12 ceases to apply

1.048   **13.** Where a reduction of benefit has been made under regulation 12 the whole of the reduction relating to any requirements to attend interviews in respect of a relevant person shall not apply—

   (a) where the relevant person subsequently takes part in an interview, as from the first day of the benefit week in which a requirement to take part in an interview was met; or

   (b) as from the date when a relevant person who failed to take part in an interview is no longer a relevant person to whom regulations 3 to 15 apply by virtue of regulation 2(3).

Good cause

1.049   **14.** Matters to be taken into account in determining whether the relevant person or, where the relevant person is a partner, the relevant person or the benefit recipient has shown good cause for the relevant person's failure to take part in an interview include—

   (a) that the relevant person misunderstood the requirement to take part in an interview due to any learning, language or literacy difficulties of the relevant person or any misleading information given to the relevant person by the officer;

   (b) that the relevant person was attending a medical or dental appointment, or accompanying a person for whom the relevant person had caring responsibilities to such an appointment, and that it would have been unreasonable, in the circumstances, to rearrange the appointment;

   (c) that the relevant person had difficulties with his normal mode of transport and that no reasonable alternative was available;

   (d) that the established customs and practices of the religion to which the relevant person belongs prevented him attending on the day or at the time fixed for the interview;

   (e) that the relevant person was attending an interview with an employer with a view to obtaining employment;

   (f) that the relevant person was pursuing employment opportunities as a self-employed earner;

   (g) that the relevant person, benefit recipient or a dependant or a person for whom the relevant person provides care suffered an accident, sudden illness or relapse of a physical or mental health condition;

   (h) that the relevant person was attending the funeral of a relative or close friend on the day fixed for the interview;

   (i) that a disability from which the relevant person suffers made it impracticable for him to attend at the time fixed for the interview.

GENERAL NOTE

1.050   The decision that a person lacks good cause for failing to attend an interview is appealable under reg.15 below. The nine grounds specified in the regulation are not exhaustive. They are an illustrative list of matters which are to be taken into account in determining whether a person has good cause for failing to attend an interview. Good cause is nowhere defined. Its precise content is a matter of judgment for adjudicating bodies in the light of all the circumstances of the case.

Appeals

15.—(1) This regulation applies to any relevant decision made under regulation 11(4) or any decision made under section 10 of the 1998 Act (decisions superseding earlier decisions) superseding such a decision.   1.051

(2) This regulation applies whether the decision is as originally made or as revised under section 9 of the 1998 Act (revision of decisions).

(3) In the case of a decision to which this regulation applies, the relevant person in respect of whom the decision was made and, where the relevant person is a partner, the benefit recipient shall have a right of appeal under section 12 of the 1998 Act (appeal to appeal tribunal) to an appeal tribunal.

Areas designated as employment zones

16. The areas designated as employment zones for the purposes of these Regulations are the five areas comprising the postcodes listed in Part 2 of the Schedule.   1.052

GENERAL NOTE

Regulations 16 to 21 deal with areas designated as employment zones. They impact upon those: (a) claiming a jobseekers allowance who have been continuously in receipt of the benefit for three months immediately preceding the direction to participate in an interview, and (b) who have participated in any employment zone programme in the previous 12 months: see reg.17.   1.053

Referral to an employment zone programme

17. An officer may direct a jobseeker to participate in an employment zone programme if the jobseeker—   1.054
  (a) has been entitled to a jobseeker's allowance for a continuous period of at least three months in the period immediately preceding the date on which the direction is made; or
  (b) has participated in an employment zone programme pursuant to these Regulations or other regulations made pursuant to section 60 of the Welfare Reform and Pensions Act 1999 (special schemes for claimants for jobseeker's allowance) in the previous 12 months but did not complete the programme.

Early entry to an employment zone programme

18. An officer may direct a jobseeker to participate in an employment zone programme before he has been entitled to a jobseeker's allowance for a continuous period of at least three months provided that—   1.055
  (a) the jobseeker has requested the direction; and
  (b) his personal circumstances place him at a significant disadvantage in obtaining employment.

Stages of employment zone programme

1.056   **19.**—(1) An employment zone programme shall consist of two stages, of which—

(a) the first stage shall last for a maximum period of four weeks;

(b) the second stage shall last for a maximum period of 26 weeks.

(2) A jobseeker begins to participate in the first stage of an employment zone programme on the day when he attends an initial interview with an officer who is an employment zone programme adviser following a direction given under regulation 17 or 18.

(3) Subject to paragraph (1)(a), the jobseeker shall cease to participate in the first stage on the day specified by an officer in a written notification to the jobseeker.

(4) A jobseeker begins to participate in the second stage of an employment zone programme on the day specified by an officer in a written notification to the jobseeker.

(5) Subject to paragraph (1)(b), the jobseeker shall cease to participate in the second stage on the day specified by an officer in a written notification to the jobseeker.

Suspension of the requirements of the Jobseekers Act 1995

1.057   **20.**—(1) During the jobseeker's participation in the first stage of an employment zone programme the condition for receipt of a jobseeker's allowance specified in section 1(2)(b) of the Jobseekers Act 1995 (the jobseeker's allowance) that the jobseeker has entered into a jobseeker's agreement which remains in force is suspended.

(2) During the jobseeker's participation in the second stage of an employment zone programme the conditions for receipt of a jobseeker's allowance specified in section 1(2) of the Jobseekers Act 1995 shall apply with the suspension of the conditions in section 1(2)(a) to (c) of that Act that the jobseeker—

(a) be available for employment;

(b) has entered into a jobseeker's agreement which remains in force; and

(c) is actively seeking employment.

Cessation and consequential provision

1.058   **21.**—(1) Where a jobseeker to whom a direction given under regulation 17 or 18 would otherwise apply informs the Secretary of State of a change of address that results in that jobseeker no longer being ordinarily resident within an area identified in Part 2 of the Schedule, then—

(a) any sanction incurred by that jobseeker under section 19 (circumstances in which a jobseeker's allowance is not payable) or 20A (denial or reduction of joint-claim jobseeker's allowance) of the Jobseekers Act 1995 as a result of his refusing or failing to participate in, or giving up a place on, an employment zone programme as specified in regulation 75(1)(a)(iii) of the Jobseeker's Allowance Regulations 1996 shall end; and

(b) regulations 19 and 20 shall cease to apply to that jobseeker unless he asks to complete an employment zone programme in which he is participating, in which case those regulations shall continue to apply until he ceases to participate in that programme.

(2) Where a jobseeker asks to complete an employment zone programme in the circumstances specified in paragraph (1) then he shall not incur a sanction under section 19 or 20A of the Jobseekers Act 1995 if, for whatever reason, he subsequently refuses or fails to participate in, or gives up his place on, the employment zone programme in which he was participating.

SCHEDULE

For the purposes of Regulation 2(3)(a) and (4)(a) the areas are parts of the following local authority wards, and small parts of neighbouring wards, as specified in the listed postcode districts—   **1.059**

(a) Part 1—
  Birkenhead, Wirral
  Castle, Hastings
  Manor, Sheffield
  Monkchester, Newcastle
  Northwood, Knowsley
  Penderry, Swansea
  Central and Northgate, Great Yarmouth;

(b) Part 2—
  Aston, Birmingham
  East India & Lansbury, Tower Hamlets
  Hutchesontown, Glasgow
  Parkhead, Glasgow
  Thorntree, Middlesbrough.

PART 1

Birkenhead, Wirral: **1.060**
  CH41 1AB, CH41 1AD, CH41 1AF, CH41 1AG, CH41 1AH, CH41 1AL, CH41 1AN, CH41 1AP, CH41 1AR, CH41 1AS, CH41 1AT, CH41 1AW, CH41 1AX, CH41 1AY, CH41 1AZ, CH41 1BA, CH41 1BB, CH41 1BD, CH41 1BG, CH41 1BJ, CH41 1BN, CH41 1BP, CH41 1BQ, CH41 1BR, CH41 1DA, CH41 1DE, CH41 1ER, CH41 1ET, CH41 1EU, CH41 1EW, CH41 1EY, CH41 1EZ, CH41 1FN, CH41 1FP, CH41 1FS, CH41 1FW, CH41 1HB, CH41 1HT, CH41 1JL, CH41 1JN, CH41 1LB, CH41 1LD, CH41 1LE, CH41 1LF, CH41 1LJ, CH41 1LP, CH41 1LQ, CH41 1LU, CH41 1LW, CH41 1LX, CH41 1LY, CH41 1ND, CH41 1NE, CH41 1NF, CH41 1NG, CH41 1NQ, CH41 1WA, CH41 1WB, CH41 1WD, CH41 1WE, CH41 1WF, CH41 1WH, CH41 1WL, CH41 1WR, CH41 1YY, CH41 1YZ, CH41 2JQ, CH41 2PH, CH41 2PX, CH41 2PZ, CH41 2QD, CH41 2QH, CH41 2QJ, CH41 2QQ, CH41 2QR, CH41 2QS, CH41 2QX, CH41 2RB, CH41 2RG, CH41 2RH, CH41 2RL, CH41 2RQ, CH41 2SB, CH41 2SE, CH41 2SH, CH41 2SX, CH41 2TF, CH41 2TJ, CH41 2TL, CH41 2TN, CH41 2TP, CH41 2TS, CH41 2TW, CH41 2TX, CH41 2TY, CH41 2TZ, CH41 2UD, CH41 2UE, CH41 2UJ, CH41 2UP, CH41 2UW, CH41 2UZ, CH41 2WB, CH41 2WD, CH41 2WU, CH41 2XE, CH41 2XF, CH41 2XJ, CH41 2XL, CH41 2XN, CH41 2XP, CH41 2XS, CH41 2YP, CH41 2ZA, CH41 2ZD, CH41 3HT, CH41 3HU, CH41 3HX, CH41 3HY, CH41 3HZ, CH41 3JA, CH41 3JD, CH41 3JE, CH41 3JF, CH41 3JU, CH41 3JY, CH41 3LH, CH41 3LL, CH41 3LU, CH41 3LY, CH41 3NE, CH41 3NG, CH41 3NJ, CH41 3NL, CH41 3NN, CH41 3NP, CH41 3NR, CH41 3NT, CH41 3NU, CH41 3NW, CH41 3NX, CH41 3NZ, CH41 3PA, CH41 3PB, CH41 3PD, CH41 3PF, CH41 3PG, CH41 3PH, CH41 3PQ, CH41 3PR, CH41 3PS, CH41 3PT, CH41 3PX, CH41 3PY, CH41 3PZ, CH41 3QB, CH41 3QD, CH41 3QE, CH41 3QF, CH41 3QG, CH41 3QH, CH41 3QJ, CH41 3QL, CH41 3QN, CH41 3QP, CH41 3QQ, CH41 3QT, CH41 3QZ, CH41 3RB, CH41 3RF, CH41 3RG, CH41 3RH, CH41 3RJ, CH41 3RQ, CH41 3RS, CH41 3RT, CH41 3RU, CH41 3RX, CH41 3RY, CH41 3SA, CH41 3SB, CH41 3SD, CH41 3SE, CH41 3SG, CH41 3SH, CH41 3SP, CH41 3SS, CH41 3ST, CH41 3SU,

CH41 3SX, CH41 3WA, CH41 3YS, CH41 3YY, CH41 3YZ, CH41 4AA, CH41 4AG, CH41 4AH, CH41 4AQ, CH41 4AU, CH41 4AX, CH41 4BB, CH41 4BE, CH41 4BG, CH41 4BH, CH41 4BQ, CH41 4BR, CH41 4BS, CH41 4BW, CH41 4BX, CH41 4BY, CH41 4BZ, CH41 4DA, CH41 4DB, CH41 4DF, CH41 4DP, CH41 4DR, CH41 4DS, CH41 4DT, CH41 4DU, CH41 4DX, CH41 4DY, CH41 4FD, CH41 4FG, CH41 4FN, CH41 4FP, CH41 4FQ, CH41 4FU, CH41 4FX, CH41 4FZ, CH41 4HE, CH41 4HF, CH41 4HG, CH41 4HH, CH41 4HN, CH41 4HW, CH41 4JB, CH41 4JF, CH41 4JG, CH41 4JH, CH41 4JJ, CH41 4JN, CH41 4JQ, CH41 4JT, CH41 4JU, CH41 4JW, CH41 4JX, CH41 4JY, CH41 4JZ, CH41 4LA, CH41 4LB, CH41 4LE, CH41 4LG, CH41 4LQ, CH41 4LR, CH41 4LW, CH41 4LX, CH41 4LY, CH41 4LZ, CH41 4NA, CH41 4NB, CH41 4NF, CH41 4NG, CH41 4NH, CH41 4NJ, CH41 4NT, CH41 4NX, CH41 4NY, CH41 4NZ, CH41 4PE, CH41 4PG, CH41 4PJ, CH41 4PL, CH41 4PN, CH41 4PR, CH41 4PS, CH41 4WA, CH41 4WB, CH41 4WD, CH41 5AA, CH41 5AD, CH41 5AE, CH41 5AG, CH41 5AH, CH41 5AJ, CH41 5AN, CH41 5AR, CH41 5AS, CH41 5AT, CH41 5AU, CH41 5BD, CH41 5BL, CH41 5BN, CH41 5BP, CH41 5BR, CH41 5BS, CH41 5BT, CH41 5BU, CH41 5BY, CH41 5DA, CH41 5DB, CH41 5DD, CH41 5DE, CH41 5DG, CH41 5DL, CH41 5DQ, CH41 5EA, CH41 5EB, CH41 5ED, CH41 5EH, CH41 5EJ, CH41 5EN, CH41 5EP, CH41 5ER, CH41 5ES, CH41 5ET, CH41 5EU, CH41 5EX, CH41 5FD, CH41 5FL, CH41 5FN, CH41 5FX, CH41 5GA, CH41 5HA, CH41 5HJ, CH41 5HL, CH41 5HN, CH41 5HS, CH41 5HW, CH41 5HZ, CH41 5JF, CH41 5LG, CH41 5LL, CH41 5LN, CH41 5LP, CH41 5LR, CH41 5LS, CH41 5LU, CH41 5LW, CH41 5LX, CH41 5LZ, CH41 5NA, CH41 5NB, CH41 5WA, CH41 5WB, CH41 5WD, CH41 5WE, CH41 5WF, CH41 5WG, CH41 5WH, CH41 5WJ, CH41 5WL, CH41 5WN, CH41 5WP, CH41 5WQ, CH41 5YW, CH41 5YY, CH41 5YZ, CH41 6AA, CH41 6AB, CH41 6AD, CH41 6AE, CH41 6AF, CH41 6AG, CH41 6AH, CH41 6AL, CH41 6AN, CH41 6AR, CH41 6AU, CH41 6AW, CH41 6AX, CH41 6AY, CH41 6AZ, CH41 6BA, CH41 6BL, CH41 6BR, CH41 6BT, CH41 6BU, CH41 6BW, CH41 6DB, CH41 6DJ, CH41 6DL, CH41 6DN, CH41 6DQ, CH41 6DX, CH41 6DY, CH41 6EB, CH41 6ED, CH41 6EE, CH41 6EJ, CH41 6EL, CH41 6EP, CH41 6EX, CH41 6HA, CH41 6HB, CH41 6HH, CH41 6HR, CH41 6HS, CH41 6HT, CH41 6HW, CH41 6JD, CH41 6JE, CH41 6JH, CH41 6JN, CH41 6LA, CH41 6LD, CH41 6LE, CH41 6LF, CH41 6LG, CH41 6LH, CH41 6LL, CH41 6LP, CH41 6LQ, CH41 6LR, CH41 6LT, CH41 6LW, CH41 6LZ, CH41 6ND, CH41 6NR, CH41 6NU, CH41 6NX, CH41 6PE, CH41 6PH, CH41 6PN, CH41 6PQ, CH41 6PT, CH41 6PU, CH41 6PW, CH41 6PX, CH41 6PY, CH41 6QD, CH41 6QH, CH41 6QJ, CH41 6QP, CH41 6QS, CH41 6QX, CH41 6QY, CH41 6RA, CH41 6RH, CH41 6RN, CH41 6RQ, CH41 6RR, CH41 6RT, CH41 6RU, CH41 6RX, CH41 6RZ, CH41 6SA, CH41 6SB, CH41 6SD, CH41 6SE, CH41 6WA, CH41 6WB, CH41 6WH, CH41 6YY, CH41 6YZ, CH41 6ZA, CH41 7HF, CH41 7HQ, CH41 7WB, CH41 8AZ, CH41 8BB, CH41 8BE, CH41 8BP, CH41 8BQ, CH41 8BR, CH41 8BS, CH41 8BW, CH41 8EE, CH41 8EG, CH41 8EL, CH41 8EP, CH41 8FL, CH41 8FR, CH41 8FU, CH41 8GE, CH41 8WB, CH41 9AB, CH41 9AF, CH41 9BU, CH41 9BX, CH41 9BY, CH41 9DA, CH41 9DB, CH41 9DD, CH41 9HH, CH41 9HR, CH41 9WB;

CH42 0WA, CH42 2EX, CH42 4RR, CH42 4RY, CH42 4RZ, CH42 4WB, CH42 6WE, CH42 6WF, CH42 7WA, CH42 7WR, CH42 8WA, CH42 8WE, CH42 8WF, CH42 8WG, CH42 8WU, CH42 9GN, CH42 9WA, CH42 9WD, CH42 9WE, CH42 9WF, CH42 9WH, CH42 9YQ;

CH43 4TF, CH43 4TL, CH43 4TN, CH43 4TP, CH43 4TR, CH43 4TW, CH43 4US, CH43 4XF, CH43 4YD, CH43 4YE, CH43 4YF, CH43 4YG, CH43 4YJ.

1.061 Castle, Hastings:

TN34 1AA, TN34 1AB, TN34 1AD, TN34 1BA, TN34 1BB, TN34 1BD, TN34 1BE, TN34 1BF, TN34 1BG, TN34 1BH, TN34 1BJ, TN34 1BL, TN34 1BN, TN34 1BP, TN34 1BQ, TN34 1BS, TN34 1BT, TN34 1BU, TN34 1BY, TN34 1BZ, TN34 1DA, TN34 1DB, TN34 1DD, TN34 1DE, TN34 1DF, TN34 1DG, TN34 1DH, TN34 1DJ, TN34 1DL, TN34 1DN, TN34 1DP, TN34 1DQ, TN34 1DR, TN34 1DS, TN34 1DT, TN34 1DU, TN34 1DW, TN34 1DY, TN34 1EA, TN34 1EB, TN34 1ED, TN34 1EE, TN34 1EF, TN34 1EH, TN34 1EJ, TN34 1EL, TN34 1EN, TN34 1EP, TN34 1EQ, TN34 1ER, TN34 1ES, TN34 1ET, TN34 1EU, TN34 1EW, TN34 1EX, TN34 1EY, TN34 1EZ, TN34 1FT, TN34 1FX, TN34 1FY, TN34 1FZ, TN34

1GA, TN34 1GB, TN34 1GD, TN34 1GE, TN34 1GF, TN34 1GG, TN34 1GH, TN34 1GJ, TN34 1GL, TN34 1GP, TN34 1GQ, TN34 1GR, TN34 1GS, TN34 1GT, TN34 1GU, TN34 1GW, TN34 1GX, TN34 1GY, TN34 1GZ, TN34 1HA, TN34 1HB, TN34 1HD, TN34 1HE, TN34 1HF, TN34 1HG, TN34 1HH, TN34 1HJ, TN34 1HL, TN34 1HN, TN34 1HP, TN34 1HR, TN34 1HS, TN34 1HT, TN34 1HU, TN34 1HW, TN34 1HX, TN34 1HY, TN34 1HZ, TN34 1JA, TN34 1JB, TN34 1JD, TN34 1JE, TN34 1JF, TN34 1JG, TN34 1JH, TN34 1JJ, TN34 1JL, TN34 1JN, TN34 1JP, TN34 1JQ, TN34 1JR, TN34 1JS, TN34 1JT, TN34 1JU, TN34 1JW, TN34 1JX, TN34 1JY, TN34 1JZ, TN34 1LA, TN34 1LB, TN34 1LD, TN34 1LE, TN34 1LF, TN34 1LG, TN34 1LH, TN34 1LJ, TN34 1LL, TN34 1LN, TN34 1LP, TN34 1LQ, TN34 1LR, TN34 1LS, TN34 1LT, TN34 1LU, TN34 1LW, TN34 1LX, TN34 1LY, TN34 1LZ, TN34 1NA, TN34 1NB, TN34 1ND, TN34 1NE, TN34 1NF, TN34 1NG, TN34 1NH, TN34 1NJ, TN34 1NL, TN34 1NN, TN34 1NP, TN34 1NQ, TN34 1NR, TN34 1NS, TN34 1NT, TN34 1NU, TN34 1NW, TN34 1NX, TN34 1NY, TN34 1PA, TN34 1PB, TN34 1PD, TN34 1PE, TN34 1PF, TN34 1PG, TN34 1PH, TN34 1PJ, TN34 1PL, TN34 1PN, TN34 1PP, TN34 1PQ, TN34 1PR, TN34 1PS, TN34 1PT, TN34 1PU, TN34 1PX, TN34 1PY, TN34 1PZ, TN34 1QA, TN34 1QB, TN34 1QD, TN34 1QE, TN34 1QF, TN34 1QG, TN34 1QH, TN34 1QJ, TN34 1QL, TN34 1QN, TN34 1QP, TN34 1QQ, TN34 1QR, TN34 1QS, TN34 1QT, TN34 1QU, TN34 1QW, TN34 1QX, TN34 1QY, TN34 1QZ, TN34 1RA, TN34 1RB, TN34 1RD, TN34 1RE, TN34 1RF, TN34 1RG, TN34 1RH, TN34 1RJ, TN34 1RL, TN34 1RN, TN34 1RP, TN34 1RQ, TN34 1RR, TN34 1RS, TN34 1RT, TN34 1RU, TN34 1RW, TN34 1RX, TN34 1RY, TN34 1RZ, TN34 1SA, TN34 1SB, TN34 1SD, TN34 1SE, TN34 1SF, TN34 1SG, TN34 1SH, TN34 1SJ, TN34 1SL, TN34 1SN, TN34 1SP, TN34 1SQ, TN34 1SR, TN34 1SS, TN34 1ST, TN34 1SU, TN34 1SW, TN34 1SX, TN34 1SY, TN34 1SZ, TN34 1TL, TN34 1UR, TN34 1UT, TN34 1WA, TN34 1WB, TN34 1WD, TN34 1WE, TN34 1WF, TN34 1WG, TN34 1WH, TN34 1WJ, TN34 1WL, TN34 1WN, TN34 1WP, TN34 1WS, TN34 1WT, TN34 1WU, TN34 1WW, TN34 1WX, TN34 1WY, TN34 1WZ, TN34 1XJ, TN34 1XW, TN34 1YQ, TN34 1YT, TN34 1ZA, TN34 1ZB, TN34 1ZE, TN34 1ZF, TN34 1ZG, TN34 1ZH, TN34 1ZJ, TN34 1ZN, TN34 1ZP, TN34 1ZQ, TN34 1ZR, TN34 1ZS, TN34 1ZT, TN34 1ZU, TN34 1ZW, TN34 1ZY, TN34 1ZZ, TN34 2FX, TN34 2GT, TN34 2SY, TN34 2TG, TN34 2UR, TN34 2WA, TN34 2WB, TN34 2WD, TN34 2YP, TN34 2ZA, TN34 2ZB, TN34 2ZD, TN34 2ZE, TN34 2ZF, TN34 2ZG, TN34 3AA, TN34 3AB, TN34 3AD, TN34 3AE, TN34 3AF, TN34 3DG, TN34 3DS, TN34 3DT, TN34 3DU, TN34 3DX, TN34 3DY, TN34 3DZ, TN34 3FL, TN34 3GR, TN34 3JW, TN34 3JZ, TN34 3QZ, TN34 3RA, TN34 3RE, TN34 3RG, TN34 3RH, TN34 3RP, TN34 3RS, TN34 3RT, TN34 3RX, TN34 3RY, TN34 3RZ, TN34 3UX, TN34 3UY, TN34 3WA, TN34 3WB, TN34 3WD, TN34 3WE, TN34 3WF, TN34 3WG, TN34 3WH, TN34 3WJ, TN34 3WQ, TN34 3WR, TN34 3WT, TN34 3WU, TN34 3WW, TN34 3WX, TN34 3WY, TN34 3ZG, TN34 3ZL, TN34 3ZQ, TN34 3ZY, TN34 3ZZ;

TN35 4BY, TN35 4BZ, TN35 4DW, TN35 4WL, TN35 4WN, TN35 4WP, TN35 4WR, TN35 4WS, TN35 4YF, TN35 4YQ, TN35 4ZA, TN35 4ZB, TN35 4ZD, TN35 4ZF, TN35 4ZG, TN35 4ZH, TN35 4ZL, TN35 4ZP, TN35 4ZR, TN35 4ZZ, TN35 5PH, TN35 5PQ, TN35 5PR, TN35 5QL, TN35 5WA, TN35 5WB, TN35 5WD, TN35 5WE, TN35 5WJ, TN35 5WS, TN35 5WU, TN35 5YX, TN35 5ZA, TN35 5ZG;

TN37 6AA, TN37 6AD, TN37 6AJ, TN37 6AL, TN37 6AN, TN37 6AP, TN37 6AR, TN37 6AS, TN37 6AT, TN37 6AU, TN37 6AW, TN37 6AY, TN37 6AZ, TN37 6BD, TN37 6BG, TN37 6BH, TN37 6BJ, TN37 6BL, TN37 6BN, TN37 6BP, TN37 6BQ, TN37 6BS, TN37 6BT, TN37 6BW, TN37 6BX, TN37 6BY, TN37 6BZ, TN37 6DB, TN37 6DD, TN37 6DE, TN37 6DF, TN37 6DG, TN37 6DH, TN37 6DJ, TN37 6DL, TN37 6DP, TN37 6DQ, TN37 6DS, TN37 6DU, TN37 6DX, TN37 6DY, TN37 6DZ, TN37 6EA, TN37 6EB, TN37 6EE, TN37 6EF, TN37 6EG, TN37 6EH, TN37 6EJ, TN37 6EL, TN37 6EN, TN37 6EP, TN37 6EQ, TN37 6ER, TN37 6ES, TN37 6ET, TN37 6EU, TN37 6EW, TN37 6EX, TN37 6EY, TN37 6EZ, TN37 6HA, TN37 6HB, TN37 6HD, TN37 6HE, TN37 6HF, TN37 6HG, TN37 6HH, TN37 6HJ, TN37 6HL, TN37 6HN, TN37 6HP, TN37 6HQ, TN37 6HR, TN37 6HS, TN37 6HT, TN37 6HU, TN37 6HW, TN37 6HX, TN37 6HY, TN37 6HZ, TN37 6JA, TN37 6JB, TN37 6JH, TN37 6JR, TN37 6JS, TN37 6JT, TN37 6JY, TN37 6JZ,

TN37 6LA, TN37 6LB, TN37 6LD, TN37 6LE, TN37 6LF, TN37 6LG, TN37 6LH, TN37 6LJ, TN37 6LL, TN37 6LP, TN37 6LQ, TN37 6LR, TN37 6LS, TN37 6LW, TN37 6NH, TN37 6NN, TN37 6QH, TN37 6QJ, TN37 6QL, TN37 6QP, TN37 6QR, TN37 6RF, TN37 6RR, TN37 6RS, TN37 6RZ, TN37 6SR, TN37 6SS, TN37 6SZ, TN37 6TA, TN37 6TF, TN37 6TN, TN37 6UF, TN37 6WS, TN37 6WT, TN37 6WZ, TN37 6XS, TN37 6ZB, TN37 6ZD, TN37 6ZF, TN37 6ZG, TN37 6ZH, TN37 6ZJ, TN37 6ZL, TN37 6ZR, TN37 6ZY, TN37 6ZZ;

TN38 0EP, TN38 0EX, TN38 0EY, TN38 0HA, TN38 0HB, TN38 0HD, TN38 0JA, TN38 0JB, TN38 0JU, TN38 0JY, TN38 0JZ, TN38 0QA, TN38 0QB, TN38 0QD, TN38 0QE, TN38 0QG, TN38 0QH, TN38 0QJ, TN38 0QL, TN38 0QN, TN38 0QP, TN38 0QQ, TN38 0QR, TN38 0QS, TN38 0QT, TN38 0RA.

1.062 Manor, Sheffield:

S12 2AA, S12 2AB, S12 2AD, S12 2SB, S12 2SN, S12 2SS, S12 2ST;

S2 1AA, S2 1AB, S2 1AG, S2 1AH, S2 1AJ, S2 1AL, S2 1AN, S2 1AP, S2 1AQ, S2 1AR, S2 1AS, S2 1AT, S2 1AU, S2 1AW, S2 1AX, S2 1AY, S2 1AZ, S2 1BA, S2 1BB, S2 1BD, S2 1BE, S2 1BF, S2 1BG, S2 1BH, S2 1BJ, S2 1BL, S2 1BN, S2 1BP, S2 1BQ, S2 1BR, S2 1BS, S2 1BT, S2 1BU, S2 1BW, S2 1BX, S2 1BY, S2 1BZ, S2 1DA, S2 1DB, S2 1DD, S2 1DE, S2 1DF, S2 1DG, S2 1DH, S2 1DJ, S2 1DL, S2 1DN, S2 1DP, S2 1DQ, S2 1DR, S2 1DS, S2 1DT, S2 1DU, S2 1DW, S2 1DX, S2 1DY, S2 1DZ, S2 1ED, S2 1EE, S2 1EF, S2 1EG, S2 1EH, S2 1EL, S2 1EN, S2 1EP, S2 1ES, S2 1ET, S2 1EU, S2 1EW, S2 1EX, S2 1EY, S2 1EZ, S2 1FA, S2 1FB, S2 1FD, S2 1FE, S2 1FF, S2 1FG, S2 1FH, S2 1FJ, S2 1FL, S2 1GF, S2 1GJ, S2 1GL, S2 1GN, S2 1GP, S2 1GQ, S2 1GR, S2 1GS, S2 1GT, S2 1GU, S2 1GW, S2 1GY, S2 1GZ, S2 1HA, S2 1HB, S2 1HD, S2 1HE, S2 1HF, S2 1HG, S2 1HH, S2 1HJ, S2 1HL, S2 1HN, S2 1HP, S2 1HQ, S2 1HR, S2 1HS, S2 1HT, S2 1HU, S2 1HW, S2 1HX, S2 1HY, S2 1HZ, S2 1JA, S2 1JB, S2 1JD, S2 1JE, S2 1JF, S2 1JG, S2 1JH, S2 1JJ, S2 1JL, S2 1JN, S2 1JP, S2 1JQ, S2 1JR, S2 1JS, S2 1JT, S2 1JU, S2 1JW, S2 1JX, S2 1JY, S2 1JZ, S2 1LA, S2 1LB, S2 1LD, S2 1LE, S2 1LF, S2 1LG, S2 1LQ, S2 1NE, S2 1NF, S2 1NG, S2 1NH, S2 1NJ, S2 1NX, S2 1NY, S2 1NZ, S2 1PA, S2 1PB, S2 1PD, S2 1PF, S2 1PG, S2 1PJ, S2 1PL, S2 1PN, S2 1PP, S2 1PQ, S2 1PR, S2 1PS, S2 1PT, S2 1PU, S2 1PW, S2 1PX, S2 1PY, S2 1PZ, S2 1QA, S2 1QB, S2 1QD, S2 1QE, S2 1QF, S2 1QG, S2 1QH, S2 1QJ, S2 1QL, S2 1QN, S2 1QP, S2 1QQ, S2 1QR, S2 1QS, S2 1QT, S2 1QU, S2 1QW, S2 1QX, S2 1QY, S2 1RA, S2 1RB, S2 1RD, S2 1RQ, S2 1RR, S2 1RZ, S2 1SD, S2 1SE, S2 1SG, S2 1SH, S2 1SJ, S2 1SL, S2 1US, S2 1WE, S2 1WG, S2 1WJ, S2 1WT, S2 1WW, S2 1WX, S2 1YL, S2 1YN, S2 1YU, S2 1YW, S2 2EY, S2 2EZ, S2 2FB, S2 2FD, S2 2FE, S2 2FF, S2 2FG, S2 2FY, S2 2FZ, S2 2GG, S2 2GH, S2 2JA, S2 2JG, S2 2JS, S2 2JT, S2 2JU, S2 2JY, S2 2JZ, S2 2LA, S2 2LD, S2 2LE, S2 2GJ, S2 2JH, S2 2JJ, S2 2JL, S2 2LB.

1.063 Monkchester, Newcastle:

NE6 1EB, NE6 1EE, NE6 1EG, NE6 1EJ, NE6 1EL, NE6 1EU, NE6 1HY, NE6 1PB, NE6 1YB, NE6 2AU, NE6 2DF, NE6 2DG, NE6 2DU, NE6 2DX, NE6 2EG, NE6 2ER, NE6 2EW, NE6 2EZ, NE6 2FT, NE6 2HF, NE6 2HG, NE6 2HX, NE6 2HY, NE6 2JA, NE6 2JB, NE6 2JD, NE6 2JE, NE6 2JH, NE6 2JL, NE6 2JN, NE6 2JP, NE6 2JQ, NE6 2JT, NE6 2JX, NE6 2JY, NE6 2LD, NE6 2LF, NE6 2LG, NE6 2LH, NE6 2LJ, NE6 2LL, NE6 2LN, NE6 2LP, NE6 2LQ, NE6 2LR, NE6 2LS, NE6 2LT, NE6 2LU, NE6 2LW, NE6 2LX, NE6 2LY, NE6 2LZ, NE6 2NA, NE6 2NB, NE6 2ND, NE6 2NF, NE6 2NG, NE6 2NJ, NE6 2NL, NE6 2NQ, NE6 2NR, NE6 2NS, NE6 2NT, NE6 2NW, NE6 2NX, NE6 2NY, NE6 2NZ, NE6 2PD, NE6 2PF, NE6 2PG, NE6 2PU, NE6 2PW, NE6 2PX, NE6 2PY, NE6 2QA, NE6 2QB, NE6 2QD, NE6 2QE, NE6 2QH, NE6 2QJ, NE6 2QL, NE6 2QP, NE6 2QR, NE6 2QS, NE6 2QT, NE6 2QW, NE6 2QX, NE6 2QY, NE6 2QZ, NE6 2RB, NE6 2RR, NE6 2RS, NE6 2RT, NE6 2RU, NE6 2RX, NE6 2SA, NE6 2SD, NE6 2SE, NE6 2SP, NE6 2SQ, NE6 2SR, NE6 2SS, NE6 2TA, NE6 2TB, NE6 2TE, NE6 2TG, NE6 2TH, NE6 2TL, NE6 2TR, NE6 2TS, NE6 2TT, NE6 2TU, NE6 2TX, NE6 2XD, NE6 2XQ, NE6 3JH, NE6 3JJ, NE6 3JL, NE6 3JN, NE6 3JP, NE6 3JT, NE6 3JU, NE6 3JY, NE6 3LD, NE6 3LE, NE6 3LH, NE6 3LJ, NE6 3LL, NE6 3LN, NE6 3LP, NE6 3LQ, NE6 3LR, NE6 3RS, NE6 3RT, NE6 3RU, NE6 3RX, NE6 3RY, NE6 3SA, NE6 3SN, NE6 3SP, NE6 3SQ, NE6 3SR.

1.064 Northwood, Knowsley:

L33 0XB, L33 0XD, L33 0XE, L33 0XF, L33 0XG, L33 0XH, L33 0XJ, L33 0XL, L33 0XN, L33 0XP, L33 0XQ, L33 0XR, L33 0XS, L33 0XT, L33 0XU, L33 0XW,

L33 0XX, L33 0XY, L33 0XZ, L33 0YA, L33 0YB, L33 0YD, L33 0YE, L33 0YF, L33 0YG, L33 0YH, L33 0YQ, L33 1DA, L33 1DB, L33 1DD, L33 1DE, L33 1DP, L33 1DR, L33 1DU, L33 1DY, L33 1DZ, L33 1EB, L33 1QW, L33 1QZ, L33 1RA, L33 1RB, L33 1RE, L33 1RF, L33 1RG, L33 1SL, L33 1SZ, L33 1TA, L33 1TB, L33 1TD, L33 1TE, L33 1TF, L33 1TG, L33 1TH, L33 1TJ, L33 1TN, L33 1TP, L33 1TQ, L33 1TR, L33 1TS, L33 1TT, L33 1TU, L33 1TW, L33 1TX, L33 1TZ, L33 1UA, L33 1UB, L33 1UD, L33 1UE, L33 1UF, L33 1UG, L33 1UH, L33 1UJ, L33 1UL, L33 1UN, L33 1UQ, L33 1UR, L33 1US, L33 1UT, L33 1UU, L33 1UW, L33 1UX, L33 1UY, L33 1WA, L33 1WB, L33 1WD, L33 1WE, L33 1WF, L33 1WU, L33 1XE, L33 1XG, L33 1XH, L33 1XJ, L33 1XQ, L33 1XS, L33 1XT, L33 1XU, L33 1XX, L33 1XY, L33 1XZ, L33 1YA, L33 1YB, L33 1YD, L33 1YE, L33 1YF, L33 1YH, L33 1YJ, L33 1YL, L33 1YN, L33 1YP, L33 1YQ, L33 1YR, L33 1YS, L33 1YT, L33 1YU, L33 1YW, L33 1YX, L33 1YZ, L33 1ZA, L33 1ZB, L33 1ZD, L33 1ZE, L33 1ZF, L33 1ZG, L33 1ZH, L33 1ZJ, L33 1ZL, L33 1ZN, L33 1ZP, L33 1ZQ, L33 1ZR, L33 1ZS, L33 1ZT, L33 1ZU, L33 1ZW, L33 1ZX, L33 1ZY, L33 5YB, L33 5YD, L33 5YE, L33 5YF, L33 5YG, L33 5YH, L33 5YJ, L33 5YL, L33 5YN, L33 5YQ, L33 5YW, L33 6UA, L33 6UB, L33 6UD, L33 6UE, L33 6UF, L33 6UH, L33 6UJ, L33 6UL, L33 6UN, L33 6UP, L33 6UR, L33 6US, L33 6XG, L33 6XH, L33 6XJ, L33 6XP, L33 6XQ, L33 6XR, L33 6YH, L33 6YJ, L33 8XA, L33 8XB, L33 8XD, L33 8XE, L33 8XG, L33 8XH, L33 8XJ, L33 8XL, L33 8XN, L33 8XP, L33 8XQ, L33 8XR, L33 8XS, L33 8XT, L33 8XU, L33 8XW, L33 8XX, L33 8XY, L33 8XZ, L33 8YA, L33 8YB, L33 8YD, L33 8YE, L33 8YF, L33 8YG, L33 8YR, L33 8YT, L33 9TB, L33 9TD, L33 9TE, L33 9TF, L33 9TG, L33 9TH, L33 9TJ, L33 9TL, L33 9TP, L33 9TQ, L33 9TR, L33 9TS, L33 9TT, L33 9TW, L33 9TX, L33 9UA, L33 9UD, L33 9UE, L33 9UG, L33 9UH, L33 9UJ, L33 9UL, L33 9UN, L33 9UR, L33 9US, L33 9UT, L33 9UU, L33 9UX, L33 9UY, L33 9UZ, L33 9XA, L33 9XB, L33 9XD, L33 9XE, L33 9XF, L33 9XG, L33 9XH, L33 9XL, L33 9XP, L33 9XQ, L33 9XS, L33 9XT, L33 9XW.

Penderry, Swansea: **1.065**

SA5 4PG, SA5 4PH, SA5 5AE, SA5 5AF, SA5 5AG, SA5 5AH, SA5 5AQ, SA5 5ED, SA5 5EE, SA5 5EF, SA5 5EG, SA5 5EH, SA5 5EJ, SA5 5EL, SA5 5EN, SA5 5EQ, SA5 5ER, SA5 5ET, SA5 5EU, SA5 5EW, SA5 5EX, SA5 5EY, SA5 5HP, SA5 5HR, SA5 5HS, SA5 5HT, SA5 5HU, SA5 5HW, SA5 5HX, SA5 5HY, SA5 5HZ, SA5 5JA, SA5 5JB, SA5 5JD, SA5 5JE, SA5 5JF, SA5 5JH, SA5 5JJ, SA5 5JN, SA5 5JP, SA5 5JQ, SA5 5JR, SA5 5JS, SA5 5JT, SA5 5JU, SA5 5JW, SA5 5JX, SA5 5JY, SA5 5JZ, SA5 5LA, SA5 5LB, SA5 5LD, SA5 5LE, SA5 5LF, SA5 5LG, SA5 5LH, SA5 5LJ, SA5 5LL, SA5 5LN, SA5 5LP, SA5 5LQ, SA5 5LW, SA5 5LX, SA5 5NA, SA5 5NB, SA5 5ND, SA5 5NE, SA5 5NG, SA5 5NH, SA5 5NL, SA5 5NN, SA5 5NP, SA5 5NQ, SA5 5NR, SA5 5NS, SA5 5NT, SA5 5NU, SA5 5NW, SA5 5NX, SA5 5NY, SA5 5PF, SA5 5PG, SA5 5PJ, SA5 5PL, SA5 5PN, SA5 5PP, SA5 5PR, SA5 5PS, SA5 5PT, SA5 5PU, SA5 5PX, SA5 5PY, SA5 5QA, SA5 5QB, SA5 5QD, SA5 5QE, SA5 5QH, SA5 5QJ, SA5 5QQ, SA5 5YA, SA5 5YD, SA5 5YE, SA5 5YF, SA5 5YG, SA5 5YH, SA5 5YL, SA5 5YP, SA5 5YR, SA5 5YT, SA5 7AA, SA5 7AB, SA5 7AD, SA5 7AE, SA5 7AF, SA5 7AG, SA5 7AH, SA5 7AJ, SA5 7AL, SA5 7AN, SA5 7AP, SA5 7AQ, SA5 7AW, SA5 7BH, SA5 7BL, SA5 7BN, SA5 7BP, SA5 7BR, SA5 7BS, SA5 7BT, SA5 7BU, SA5 7BX, SA5 7EA, SA5 7ED, SA5 7EG, SA5 7EH, SA5 7EL, SA5 7EP, SA5 7EQ, SA5 7HH, SA5 7JN, SA5 7JP, SA5 7JS, SA5 7JT, SA5 7JU, SA5 7JW, SA5 9AA, SA5 9AB, SA5 9AD, SA5 9AE, SA5 9AF, SA5 9AG, SA5 9AJ, SA5 9AL, SA5 9AN, SA5 9AQ, SA5 9AW, SA5 9BE, SA5 9BG, SA5 9BJ.

Central and Northgate, Great Yarmouth: **1.066**

NR30 1AB, NR30 1DX, NR30 1DY, NR30 1EH, NR30 1ES, NR30 1HF, NR30 1HG, NR30 1HH, NR30 1HJ, NR30 1HL, NR30 1HN, NR30 1HP, NR30 1HQ, NR30 1HR, NR30 1HS, NR30 1HT, NR30 1HU, NR30 1HW, NR30 1HX, NR30 1HY, NR30 1JA, NR30 1JB, NR30 1JD, NR30 1JE, NR30 1JL, NR30 1JN, NR30 1JP, NR30 1JR, NR30 1LD, NR30 1LE, NR30 1LF, NR30 1LH, NR30 1LJ, NR30 1LL, NR30 1LN, NR30 1LP, NR30 1LS, NR30 1LT, NR30 1LU, NR30 1LW, NR30 1LX, NR30 1LZ, NR30 1NP, NR30 1NR, NR30 1NT, NR30 1NY, NR30 1NZ, NR30 1PA, NR30 1PB, NR30 1PD, NR30 1PE, NR30 1PF, NR30 1PG, NR30 1PH, NR30 1PJ, NR30 1PQ, NR30 1RH, NR30 1RJ, NR30 1RL, NR30 1RN, NR30 1RP, NR30 1RQ, NR30 1RR, NR30 1RS, NR30 1RT, NR30 1RU, NR30 1RW, NR30 1SA, NR30 1SY, NR30 1SZ, NR30 2AA, NR30 2AB, NR30 2AD, NR30 2AE, NR30 2AF, NR30 2AG, NR30

2AH, NR30 2AJ, NR30 2AL, NR30 2AN, NR30 2AP, NR30 2AQ, NR30 2AR, NR30 2AS, NR30 2AT, NR30 2AU, NR30 2AW, NR30 2AX, NR30 2AZ, NR30 2BA, NR30 2BB, NR30 2BD, NR30 2BE, NR30 2BH, NR30 2BJ, NR30 2BL, NR30 2BN, NR30 2BP, NR30 2BQ, NR30 2BS, NR30 2BT, NR30 2BU, NR30 2BW, NR30 2BX, NR30 2BY, NR30 2BZ, NR30 2DA, NR30 2DB, NR30 2DD, NR30 2DE, NR30 2DF, NR30 2DG, NR30 2DH, NR30 2DJ, NR30 2DL, NR30 2DN, NR30 2DP, NR30 2DQ, NR30 2DR, NR30 2DS, NR30 2DU, NR30 2DW, NR30 2DX, NR30 2DY, NR30 2DZ, NR30 2EA, NR30 2EB, NR30 2ED, NR30 2EE, NR30 2EF, NR30 2EG, NR30 2EH, NR30 2EJ, NR30 2EL, NR30 2EN, NR30 2EP, NR30 2EQ, NR30 2ER, NR30 2ES, NR30 2EU, NR30 2EW, NR30 2EX, NR30 2EZ, NR30 2GZ, NR30 2HA, NR30 2HB, NR30 2HD, NR30 2HE, NR30 2HF, NR30 2HG, NR30 2HJ, NR30 2HL, NR30 2HN, NR30 2HP, NR30 2HQ, NR30 2HR, NR30 2HS, NR30 2HT, NR30 2HU, NR30 2HW, NR30 2HX, NR30 2HY, NR30 2HZ, NR30 2JA, NR30 2JB, NR30 2JD, NR30 2JE, NR30 2JF, NR30 2JG, NR30 2JH, NR30 2JJ, NR30 2JL, NR30 2JN, NR30 2JP, NR30 2JQ, NR30 2JR, NR30 2JS, NR30 2JT, NR30 2JU, NR30 2JW, NR30 2JX, NR30 2JY, NR30 2JZ, NR30 2LA, NR30 2LB, NR30 2LD, NR30 2LE, NR30 2LF, NR30 2LG, NR30 2LH, NR30 2LJ, NR30 2LL, NR30 2LN, NR30 2LP, NR30 2LQ, NR30 2LR, NR30 2LS, NR30 2LT, NR30 2LU, NR30 2LW, NR30 2LX, NR30 2LY, NR30 2LZ, NR30 2NA, NR30 2NB, NR30 2ND, NR30 2NE, NR30 2NF, NR30 2NG, NR30 2NH, NR30 2NJ, NR30 2NN, NR30 2NP, NR30 2NQ, NR30 2NR, NR30 2NS, NR30 2NT, NR30 2NU, NR30 2NW, NR30 2NX, NR30 2NY, NR30 2NZ, NR30 2PA, NR30 2PB, NR30 2PD, NR30 2PE, NR30 2PF, NR30 2PG, NR30 2PH, NR30 2PJ, NR30 2PL, NR30 2PN, NR30 2PP, NR30 2PQ, NR30 2PR, NR30 2PS, NR30 2PT, NR30 2PU, NR30 2PW, NR30 2PX, NR30 2PY, NR30 2PZ, NR30 2QA, NR30 2QB, NR30 2QD, NR30 2QE, NR30 2QF, NR30 2QG, NR30 2QH, NR30 2QJ, NR30 2QN, NR30 2QP, NR30 2QR, NR30 2QS, NR30 2QT, NR30 2QU, NR30 2QW, NR30 2QX, NR30 2QY, NR30 2QZ, NR30 2RA, NR30 2RE, NR30 2RG, NR30 2RH, NR30 2RJ, NR30 2RL, NR30 2RN, NR30 2RP, NR30 2RQ, NR30 2RR, NR30 2RS, NR30 2RT, NR30 2RU, NR30 2RW, NR30 2RX, NR30 2RY, NR30 2RZ, NR30 2SA, NR30 2SB, NR30 2SD, NR30 2SE, NR30 2SF, NR30 2SG, NR30 2SH, NR30 2SJ, NR30 2SL, NR30 2SN, NR30 2SP, NR30 2SQ, NR30 2SR, NR30 2ST, NR30 2SW, NR30 2SX, NR30 2SY, NR30 2SZ, NR30 2TA, NR30 2XA, NR30 3AA, NR30 3AB, NR30 3AD, NR30 3AE, NR30 3AF, NR30 3AG, NR30 3AH, NR30 3AJ, NR30 3AL, R30 3AN, NR30 3AQ, NR30 3AS, NR30 3AT, NR30 3AU, NR30 3AW, NR30 3AX, NR30 3AY, NR30 3AZ, NR30 3BA, NR30 3BB, NR30 3BD, NR30 3BE, NR30 3BG, NR30 3BH, NR30 3BJ, NR30 3BL, NR30 3BN, NR30 3BP, NR30 3BQ, NR30 3BS, NR30 3BT, NR30 3BU, NR30 3BW, NR30 3BX, NR30 3BY, NR30 3BZ, NR30 3DA, NR30 3DB, NR30 3DD, NR30 3DG, NR30 3DL, NR30 3DN, NR30 3EH, NR30 3HA, NR30 3HB, NR30 3HE, NR30 3HF, NR30 3HG, NR30 3HH, NR30 3HJ, NR30 3HL, NR30 3HN, NR30 3HP, NR30 3HQ, NR30 3HR, NR30 3HS, NR30 3HT, NR30 3HU, NR30 3HW, NR30 3HX, NR30 3HY, NR30 3HZ, NR30 3JA, NR30 3JB, NR30 3JD, NR30 3JE, NR30 3JF, NR30 3JG, NR30 3JH, NR30 3JJ, NR30 3JL, NR30 3JN, NR30 3JP, NR30 3JQ, NR30 3JR, NR30 3JS, NR30 3JT, NR30 3JU, NR30 3JW, NR30 3JZ, NR30 3LA, NR30 3LB, NR30 3LD, NR30 3LE, NR30 3LF, NR30 3LG, NR30 3LH, NR30 3LJ, NR30 3LQ, NR30 3LR, NR30 3NR, NR30 3NW, NR30 3RA, NR30 3RB, NR30 3RD, NR30 3RE, NR30 3RF, NR30 3RG, NR30 3RJ, NR30 3RL, NR30 3RQ, NR30 3RR, NR30 3RT, NR30 3WB, NR30 3WF, NR30 3WG, NR30 4HF.

PART 2

1.067 Aston, Birmingham:
B18 5AD, B18 5AE, B18 5AN, B18 5AQ, B18 5AR, B18 5AS, B18 5AT, B18 5AU, B18 5AX, B18 5AY, B18 5BA, B18 5BB, B18 5BD, B18 5BE, B18 5BH, B18 5BJ, B18 5BL, B18 5BP, B18 5BQ, B18 5BX, B18 5BY, B18 5DJ, B18 5DR, B18 5DY, B18 5DZ, B18 5EN, B18 5HB, B18 5HD, B18 5HR, B18 5HS, B18 5HY, B18 5HZ, B18 5JH, B18 5JN, B18 5LN, B18 5LQ, B18 5LT, B18 5LU, B18 5NL, B18 5NN, B18 5NP, B18 5NU, B18 5NW, B18 5PH, B18 5PJ, B18 5PL, B18 5PN, B18 5PQ, B18 5PW, B18 5PZ, B18 5QA, B18 5QB, B18 5QD, B18 5QE, B18 5QG, B18 5QH, B18 5QJ, B18 5QL, B18 5QN, B18 5QP, B18 5QQ, B18 5QR, B18 5QS, B18 5QT, B18 5QU, B18 5QX, B18 5QY, B18 5QZ, B18 5RB, B18 5RD, B18 5RH, B18 5RJ, B18 5RL, B18

5RP, B18 5RR, B18 5RT, B18 5RU, B18 5RW, B18 5RX, B18 5RY, B18 5SA, B18 5SB, B18 5SD, B18 5SF, B18 5UA, B18 6PP, B18 7RP;

B19 1DP, B19 1DS, B19 1EU, B19 2DA, B19 2JX, B19 2JY, B19 2LA, B19 2LF, B19 2NH, B19 2NL, B19 2NN, B19 2NP, B19 2NS, B19 2NT, B19 2NU, B19 2NX, B19 2NY, B19 2NZ, B19 2PA, B19 2PB, B19 2PX, B19 2PY, B19 2QA, B19 2QB, B19 2QD, B19 2QE, B19 2QG, B19 2QH, B19 2QJ, B19 2RR, B19 2RT, B19 2RU, B19 2RX, B19 2RY, B19 2RZ, B19 2SA, B19 2SB, B19 2SF, B19 2SG, B19 2SH, B19 2SJ, B19 2SL, B19 2SN, B19 2SP, B19 2SQ, B19 2SS, B19 2SW, B19 2TX, B19 2TY, B19 2TZ, B19 2UA, B19 2UD, B19 2UE, B19 2UF, B19 2UG, B19 2UY, B19 2UZ, B19 2WA, B19 2WB, B19 2XA, B19 2XB, B19 2XD, B19 2XF, B19 2XH, B19 2XJ, B19 2XL, B19 2XN, B19 2XP, B19 2XQ, B19 2XR, B19 2XS, B19 2XT, B19 2XU, B19 2YD, B19 2YE, B19 2YF, B19 2YG, B19 2YH, B19 2YJ, B19 2YL, B19 2YN, B19 2YP, B19 2YQ, B19 2YR, B19 2YS, B19 2YT, B19 2YU, B19 2YW, B19 2YX, B19 2YY, B19 2ZL, B19 2ZR, B19 2ZY, B19 3AA, B19 3AE, B19 3AG, B19 3AH, B19 3AJ, B19 3AP, B19 3AQ, B19 3AS, B19 3AT, B19 3AU, B19 3AX, B19 3AY, B19 3AZ, B19 3BA, B19 3BB, B19 3BL, B19 3BN, B19 3BP, B19 3BS, B19 3BT, B19 3BU, B19 3BW, B19 3BX, B19 3BY, B19 3BZ, B19 3DA, B19 3ES, B19 3ET, B19 3HA, B19 3HB, B19 3HD, B19 3HE, B19 3HF, B19 3HH, B19 3HJ, B19 3HL, B19 3HN, B19 3HP, B19 3HQ, B19 3HR, B19 3HS, B19 3HT, B19 3HU, B19 3HW, B19 3HX, B19 3JA, B19 3JB, B19 3JD, B19 3JE, B19 3JG, B19 3JH, B19 3JJ, B19 3JL, B19 3JN, B19 3JQ, B19 3JR, B19 3JT, B19 3JX, B19 3JY, B19 3LA, B19 3LB, B19 3LD, B19 3LE, B19 3LF, B19 3LG, B19 3LH, B19 3LJ, B19 3LL, B19 3LN, B19 3LQ, B19 3LR, B19 3LS, B19 3LT, B19 3LU, B19 3LW, B19 3LX, B19 3LY, B19 3LZ, B19 3NA, B19 3NB, B19 3ND, B19 3NE, B19 3NF, B19 3NG, B19 3NH, B19 3NJ, B19 3NL, B19 3NN, B19 3NP, B19 3NQ, B19 3NR, B19 3NS, B19 3NT, B19 3NU, B19 3NW, B19 3NX, B19 3NY, B19 3NZ, B19 3PA, B19 3PB, B19 3PD, B19 3PE, B19 3PF, B19 3PH, B19 3PL, B19 3PN, B19 3PP, B19 3PQ, B19 3PR, B19 3PS, B19 3PT, B19 3PU, B19 3PX, B19 3PY, B19 3PZ, B19 3QA, B19 3QB, B19 3QD, B19 3QE, B19 3QF, B19 3QG, B19 3QH, B19 3QL, B19 3QN, B19 3QP, B19 3QS, B19 3QT, B19 3QU, B19 3QW, B19 3QY, B19 3QZ, B19 3RA, B19 3RB, B19 3RD, B19 3RG, B19 3RH, B19 3RL, B19 3RN, B19 3RQ, B19 3RR, B19 3RS, B19 3RT, B19 3RY, B19 3RZ, B19 3SA, B19 3SB, B19 3SD, B19 3SE, B19 3SF, B19 3SH, B19 3SJ, B19 3SL, B19 3SN, B19 3SP, B19 3ST, B19 3SU, B19 3SW, B19 3SY, B19 3TA, B19 3TB, B19 3TD, B19 3TE, B19 3TG, B19 3TH, B19 3TL, B19 3TN, B19 3TS, B19 3TZ, B19 3UA, B19 3UB, B19 3UD, B19 3UJ, B19 3UL, B19 3UN, B19 3UP, B19 3UR, B19 3UW, B19 3UX, B19 3UY, B19 3UZ, B19 3WB, B19 3XA, B19 3XB, B19 3XD, B19 3XE, B19 3XF, B19 3XG, B19 3XH, B19 3XJ, B19 3XL, B19 3XN, B19 3XP, B19 3XQ, B19 3XR, B19 3XU, B19 3XX, B19 3YS;

B3 1AF, B3 1AG, B3 1AH, B3 1AJ, B3 1AL, B3 1AQ, B3 1ET, B3 1HA, B3 1HB, B3 1HL, B3 1HN, B3 1QT, B3 1RB, B3 1RJ, B3 1RL;

B4 6AQ, B4 6BA, B4 6HA, B4 6HE, B4 6HJ, B4 6HW, B4 6LE, B4 6LG, B4 6LJ, B4 6LL, B4 6LR, B4 6NU, B4 6TA, B4 7BA, B4 7BB, B4 7DS;

B6 4DR, B6 4EH, B6 4EJ, B6 4EL, B6 4EN, B6 4EP, B6 4ER, B6 4ES, B6 4ET, B6 4EX, B6 4EY, B6 4EZ, B6 4HA, B6 4HG, B6 4HJ, B6 4HL, B6 4HN, B6 4HP, B6 4HQ, B6 4HT, B6 4HU, B6 4HX, B6 4HZ, B6 4JA, B6 4JB, B6 4JD, B6 4JF, B6 4JG, B6 4JN, B6 4LA, B6 4LD, B6 4LE, B6 4LF, B6 4LH, B6 4LL, B6 4LN, B6 4NG, B6 4NJ, B6 4NL, B6 4NQ, B6 4NR, B6 4NT, B6 4NX, B6 4QT, B6 4QX, B6 4QY, B6 4QZ, B6 4RA, B6 4RB, B6 4RG, B6 4RH, B6 4RJ, B6 4SP, B6 4SX.

East India & Lansbury, Tower Hamlets: 1.068

E14 0BD, E14 0EA, E14 0EB, E14 0ED, E14 0EG, E14 0HH, E14 0HJ, E14 0HP, E14 0NN, E14 0NP, E14 0NR, E14 0NS, E14 0NT, E14 0NU, E14 0NW, E14 0NX, E14 0NY, E14 0PD, E14 0PE, E14 0PF, E14 0PG, E14 0PJ, E14 0PQ, E14 0QA, E14 0QB, E14 0QD, E14 0QJ, E14 0QP, E14 0QR, E14 0QS, E14 0QT, E14 0QU, E14 0QX, E14 0QY, E14 0RB, E14 0SA, E14 0SD, E14 0SE, E14 0SF, E14 0SG, E14 0SH, E14 0SJ, E14 0UB, E14 0UD, E14 0UE, E14 0UF, E14 0UG, E14 0UH, E14 0UJ, E14 0UQ, E14 0UW, E14 0WB, E14 0YQ, E14 3FG, E14 3LZ, E14 3PL, E14 3SL, E14 3WP, E14 3WR, E14 3WS, E14 3WT, E14 3WU, E14 3WX, E14 3WY, E14 3WZ, E14 3XE, E14 3XF, E14 3XN, E14 3XQ, E14 3XR, E14 3XS, E14 3XT, E14 3XW, E14 3XZ, E14 3YA, E14 3YB, E14 3YE, E14 3YF, E14 3YG, E14 3YL, E14 3YP, E14 3YR, E14 3YT, E14 3YU, E14 3YW, E14 3YX, E14 3YZ, E14 3ZD, E14 3ZH, E14 3ZP, E14 3ZQ, E14 4AR, E14 4HZ, E14 4UB, E14 4UE, E14 4UL, E14 4WA, E14 4WJ, E14

4WQ, E14 5BA, E14 5BE, E14 5BN, E14 5BW, E14 5BY, E14 5FB, E14 5FE, E14
5FF, E14 5FG, E14 5FH, E14 5FL, E14 5FP, E14 5FQ, E14 5FR, E14 5FT, E14 5FX,
E14 5FZ, E14 5UA, E14 5UU, E14 5UX, E14 5UY, E14 5WA, E14 5WL, E14 5WP,
E14 5WZ, E14 5XF, E14 5XL, E14 6AA, E14 6AB, E14 6AD, E14 6AE, E14 6AF, E14
6AG, E14 6AH, E14 6AJ, E14 6AL, E14 6AN, E14 6AP, E14 6AQ, E14 6AR, E14
6AS, E14 6AT, E14 6AU, E14 6AW, E14 6AY, E14 6BA, E14 6BD, E14 6BE, E14
6BG, E14 6BH, E14 6BL, E14 6BN, E14 6BP, E14 6BQ, E14 6BS, E14 6BT, E14
6BU, E14 6BW, E14 6BX, E14 6BY, E14 6BZ, E14 6DA, E14 6DB, E14 6DE, E14
6DF, E14 6DG, E14 6DH, E14 6DJ, E14 6DL, E14 6DN, E14 6DP, E14 6DR, E14
6DS, E14 6DT, E14 6DU, E14 6DW, E14 6DX, E14 6DY, E14 6DZ, E14 6EA, E14
6EB, E14 6ED, E14 6EE, E14 6EF, E14 6EG, E14 6EH, E14 6EJ, E14 6EL, E14 6EP,
E14 6EQ, E14 6ER, E14 6ES, E14 6ET, E14 6EU, E14 6EX, E14 6EY, E14 6EZ, E14
6GQ, E14 6GR, E14 6HA, E14 6HB, E14 6HD, E14 6HE, E14 6HF, E14 6HG, E14
6HH, E14 6HJ, E14 6HL, E14 6HN, E14 6HP, E14 6HQ, E14 6HR, E14 6HS, E14
6HT, E14 6HU, E14 6HW, E14 6HX, E14 6JA, E14 6JE, E14 6JF, E14 6JG, E14 6JH,
E14 6JJ, E14 6JL, E14 6JN, E14 6JP, E14 6JR, E14 6JS, E14 6JT, E14 6JW, E14 6JX,
E14 6JY, E14 6LA, E14 6LB, E14 6LD, E14 6LE, E14 6LF, E14 6LG, E14 6LH, E14
6LJ, E14 6LL, E14 6LN, E14 6LP, E14 6LR, E14 6LS, E14 6LT, E14 6LU, E14 6LW,
E14 6LX, E14 6LY, E14 6LZ, E14 6NA, E14 6NB, E14 6ND, E14 6NE, E14 6NF,
E14 6NG, E14 6NL, E14 6NN, E14 6NP, E14 6NS, E14 6NT, E14 6NY, E14 6NZ,
E14 6PF, E14 6PG, E14 6SE, E14 6SH, E14 6SN, E14 6SQ, E14 6SR, E14 6ST, E14
6SU, E14 6SW, E14 6SX, E14 6SY, E14 6SZ, E14 6TA, E14 6TB, E14 6WA, E14
6WB, E14 6WJ, E14 6WP, E14 6WQ, E14 6XA, E14 6XB, E14 6XD, E14 6XF, E14
6XQ, E14 6XZ, E14 6YA, E14 6YN, E14 6YQ, E14 6YZ, E14 6ZQ, E14 7AE, E14
7DB, E14 7DH, E14 7DJ, E14 7DL, E14 7DN, E14 7DR, E14 7DS, E14 7DT, E14
7DU, E14 7DW, E14 7DX, E14 7DY, E14 7DZ, E14 7EA, E14 7EB, E14 7ED, E14
7EE, E14 7EF, E14 7EG, E14 7EP, E14 7EQ, E14 7GD, E14 7GW, E14 7HN, E14
7XB, E14 7XJ, E14 7XS, E14 7XZ, E14 7YB, E14 7YQ, E14 7YZ, E14 8DT, E14
8ED, E14 8ER, E14 8EX, E14 8EZ, E14 8FB, E14 8FD, E14 8FF, E14 8FG, E14
8FH, E14 8FP, E14 8FX, E14 8FY, E14 8FZ, E14 8GA, E14 8GX, E14 8HB, E14 8JA,
E14 8QP, E14 8RF, E14 8XA, E14 8XF, E14 8XH, E14 8XT, E14 8XY, E14 8YB, E14
8YE, E14 8YF, E14 8YG, E14 8YP, E14 8YQ, E14 8YT, E14 8YZ, E14 9AG, E14 9AP,
E14 9AZ, E14 9BF, E14 9BQ, E14 9DA, E14 9DN, E14 9DP, E14 9DX, E14 9DY,
E14 9ED, E14 9ER, E14 9GU, E14 9HH, E14 9HR, E14 9HS, E14 9LE, E14 9LZ,
E14 9NF, E14 9YH, E14 9ZA, E14 9ZE, E14 9ZH, E14 9ZN, E14 9ZQ, E14 9ZR,
E14 9ZT, E14 9ZW, E14 9ZY;

E16 1BX, E16 1JY, E16 1RF, E16 1RG, E16 1RJ, E16 1RP, E16 1RT, E16 1RX, E16
1RY, E16 1XQ, E16 1YB, E16 1YF, E16 1YQ, E16 2EP, E16 2EU, E16 2NT, E16
2UT, E16 2UZ, E16 2WA, E16 2WH, E16 3DG, E16 3EP, E16 3FH, E16 3FJ, E16
3FN, E16 3FP, E16 3FR, E16 3FS, E16 3FT, E16 3FX, E16 3UN, E16 3WD, E16
3WQ, E16 3WU, E16 4FY, E16 4TS, E16 4TZ, E16 4UD, E16 4UE, E16 4UF, E16
4UG, E16 4UH, E16 4UP, E16 4WA, E16 4WB, E16 4WE, E16 4WG, E16 4WL, E16
4WQ;

E3 3DR, E3 3QJ, E3 3QP, E3 3QR, E3 3RE, E3 3RJ, E3 3RN, E3 3RP, E3 3RR, E3
3RS, E3 3RT, E3 3RU, E3 3RX, E3 3RZ, E3 3SP, E3 3SW, E3 4AX, E3 4AY.

1.069 Hutchesontown, Glasgow:

G41 1PS, G41 1PT, G41 1PU, G41 1PX, G41 1PY, G41 1PZ, G41 1QB, G41 1RB,
G41 1RD, G41 1RL, G41 1TL;

G42 7AR, G42 7AS, G42 7AT, G42 7AY, G42 7BE, G42 7BH;

G5 0BL, G5 0BN, G5 0BW, G5 0DL, G5 0DN, G5 0DW, G5 0JP, G5 0JR, G5 0JW,
G5 0LA, G5 0LT, G5 0LU, G5 0NA, G5 0ND, G5 0NE, G5 0NF, G5 0NG, G5 0NH,
G5 0NJ, G5 0NL, G5 0NN, G5 0NP, G5 0NQ, G5 0NR, G5 0NS, G5 0NT, G5 0NU,
G5 0NW, G5 0NY, G5 0NZ, G5 0PA, G5 0PB, G5 0PD, G5 0PH, G5 0PJ, G5 0PL,
G5 0PN, G5 0PP, G5 0PQ, G5 0PR, G5 0PS, G5 0PU, G5 0PW, G5 0PX, G5 0PY, G5
0PZ, G5 0QA, G5 0QB, G5 0QD, G5 0QE, G5 0QF, G5 0QH, G5 0QJ, G5 0QW, G5
0RB, G5 0RG, G5 0RL, G5 0RQ, G5 0SB, G5 0SD, G5 0SE, G5 0SF, G5 0YL, G5
0YP, G5 0YT, G5 0YU, G5 0YX, G5 0YZ, G5 9AP, G5 9AS, G5 9AT, G5 9AU, G5
9BP, G5 9BS, G5 9BT, G5 9BU, G5 9BW, G5 9BX, G5 9BY, G5 9BZ, G5 9DB, G5
9DS, G5 9DW, G5 9EJ, G5 9EP, G5 9ER, G5 9EW, G5 9JE, G5 9JF, G5 9JH, G5 9JJ,
G5 9JL, G5 9LQ, G5 9NE, G5 9NF, G5 9NH, G5 9NL, G5 9NR, G5 9NS, G5 9NT,
G5 9NZ, G5 9PA, G5 9PB, G5 9PD, G5 9PE, G5 9PF, G5 9PS, G5 9QA, G5 9QB,

G5 9QH, G5 9QJ, G5 9QQ, G5 9QS, G5 9QX, G5 9QZ, G5 9RB, G5 9TA, G5 9TS, G5 9TT, G5 9TW, G5 9XA, G5 9XB, G5 9ZR, G5 0JD, G5 0JS.

Parkhead, Glasgow:
1.070
G31 1JX, G31 1JY, G31 1JZ, G31 1LB, G31 1LL, G31 1LQ, G31 1LR, G31 1LZ, G31 1NP, G31 1NQ, G31 1NY, G31 1NZ, G31 1PD, G31 1PG, G31 1PJ, G31 1PQ, G31 3SX, G31 3SY, G31 3SZ, G31 3TH, G31 3TJ, G31 3TL, G31 3 TN, G31 3TW, G31 4BH, G31 4BN, G31 4BT, G31 4DJ, G31 4DN, G31 4DR, G31 4DS, G31 4DX, G31 4EB, G31 4EG, G31 4EH, G31 4EL, G31 4EQ, G31 4EU, G31 4EX, G31 4HB, G31 4HE, G31 4HG, G31 4HL, G31 4HR, G31 4HU, G31 4HX, G31 4HZ, G31 4JU, G31 4JX, G31 4JY, G31 4JZ, G31 4LA, G31 4LD, G31 4LH, G31 4LS, G31 4LT, G31 4LU, G31 4LX, G31 4LY, G31 4LZ, G31 4NA, G31 4NB, G31 4ND, G31 4NE, G31 4NF, G31 4NG, G31 4NH, G31 4NJ, G31 4NL, G31 4NN, G31 4NP, G31 4NQ, G31 4NT, G31 4NW, G31 4PE, G31 4PJ, G31 4PL, G31 4PN, G31 4PP, G31 4PR, G31 4PS, G31 4PT, G31 4PW, G31 4QZ, G31 4ST, G31 4SZ, G31 4TA, G31 4TB, G31 4TF, G31 4TL, G31 4TP, G31 4TR, G31 4TS, G31 4UG, G31 4UH, G31 4UN, G31 4UR, G31 4UT, G31 4UW, G31 4UX, G31 4UY, G31 4UZ, G31 4XA, G31 4XB, G31 4XD, G31 5AD, G31 5AE, G31 5AF, G31 5AL, G31 5AR, G31 5AS, G31 5BA, G31 5BH, G31 5BJ, G31 5BL, G31 5BN, G31 5BS, G31 5BT, G31 5BU, G31 5BW, G31 5BY, G31 5DA, G31 5DB, G31 5DD, G31 5DE, G31 5DF, G31 5DG, G31 5EH, G31 5EL, G31 5ES, G31 5ET, G31 5EU, G31 5EW, G31 5EX, G31 5EY, G31 5HB, G31 5HD, G31 5HE, G31 5HH, G31 5HJ, G31 5HN, G31 5HP, G31 5HW, G31 5JL, G31 5JS, G31 5JT, G31 5JX, G31 5LA, G31 5LB, G31 5LD, G31 5LF, G31 5LG, G31 5LL, G31 5LN, G31 5LP, G31 5LQ, G31 5LR, G31 5LS, G31 5LT, G31 5LU, G31 5LW, G31 5NA, G31 5NG, G31 5NJ, G31 5NR, G31 5NU, G31 5NW, G31 5NX, G31 5NZ, G31 5PN, G31 5PZ, G31 5QG, G31 5QY, G31 5RA, G31 5RB;

G32 6BW, G32 6BX, G32 6DG, G32 6DH, G32 6DJ, G32 6DQ, G32 6DR, G32 6DS, G32 6EH, G32 6EJ, G32 6EL, G32 6EN, G32 6EP, G32 6EQ, G32 6ER, G32 6ES, G32 6ET, G32 6EW, G32 7EA;

G40 3HW.

Thorntree, Middlesbrough:
1.071
TS3 8DN, TS3 8EN, TS3 8EP, TS3 8ER, TS3 8ES, TS3 8ET, TS3 8EU, TS3 8EW, TS3 8HB, TS3 8HD, TS3 8HE, TS3 8HH, TS3 8HJ, TS3 8HL, TS3 8HQ, TS3 8HR, TS3 8HU, TS3 8HZ, TS3 8JA, TS3 8JB, TS3 8JD, TS3 8JE, TS3 8JL, TS3 8JN, TS3 8JP, TS3 8JR, TS3 8JS, TS3 8JT, TS3 8JW, TS3 8JX, TS3 8JY, TS3 8JZ, TS3 8LA, TS3 8LB, TS3 8LD, TS3 8LE, TS3 8LF, TS3 8LG, TS3 8LH, TS3 8LJ, TS3 8LL, TS3 8LN, TS3 8LP, TS3 8LQ, TS3 8LS, TS3 8LT, TS3 8LU, TS3 8LW, TS3 8LX, TS3 8LY, TS3 8LZ, TS3 8NA, TS3 8NB, TS3 8ND, TS3 8NE, TS3 8NF, TS3 8NG, TS3 8NH, TS3 8NL, TS3 8NP, TS3 8NQ, TS3 8PD, TS3 8QD, TS3 8RL, TS3 8YT, TS3 8YU, TS3 8YX, TS3 9AR, TS3 9AT, TS3 9AX, TS3 9AY, TS3 9AZ, TS3 9BA, TS3 9BB, TS3 9BE, TS3 9BG, TS3 9BH, TS3 9BJ, TS3 9BL, TS3 9BN, TS3 9BP, TS3 9BQ, TS3 9BS, TS3 9BT, TS3 9BU, TS3 9BW, TS3 9BX, TS3 9BY, TS3 9BZ, TS3 9DA, TS3 9DB, TS3 9DD, TS3 9DE, TS3 9DF, TS3 9DP, TS3 9DS, TS3 9DT, TS3 9DU, TS3 9DW, TS3 9DX, TS3 9DY, TS3 9DZ, TS3 9EA, TS3 9ED, TS3 9EE, TS3 9EF, TS3 9EG, TS3 9EH, TS3 9EJ, TS3 9EL, TS3 9EN, TS3 9EP, TS3 9EQ, TS3 9ER, TS3 9ES, TS3 9ET, TS3 9EU, TS3 9EW, TS3 9EZ, TS3 9HA, TS3 9HB, TS3 9HD, TS3 9HE, TS3 9HF, TS3 9HG, TS3 9HH, TS3 9HJ, TS3 9HL, TS3 9HN, TS3 9HP, TS3 9HQ, TS3 9HR, TS3 9HS, TS3 9HT, TS3 9HU, TS3 9HW, TS3 9HX, TS3 9HY, TS3 9HZ, TS3 9JA, TS3 9JB, TS3 9JD, TS3 9JE, TS3 9JF, TS3 9JG, TS3 9JH, TS3 9JJ, TS3 9JL, TS3 9JN, TS3 9JP, TS3 9JQ, TS3 9JR, TS3 9JS, TS3 9JT, TS3 9JU, TS3 9JW, TS3 9JX, TS3 9JY, TS3 9JZ, TS3 9LA, TS3 9LB, TS3 9LD, TS3 9LE, TS3 9LF, TS3 9LG, TS3 9LH, TS3 9LJ, TS3 9LL, TS3 9LN, TS3 9LP, TS3 9LQ, TS3 9LU, TS3 9LW, TS3 9LX, TS3 9LY, TS3 9NA, TS3 9NB, TS3 9ND, TS3 9NE, TS3 9NF, TS3 9NG ,TS3 9NH, TS3 9NJ, TS3 9NL, TS3 9NN, TS3 9NP, TS3 9NQ, TS3 9NS, TS3 9NT, TS3 9NW, TS3 9NX, TS3 9PA, TS3 9PD, TS3 9PL, TS3 9PS, TS3 9PT, TS3 9PU, TS3 9PX, TS3 9PZ, TS3 9QA, TS3 9QB, TS3 9QD, TS3 9QE, TS3 9QH, TS3 9QL, TS3 9QN, TS3 9QP, TS3 9QW, TS3 9RA, TS3 9RB, TS3 9RD, TS3 9RE, TS3 9RF, TS3 9RG, TS3 9RH, TS3 9RJ, TS3 9RL, TS3 9RN, TS3 9RP, TS3 9RQ, TS3 9RR, TS3 9RW, TS3 9WZ, TS3 9YW, TS3 9YX, TS3 9YZ.

Tax Credits (Provision of Information) (Evaluation and Statistical Studies) (Northern Ireland) Regulations 2004

(S.I. 2004 No. 1414)

Made	*24th May 2004*
Laid before Parliament	*24th May 2004*
Coming into force	*14th June 2004*

The Commissioners of Inland Revenue, in exercise of the powers conferred upon them by sections 65(2) and 67 of, and paragraph 4(2) of Schedule 5 to, the Tax Credits Act 2002 make the following Regulations:

Citation, commencement and extent

1.072   **1.** These Regulations may be cited as the Tax Credits (Provision of Information) (Evaluation and Statistical Studies) (Northern Ireland) Regulations 2004, shall come into force on 14th June 2004 and extend only to Northern Ireland.

Purposes for which information may be provided

1.073   **2.** The purposes of conducting evaluation and statistical studies about community relations, education and employment of persons in Northern Ireland under the age of 18, are prescribed under paragraph 4 of Schedule 5 to the Tax Credits Act 2002 (provision of information by the Board of Inland Revenue for evaluation and statistical studies).

Tax Credits (Provision of Information) (Functions Relating to Health) (Scotland) Regulations 2004

(S.I. 2004 No. 1895 (S.6))

Made	*20th July 2004*
Laid before Parliament	*21st July 2004*
Coming into force	*11th August 2004*

The Commissioners of Inland Revenue, in exercise of the powers conferred upon them by sections 65(2) and 67 of, and paragraph 9 of Schedule 5 to, the Tax Credits Act 2002, make the following Regulations:

Citation, commencement and extent

1. These Regulations may be cited as the Tax Credits (Provision of Information) (Functions Relating to Health) (Scotland) Regulations 2004, shall come into force on 11th August 2004 and extend only to Scotland.   1.074

Purpose for which information may be provided

2.—(1) The purpose of conducting surveys of the health of children and young people under the age of 17 and their families, by the Scottish Ministers or persons providing services to them, or exercising functions on behalf of them, is prescribed under paragraph 9 of Schedule 5 to the Tax Credits Act 2002 (provision of information by the Board of Inland Revenue for health purposes).   1.075

(2) Nothing in these Regulations affects the operation of the Tax Credits (Provision of Information) (Functions Relating to Health) Regulations 2003 or the Tax Credits (Provision of Information) (Functions Relating to Health) (No. 2) Regulations 2003.

PART II

UPDATING MATERIAL
VOLUME I

NON-MEANS TESTED BENEFITS

pp.56–57, *annotation to Social Security Contributions and Benefits Act 1992, s.30DD (incapacity benefit: reduction for pension payments*

CIB/683/2003 has been reported as *R(IB) 1/04.*   2.001

p.58, *annotation to Social Security Contributions and Benefits Act 1992, s.30E (incapacity benefit: reduction for councillor's allowance)*

With effect from October 1, 2004, the prescribed amount is £78.00   2.002
(see update to p.664, below).

p.67, *annotation to Social Security Contributions and Benefits Act 1992, s.38: widow's pension*

The decision in *CG/1467/2001* has been reported as *R(G) 2/04.*   2.003

p.71, *annotation to Social Security Contributions and Benefits Act 1992, s.39C: requirement of marriage for bereavement benefits*

In *R(G) 1/04* a claim to bereavement benefits was made by a woman   2.004
following the death of her long-term partner. Her claim was made firstly
on the ground that there should be a marriage presumed after long-term
cohabitation or, alternatively, that the words of ss.36 to 38 should be
construed in the light of the Human Rights Act to extend to such a
common law marriage. The Commissioner rejected both arguments.
There could be no room for presumption of marriage where the parties
had expressly decided against marrying. Nor was it necessary to construe
the Benefits Act in accordance with the Human Rights Act because the
decision refusing benefit, and now under appeal, was made before that
Act came into force. Even if it had been necessary to so construe the
Benefits Act it would be impossible to read those words in any way other
than to require there to have been a valid marriage. Finally, it would not
have been open to the Commissioner to make a declaration of incompatibility and in any case the *Shackell* case showed that there was no
discrimination in the different treatment of married and unmarried
couples.

p.77, *annotation to Social Security Contributions and Benefits Act 1992, ss.36–39C: effect of Forfeiture Act 1982 on entitlement to benefits consequent on death of spouse*

In *R(FG) 1/04* the claimant had been convicted of soliciting her   2.005
husband's murder (an offence under the Offences Against the Person
Act, 1861). She claimed a widow's pension after her release from prison.
The Commissioner held that the forfeiture rule applied to her claim
because she had "unlawfully counselled" her husband's death within
s.1(2) of the Forfeiture Act 1982, but that it was not caught by s.5 of that
Act which proscribed any relief where the claimant was convicted of
murder. This meant that it was open to the Commissioner to modify the
effect of forfeiture. On the facts of this case however, he held that no

modification was appropriate because she had been closely and directly involved in the murder.

pp.88–91, *annotation to Social Security Contributions and Benefits Act 1992, s.44: effect of a guaranteed minimum pension under Pension Schemes Act 1993*

2.006   A Category A retirement pension consists of two elements; basic pension under subs.(3)(a) and an additional pension under subs.(3)(b). Claimants who at some time had pensions based upon a contracted out provision (introduced originally under the Social Security Pensions Act 1975) will be entitled to a guaranteed minimum pension (GMP) under that scheme. Where a person is entitled to both a retirement pension and a GMP there is provision for offsetting, under subs.3(b), the amount of either the GMP, or the amount of the additional pension for certain years, whichever is the less. This provision is found in Pension Schemes Act 1993, s.46 and see the notes following that section.

pp.96–97, *annotation to Social Security Contributions and Benefits Act 1992, s.47(3): effect of a guaranteed minimum pension on entitlement to retirement pension*

2.007   Note that under s.46 of the Pensions Schemes Act 1993, the amount of any retirement pension is reduced by the guaranteed minimum pension to which the claimant may be entitled. See notes to that section.

pp.137, *annotation to Social Security Contributions and Benefits Act 1992, s.72*

2.008   The decision of the Court of Appeal recorded at [2004] EWCA Civ. 16, has now been reported as *R(DLA) 1/04.*

p.138, *annotation to Social Security Contributions and Benefits Act 1992, s.72*

2.009   The first reference to *R(DLA) 10/02* should be amended to read *R(DLA) 9/02.*

p.155, *annotation to Social Security Contributions and Benefits Act 1992, s.72: the cooking test*

2.010   The use of a microwave oven as an ordinary means of cooking food that has been prepared by the claimant, rather than as a means of reheating meals prepared by others, has been accepted in *CDLA/ 2367/2004.*

In *CDLA/1471/2004,* Commissioner Jacobs had to consider whether a risk of self-harming could cause the claimant to be unable to cook a main meal for himself, presumably because he could not be trusted to be in possession of sharp knives or, possibly, to have access to hot surfaces. An argument was put on behalf of the Secretary of State that, as the cooking test was of an hypothetical ability to cook, it was sufficient that the claimant could have been able to cook were he able to have the means to do so. The Commissioner rejects this argument. The test, he says, was hypothetical only in the sense that the claimant's need to cook, or his inclination to do so, were irrelevant in determining his ability to cook a main meal. In other words anything that derives from the claimant's mental or physical condition and prevents him from cooking can be a disability for this purpose and that includes the safety risk arising from a propensity for self-harm.

This decision is in conflict with that of Commissioner May in *CSDLA/ 854/2003*. There, the claimant had alleged that he was unable to cook because he suffered nausea when either preparing or even eating cooked food. The Tribunal rejected his claim because they did not believe his evidence and his appeal to the Commissioners failed too because they had made no error of law in rejecting evidence that they had found to be implausible. However, the interest in the case lies in the question raised by the Commissioner (and referred to the parties for their comment) as to whether, had his evidence been accepted, it would have qualified him under s.72. In this case the Commissioner accepted an argument from the Secretary of State that, in accordance with the *Moyna* decision, the test is of the claimant's hypothetical ability to cook only: "a thought experiment to calibrate the severity of the disability". In Commissioner May's view this meant a test of capacity to do the job, and a feeling of nausea, while unpleasant, did not, in his view, make the claimant incapable of cooking.

While these cases may be reconciled (in the first the claimant could   2.011
not be permitted to approach the task of cooking safely, in the second the nausea was assumed to be only a matter of suffering some unpleasantness) there is clearly further ground to be explored—what if the nausea were so extreme as to make the claimant unwell, or what if the smells of cooking induced an attack of asthma—presumably then the illness or the asthma would be the disability.

An inability to concentrate sufficiently to accomplish cooking tasks safely has been accepted, at least in principal, to be sufficient in *CSDLA/ 430/2004*.

pp.156–160, *annotation to Social Security Contributions and Benefits Act 1992, s.72(1): meaning of "frequent throughout the day" and "prolonged or repeated" at night*

In *CDLA/492/2004* Judge G. R. Hickinbottom, the Chief Commis-   2.012
sioner, has carried the approach to interpretation that was set by the House of Lords in *Moyna* across to the rest of the criteria for qualification for DLA care component in s.72(1). This means, he says, that decision makers and tribunals must take a broad view of the matter, reading the words of the section in their context so as to identify the correct legal test and then deciding each case as a question of fact according to whether it falls on one side of that line of the other. Thereafter, an appeal on points of law could only interfere with their

decision if either they have identified the wrong legal line or if they have reached a conclusion which is "outside the bounds of reasonable judgment", *i.e.* irrational.

Judge Hickinbottom goes on to point out that the oft quoted guidance taken from the judgment of Lord Denning in *R. v National Insurance Commissioner Ex p. Secretary of State for Social Services* [1981] 1 W.L.R. 1017, on the meaning of these phrases, was not only *obiter*, but was only a limited attempt to identify some fairly obvious characteristics of the words used, and must not be regarded as providing anything like definitions—as he suggests commentators appear to have done. He also takes to task certain Commissioners for attempting to paraphrase the sections in alternative words to explain their meaning.

The test of "frequently throughout the day", he suggests, is not to be approached in two stages—how often and over what period—but is to be treated as a single composite impression. Again, frequency is not just a question of number, but may be affected by the nature and duration of the occurrences, thus disagreeing with Commissioner Parker in *CSDLA/590/2000*. By way of example he contrasts the meaning of frequent when used in relation to an ice age with its use in relation to a train timetable; or again, a long distance train service every hour might be regarded as frequent when an hourly local service was not. As well, he points out that, although the scheme of s.72(1) is not necessarily one of gradation, in as much as the qualifying conditions in each of the three paragraphs are quite distinct and different, the context requires a recognition that Parliament can hardly have intended that a claimant should qualify for the middle-rate benefit on a lesser requirement for care than was necessary to gain the lowest rate of benefit.

2.013   All of this makes good sense. But it may make things difficult for tribunals for two reasons. First, tribunals must give reasons to support their decision. Often, an attempt to explain a decision will consist of rephrasing the statute to explain the line the tribunal is taking. If tribunals are not to rephrase the section to explain what they take to be its meaning, will it suffice for a tribunal to say, *e.g.* "we find this to be frequent attention because we think it is"? Secondly, decisions that are treated as findings of fact and appealable to a Commissioner only when they are grossly unreasonable may result in inequitable chaos. For example, in one of the cases that was considered in this appeal the Judge concluded, as had the tribunal, that an epileptic claimant who regularly required attention, at night, once or twice a week for up to 20 minutes on each occasion, did not satisfy the test of requiring "prolonged attention" throughout the period of his claim. Taking a broad view of the matter, and in particular the length of the fits and the pattern on an unpredictable but regular basis, he concluded that the claimant's need did not constitute prolonged attention throughout the relevant period. But what if a more generously inclined tribunal on a similar case were to conclude that it did? Would that be so unreasonable as to be appealable? (It could not be said to be out of line with the treatment of a lowest-rate claimant because the drafting of the section envisages that night-time care will be treated differently.) But if it is not appealable, then will it not be inequitable for the first claimant?

p.159, *annotation to Social Security Contributions and Benefits Act 1992, s.72: meaning of "night"*

The decision in *CSA/322/2003* is now reported as *R(A) 1/04.*   2.014

p.160, *annotation to Social Security Contributions and Benefits Act 1992, s.72*

The decision in *CDLA/3324/2001* has been reported as *R(DLA)*   2.015
11/02.

p.161, *annotation to Social Security Contributions and Benefits Act 1992, s.72(4)*

A claimant who qualifies for the lowest rate of care component as well   2.016
as the middle rate can be paid only at the middle rate. This is illustrated
by the decision in *CDLA/2495/2004.*

p.162, *annotation to Social Security Contributions and Benefits Act 1992, s.72(b): attention and supervision of a disabled child, decision CDLA/3737/2002*

An appeal against this decision was dismissed by the Court of Appeal   2.017
and is now reported as *R(DLA) 1/04.* The Secretary of State argued,
inter alia, that the time spent by a teacher at school with a pupil could not
be regarded as attention for the purposes of s.72. The Court refused to
enter into the merits of this argument because that ground of appeal had
not been put before the Commissioner, despite his having given a provisional indication of his thinking before reaching his final decision. The
Court of Appeal did suggest that the fact that this point had not been
fully argued before the Commissioner might detract from the value of his
decision as a precedent. We may well look forward to a further test case,
or to statutory amendment. The Court of Appeal also took the opportunity to remind us (and themselves) of the need for caution when the
ordinary courts enter upon a field where the process of adjudication
(including two levels of appeal) has been entrusted to a specialist
system.

p.162, *annotation to Social Security Contributions and Benefits Act 1992, s.72(6)*

Where a claim is made on behalf of a child, and it is based on the care   2.018
and attention necessary to clean and wash as a result of the child not
having developed control over their bowel or bladder, it may seem that
the most obvious question is whether the child satisfies the requirement
set in subs.(6) namely, is that attention substantially in excess of the
normal requirements for a child of his age. But, as has been pointed out
in *CSDLA/555/01,* and now again in *CDLA/4149/2003,* there is another
question that needs to be decided first—is there evidence that the child's
condition is the result of any physical or mental disability? The fact that
a child is late in developing control of the bowels, etc. is not, in itself,

evidence of disability, and nocturnal enuresis may continue in a normal child for several years. In this case a claim for a child of six failed because the evidence did not necessarily show a disability even though she wet and sometimes fouled herself on most nights of the week. But the Commissioner did add that as she grew older a continuing failure to develop control might become some evidence of disability that might then be supported by medical evidence.

p.167, *annotation to Social Security Contributions and Benefits Act 1992, s.73(1)(d): meaning of guidance and supervision*

2.019   In *R(DLA) 3/04* Commissioner Rowland considered the case of a claimant who, because of her state of anxiety and depression, suffered severe panic attacks if she tried to walk out on her own. She could only walk for any significant distance if she was accompanied by one of her family who would provide continuous reassurance and encouragement. The Commissioner held that this level of support could constitute guidance and supervision. He went on to hold that her claim was not precluded by reg.12(7) of the Disability Living Allowance Regulations because her state of anxiety was a symptom of a mental disability provided for under reg.12(8).

pp.188–189, *annotation to Social Security Contributions and Benefits Act 1992, s.83: pension increase (wife)*

2.020   For a decision on the computation of earnings in respect of a wife for whom an increase of retirement pension had been claimed, see *CP/3017/2004*. This decision is summarised in detail in relation to reg.9 of the Computation of Earnings Regulations.

pp.343–345, *annotation to Pensions Schemes Act 1993, s.46: effect of guaranteed minimum pension on payment of retirement pension*

2.021   The complexities arising from the calculations of benefit entitlement under s.46, and of the appeal structure to be followed in connection with such entitlement, are explored and explained by Commissioner Williams in *R(P) 1/04.*
    The claimant was entitled to a guaranteed minimum pension (GMP). Under s.46 his state retirement pension was reduced by the amount of his GMP, but responsibility for calculation of GMP, and any appeal consequent thereon was the responsibility of the Inland Revenue. The Commissioner explains that to decide any appeal against the determination of a claim for state retirement pension, a tribunal must first ascertain what amount has been determined to be due for the GMP. Unless that sum has been formally notified to the claimant, and any appeal that he makes to the Board has been disposed of, the Secretary of State for Work & Pensions, and hence any, tribunal hearing an appeal from his decision, cannot proceed with the calculation of his relevant pension. Although it was unnecessary to do so in this appeal, the Commissioner also decided (at the invitation of the parties) that where a claimant is entitled to more than one GMP the function of the Inland Revenue is only to calculate

the amount of each individual pension and communicate those to the DWP. It remains the function of Secretary of State there, to aggregate those sums once he is satisfied that they qualify as GMP pensions, and then calculate the resulting entitlement to retirement pension. Any Tribunal faced with one of these appeals will benefit from reading this decision and the appendices attached.

The operation of the section has been further explored by Commissioner Mesher in *CP/1318/2001*. There, the claimant had argued for the offsetting of the GMP from his retirement pension to be limited to the amount of GMP earned in the years for which he had been contracted out for earnings-related pension and to exclude the effect of any offsetting on the additional pension earned when contracted in. He said that promises made by the Government spokesman at the time of the introduction of SERPS in 1975 compelled this interpretation of the legislation. The Commissioner rejected his argument. The meaning of the legislation, he said, was clear: it required the offsetting to be against the whole of the retirement pension payable including the additional pension earned in years when the claimant was contracted in. This case (and *CP/1412/2002*, heard with it) deals also with the application of subs.(3) of this section, where the claimant is entitled also to transitional invalidity allowance surviving from the shift to incapacity benefit in 1995. The provisions in this case require that the entitlement to GMP be deducted as well from the amount of any such invalidity allowance. What at first seemed to the Commissioner to be an instance of double recovery turned out, upon tracing the history of the matter, to have been in accordance with the purpose of the legislation and, therefore the correct interpretation to be applied.

A demonstration of how a claimant's entitlement to additional pension **2.022** could be swallowed entirely by the offsetting procedure is provided by *CP/281/2002*. In this case the claimant, who retired early, had asked for and received, a forecast of his pension entitlement more than three years before his claim could be made. The forecast showed a possible entitlement to additional pension of £3.34, but by the time his claim was made his GMP had increased significantly and was now more than the additional pension to which he was entitled. Although the claimant's total pension was now slightly more than the forecast, the additional pension payable was nil since a deduction of the lesser sum (his additional pension) from his additional pension left precisely nothing. The claimant had appealed because he thought he had been robbed of an amount that the forecast had said was already earned. The appeal was dismissed.

The case also demonstrates a point made by Commissioner Mesher in the case above, (having been raised originally in *R(P) 1/04*), that the GMP can never reduce the amount of basic pension because it is only the lesser of the two sums that is deducted. The maximum deduction is therefore never more than the amount of the additional pension.

pp.418–420, *annotation to Computation of Earnings Regulations 1996, reg.4: notional earnings*

CIB/1650/2002 is now reported as *R(IB) 7/03*.   **2.023**

pp.424–426, *annotation to Computation of Earnings Regulations 1996, reg. 9: earnings of employed earners*

2.024   The claimant in *CP/3017/2004* had made an advance claim for an increase of his retirement pension in respect of his wife. She had earnings and the decision-maker had determined that these were in excess of the specified figure with the result that the claimant had no entitlement to the increase. The appeal tribunal confirmed the decision, but the Commissioner found that they had erred in law and substituted his own decision awarding the increase. The claimant's wife worked as a sales promoter of a variety of goods in supermarkets. She made the planning arrangements for promotional visits to the supermarkets from home and attended at supermarkets in the region to ensure the successful operation of the promotion. She received expenses relating to travel (including travel from home), maintenance of her car and car parking. The Commissioner concluded that, in the particular circumstances of this case, the expenses were to be excluded from the calculation of the earnings of the claimant's wife under reg.9(3), which trumped the provisions in reg.9(1)(f)(i).

pp.451–453, *annotation to the Dependency Regulations 1977, reg. 8: earnings rules for increases for adult dependants*

2.025   In *CP/3017/2004* the Commissioner said:

"6. Before going on to mention the legislative provisions that set out rules for calculating earnings for the purposes of benefits including retirement pension, there is one oddity arising from regulation 8(2) of the Dependency Regulations to be examined. Regulation 8(2) lays down a test to be applied week by week for each week of payment of retirement pension (see the definition in regulation 8(7)(a)), which test depends on the spouse's earnings in the previous week. The application of a week by week test seems to be reinforced by section 92 of the Social Security Contributions and Benefits Act 1992, which applies where an award of an increase has been made and causes the award to continue in force even though entitlement is interrupted by a week or weeks in which the spouse's earnings exceed the limit. In the present case, the first week of payment of retirement pension to the claimant would have been that beginning on Monday 31 May 2004. It might be said that at the date of the decision in question there could have been absolutely no evidence of what the wife's earnings would be in the week commencing Monday 24 May 2004 or in any subsequent week. How therefore could a decision be given disallowing an increase?

7. The main answer stems from regulation 15(1) of the Claims and Payments Regulations and the decision of the Tribunal of Commissioners in *CDLA/2751/2003* and others, about advance renewal claims for disability living allowance (DLA). It was held there that the legislative power to make an award of DLA in advance of the start date of the period of the award carried with it the power to disallow the claim in advance. The same must also apply to regulation 15(1), so that

there is a power to disallow a claim for an increase of retirement pension for a wife up to four months before a claimant might become entitled to the pension. Then, in accordance with section 8(2) of the Social Security Act 1998 as explained by the Tribunal of Commissioners, in making such a decision the Secretary of State would be prohibited from taking into account any changes of circumstances anticipated to occur after the date of the decision. Equally, on appeal, an appeal tribunal would be prohibited from taking into account any actual changes of circumstances after that date (Social Security Act 1998, section 12(8)(b)). The Tribunal of Commissioners seems to have thought that if there was change of circumstances in favour of a claimant between the date of the decision and the date from which the disallowance of the claim took effect, there could be a supersession on the ground of relevant change of circumstances (Social Security and Child Support (Decisions and Appeals) Regulations 1999, regulation 6(2)(a)(i)). However, there is a problem with that view because regulation 6(2)(a)(i), as amended with effect from 5 May 2003, allows supersession only where there has been a relevant change of circumstances since the decision to be superseded "had effect". That seems to rule out a supersession for a change occurring between the date of an advance decision and its effective date. A claimant would thus be restricted to making a fresh claim, on the basis of the changed circumstances, from some date after the effective date of the disallowing decision.

8. In paragraph 24 of *CDLA/2751/2003* and others, the Tribunal of Commissioners did suggest that, in some cases where there was likely to be a significant change of circumstances before the start date of the period covered by a claim, it might well be good practice to defer making a decision until it was known whether that change had actually materialised. It seems to me that the present case is one where that course should have been taken. It was plain from the evidence provided that the claimant's wife's earnings fluctuated a great deal from one pay period to another. And the nature of the case is different from that of a person suffering some potentially disabling or incapacitating condition, where in most cases there can be a sensible prediction about how the condition might progress in the future. It was simply unknown on 3 March 2004 what the claimant's wife's earnings might be in the week prior to 31 May 2004. Quite apart from the doubts that I explain below about the averaging process carried out by the officer, it would have been better to have waited until close to 28 May 2004 and then considered the current evidence about the wife's earnings. I do not think that there would have been any difficulty in making an advance decision on the claimant's own retirement pension entitlement, but deferring the decision on the increase. However, that did not happen. A decision disallowing the increase was made on 3 March 2004 and I must deal with the consequences."

In para.21 of his decision, the Commissioner concluded: 2.026

"21. If I adopt the same method as the officer who made the decision of 3 March 2004 and take an average of the seven payslips, counting only the taxable pay, the result is £32.59 per week. With the addition of the weekly amount of the wife's occupational pension, the total earnings are well below the limit in regulation 8(2) of the Dependency Regulations. I have doubts about the use of averaging under regulation 8(3) of the Computation of Earnings Regulations. That provision allows averaging over a recognisable cycle of work or some other period that will allow average weekly earnings to be identified more accurately. But, for the reasons given in paragraph 6 above, the Dependency Regulations may properly work on the amount of actual earnings received week by week (with payments received at other intervals spread according to the rules in regulation 8(1) and (2) of the Computation of Earnings Regulations). If so, the use of an average figure might not be appropriate at all. But I do not have to decide the issue. I have already shown that the result of averaging under regulation 8(3) is in favour of the claimant. If I do not apply regulation 8(3), the circumstances as at 3 March 2004 were that, for six of the payments in evidence, the weekly equivalent of the earnings received was below the limit, usually well below. It was only in respect of the payment received on 14 December 2003 that the weekly equivalent (£98) was over the limit. There might well have been unusual circumstances in the run-up to Christmas. Looking at that evidence, and not knowing what earnings had been received immediately before 3 March 2004, I have no difficulty in concluding that the level of the wife's earnings to be taken into account in respect of the period from 28 May 2004 onwards is below the limit in regulation 8(2) of the Dependency Regulations. Thus, on either approach, the claimant's appeal succeeds and he is to be awarded the increase of retirement pension."

pp.499–506, *annotation to Persons Abroad Regulations 1975, reg.2: modification of the Act in relation to incapacity benefit, severe disablement allowance, unemployability supplement and maternity allowance*

2.027   *CDLA/2089/2004* concerned the interpretation of differently worded reg.2(2)(d) and (e) of the Disability Living Allowance Regulations on temporary absence from Great Britain, but the point the Commissioner makes may well have relevance when the provisions of this regulation are considered. The Commissioner rules that the continuation of benefit payment is based on two facts: first, that the absence from Great Britain must be for a temporary purpose, and secondly, that the absence has not lasted for more than 26 weeks. The period of 26 weeks does not define the word "temporary"; it merely limits to a maximum of 26 weeks the period during which benefit can remain in payment if the absence is temporary (provided that any other conditions set out in the regulations are satisfied).

p.539, *Attendance Allowance Regulations 1991, reg.7: omission of paras 3 and 4*

2.028   The text of this regulation should be amended by omitting paras (3) and (4). This amendment was effected by reg.2(2)(b) of the Social

Security (Attendance Allowance and Disability Living Allowance) (Amendment) Regulations 2003 (SI 2003/2259) with effect from October 6, 2003.

pp.540–541, *annotation to Attendance Allowance Regulations 1991, regs 7 and 8: disqualification where claimant is in certain accommodation*

The treatment of a claimant for whom the cost of accommodation is being met by a Local Authority on a temporary basis and subject to repayment by the claimant, was considered again in *CDLA/5106/2001*. In this case the cost of the accommodation was met initially by the Local Authority, but first a contribution was required, and then an obligation to repay in full under s.22 of the 1948 Act. By the time of the hearing, full repayment had been made. Commissioner Turnbull, nevertheless, held that she was disqualified from receiving benefit because her accommodation was provided in accordance with reg.7(1)(a) and the claimant was not exempted by reg.8(6)(b) until she ceased to be entitled to Income Support because she was not, until then, meeting the whole of the cost of accommodation from her own resources. Although the Commissioner makes no reference to *R(A) 1/02*, his decision accords with that case because there, too, the claimant was disqualified for part of the period in question because she was then in receipt of Income Support. It does not appear that in either case an argument was made that the claimant's entitlement to Income Support should be regarded as a part of her own resources. 2.029

p.548, *annotation to Disability Living Allowance Regulations 1991, reg.2(2)(d)*

The meaning of para.(2)(d) is explained in *CDLA/2089/2004*. To retain entitlement to benefit, at least for a time when abroad, the claimant must show that their absence is temporary and that it lasts for less than six months. But these are separate requirements. Absence for more than six months does not meant that the claimant's absence was not temporary. The six-month limitation operates as a separate disqualification beyond which benefit will not be paid even though the absence was at its inception, and may remain, temporary. 2.030

p.557, *annotation to Disability Living Allowance Regulations 1991, reg.9(1)(b)*

In *CDLA/870/2004* (to be reported as *R(DLA) 6/04*) the claimant was accommodated on week days in residential accommodation run by the local authority. This accommodation was provided under the Mental Health Act 1983. The Commissioner holds that the situation is covered by sub-para.(b) of reg.9(1). The Mental Health Act 1983 is not mentioned specifically in sub-para.(a), nor is it listed in the DM guidance, but s.117 of that Act requires the local authority in exercise of its social 2.031

services function to provide after-care for persons who are under supervision. The question to be answered therefore was whether persons released from hospital, but still receiving after-care under supervision, are persons under a disability within the meaning of reg.9. The Commissioner had no doubt that they were.

p.565, *annotation to Disability Living Allowance Regulations 1991, reg.12*

2.032   The reference to *CDLA/3223/2003* should be amended to read *CDLA/3323/2003*.

In this decision Commissioner Rowland considered the case of a claimant who suffered an accident injuring his back and resulting in him being unable to walk. By the time of the claim, however, the medical examination showed no continuing lesion of the back and the medical report concluded that the inability to walk was entirely psychosomatic. The doctors agreed that the claimant was not malingering. The Commissioner found that his inability to walk was a manifestation of his physical condition as a whole and that it mattered not that the cause of that physical condition was itself mental rather than physical. In his view (in which he was following a view expressed by Commissioner Walker in *CSDLA/265/1997*) the purpose of confining an inability to walk to a physical and not a mental condition was to exclude claims by those suffering from agoraphobia, depression, etc. when they might be able to walk but be unwilling to do so. In his view there could be no purpose in Parliament, having intended to provide a benefit for people unable to walk, excluding claimants like the present who could not make their legs work.

The other decision referred to in the main volume was *CDLA/3612/2003*. In this case Commissioner Parker reached the opposite conclusion to that above. The claimant suffered from a number of conditions, but none of them should have affected her ability to walk. The tribunal that heard her case concluded that her "perceptions of pain and inability to function were genuinely held by her," but they accepted the evidence of the EMP that her problems with walking were psychological rather than physical. They rejected her claim and their decision was upheld by the Commissioner. Commissioner Parker made a thorough examination of the decisions from *Harrison* (*R(M) 1/88*) to the present and reasserts the requirement that the inability to walk must be caused by, or at least derive from, some physical condition. This area is now to be considered by a Tribunal of Commissioners in *CDLA/2789/2004* and *CDLA/2899/2004*.

p.569, *annotation to Disability Living Allowance Regulations 1991, reg.12*

2.033   The decision in *CDLA/2139/2003* has now been reported as *R(DLA) 4/04*.

In this decision Commissioner Bano held that a claimant who suffered pain all of the time, and whose pain was not made worse by attempting to walk, could still qualify if it was the pain that made it impossible or difficult for the claimant to walk.

pp.569–570, *annotation to Disability Living Allowance Regulations 1991, reg.12: the could not/would not walk test*

The distinction that was drawn by the Tribunal of Commissioners in   2.034
R(M) 3/86 between a claimant (in most cases of this sort, a child) who could not walk and a claimant who would not walk was based upon the simple question of whether such a person could be made to move by coaxing or by bribery. The Commissioners' conclusion was that if the child could be persuaded to move, it followed that the disablement was a matter of volition and could not then be the result of his physical condition.

A series of subsequent cases have questioned this conclusion. They are summarised, and the counter-argument put most powerfully, in *CDLA/ 4565/2003* by Deputy Commissioner McGavin. There a child suffered from Williams syndrome, a rare condition that caused both learning difficulties and behavioural problems as well as some physical symptoms. But like some claimants suffering from Downs Syndrome, autism and brain damage, though she could walk in a physical sense, she might then sit or lie down, and might become aggressive if her wishes were thwarted.

The Commissioner points out that in the case of claimants such as these, to describe their behaviour as simply that of a naughty child (as the can't walk/won't walk test would seem to compel him to do) flies in the face of all the medical evidence provided and of the combined experience of the claimants' carers. As the Commissioner in *CM/98/1989* (a case concerning the claim of an 18-year-old man with brain damage) put the matter:

> "If . . . the relevant behavioural problems have nothing to do with physical damage what do they derive from? In the case of this 18-year-old are the tribunal suggesting that his behaviour was that of a naughty child who just would not walk when required? And, if they were, is not the fact that a brain damaged 18-year-old behaves like a child something to do with the brain damage?"

In the present case the Commissioner suggests that a tribunal should not conclude that a claimant who can be persuaded to move must be regarded as capable of walking, but instead should look at the medical evidence from which they might conclude that the refusal to walk was still a consequence of the malfunctioning of the brain, rather than simply wilful naughtiness. If so, then a refusal to walk that was frequent, sustained and not easily overcome could still constitute an inability to walk.

pp.572–574, *annotation to Disability Living Allowance Regulations 1991, reg.12*

The difficulty experienced by a claimant seeking the higher rate of   2.035
mobility component under paras (5) and (6) is further demonstrated by Commissioner Williams in *CDLA/1545/2004*. This case concerned a

claimant suffering from Tourettes syndrome. The claimant had originally been allowed both the higher rate of care component and the higher rate of mobility. This appeal was from a renewal decision in which he had been allowed the highest rate of care, but only the lower rate of mobility. The appeal was allowed because, in the view of the Commissioner the tribunal had failed to explain why they were deciding against him with regard to mobility on the current claim, when the claimant's condition had not been found to have changed. (See the decision of Commissioner Howell in *R(M) 1/96* as to the need for a DM to make clear why a different conclusion had been reached on the renewal claim.) The Commissioner in this case makes a useful review of the decisions on these paragraphs so far, and concludes that the appeal should be sent back to a fresh tribunal for them to consider the medical evidence as to whether the requirements of reg.12(5) were satisfied. The evidence for the decision currently under appeal was unclear—the consultant confirmed moderate learning difficulties, but said they were of "non specific cause" going on to refer to Tourettes syndrome and mental health problems. The same or similar evidence had been accepted as qualifying the claimant by a DM on the original claim. The Commissioner thought the tribunal should have at least considered the earlier evidence to explain why the current decision was different, and that, if the evidence was unclear, perhaps they should have asked for a further opinion. On para.(6) the medical evidence was equally ambivalent. The consultant firstly answered yes to the question did the claimant require regular restraint but, in expanding upon that answer, appeared to be saying no, only to be followed by further information that might have confirmed the first impression. This last information was that the claimant was responding well to a strategy of enhanced supervision by two care helpers. The Commissioner thought that the new tribunal should enquire further into that, although it is not clear whether in suggesting this approach he was disagreeing with the decision in *R(DLA) 7/02* where it was said that supervision which precluded the need for intervention or removed the element of unpredictable behaviour could not entitle the claimant to benefit because he would not then satisfy the words of sub-paras (b) or (c). In the event, though, the non compliance with para.(6) had to be returned to the new tribunal because it appeared to have been raised in the decision only by the tribunal itself, and it was not clear that it had been put to the claimant's representative for him to deal with it.

p.574, *annotation to Disability Living Allowance Regulations 1991, reg.12(7) and 12(8): disqualification on grounds of fear and anxiety*

2.036   The operation of these paragraphs has been considered in *R(DLA) 3/04* where the claimant was unable to walk outside for any distance unless she was accompanied by a member of her family who could, by giving her reassurance and encouragement, prevent her from having panic attacks. These attacks were a symptom of a severe state of anxiety and depression from which she was suffering. Commissioner Rowland allowed her appeal, finding that although her inability to walk outside clearly arose from fear and anxiety it was equally clear that, in her case, that anxiety was a symptom of her mental illness. The wording of para.(8) did not require that the mental disability should be some illness other than the anxiety itself.

These paragraphs were also considered in *CSDLA/430/2004*. There, the claimant suffered from asthma and also a chronic anxiety state that made him reluctant to walk outside alone for fear of suffering an asthma attack. Commissioner Parker, in allowing an appeal, points out that in this case there are really two separate questions to be answered. The first, (referring to para.(8)) is whether the anxiety attack was a symptom of mental illness and whether it was so severe as to prevent him walking unaccompanied. The second, and wholly separate question, (in accordance with s.73(1)(d)) was whether real asthma attacks did occur that disabled him, so as to make it necessary for him to be accompanied for the purpose of supervision for most of the time.

p.574, *annotation to Disability Living Allowance Regulations 1991, reg.12*

The decision in *CDLA/6701/1999* is reported as *R(DLA) 7/02*.　　2.037

p.664, *amendment to the Incapacity Benefit Regulations 1994 reg.8 (limit of earnings from councillor's allowance)*

With effect from October 1, 2004, reg.3 of the Social Security (Inca-　2.038 pacity) (Miscellaneous Amendments) Regulations 2004 (SI 2004/2301) substituted for the amount of £72.00 an amount of £78.00.

pp.698–700, *annotation to Incapacity for Work (General) Regulations 1995, reg.8 (person may be called for a medical examination): the matter of "good cause"*

The Northern Ireland decision *C11/03–04(IB)* is a useful reminder of　2.039 the need to ascertain the precise facts and be careful in applying to them the concept of "good cause". The case concerned a common "defence", where the claimant alleged he had never received a particular letter sent by the Department, a typical case of conflict of evidence. Deputy Commissioner Powell thought that sometimes it is right to reject such allegations in a robust manner, for example, where the excuse extends to a number of letters, or is coupled with suspicious circumstances, or if the non-receipt of mail is selective so that only certain letters are not received. The case before him, however, concerned a rather different situation—the uncontradicted evidence of the claimant, who did not attend the appeal hearing, of the non-receipt of a single letter in plausible circumstances, namely, a communal delivery of mail to particular premises and the possibility that another went through it before the claimant had a chance to do so. The Commissioner could not see how an effective challenge could be mounted to the claim and that, in these circumstances, the claimant had established good cause.

pp.702–703, *annotation to Incapacity for Work (General) Regulations 1995, reg.10 (certain persons with a severe condition to be treated as incapable of work: para.(2)(e)(iii)*

2.040   This provides that someone with an "active and progressive form of polyarthritis" must be treated as incapable of work. In *CIB/4033/2003*, Commissioner Jacobs held that this did not embrace osteoarthritis. He first considered the expression as a whole, the language used and its relation to the use of medical terminology in other cases, and stated:

> "The language used is not the language that I usually find associated with osteoarthritis. That form of arthritis may affect a number of joints and it may involve inflammation. But I have never heard the word 'active' used in connection with it. 'Symptomatic' and 'asymptomatic', yes, but not 'active'. Active suggests that the condition may exist without being active. I have heard of rheumatoid arthritis being in remission and, therefore, not active, but I have never heard of this in a case of osteoarthritis. Quite the contrary, I regularly see evidence that osteoarthritis will inevitably deteriorate. Deteriorate, notice, not progress. This suggests that the Secretary of State's argument is correct that osteoarthritis is not an exempt condition" (para.15).

He then checked that provisional conclusion against an admittedly not comprehensive internet search of medical literature, forming as a result the confirmatory impression that the expression in medical usage does not cover osteoarthritis.

p.718, *amendment to the Incapacity Benefit (General) Regulations 1995, reg.17(2)(a) (earnings limit for exempt work)*

2.041   With effect from October 1, 2004, reg.4 of the Social Security (Incapacity) (Miscellaneous Amendments) Regulations 2004 (SI 2004/2301) substituted for the amount of £72.00 an amount of £78.00.

pp.722–723, *annotation to Incapacity for Work (General) Regulations 1995, reg.17 (exempt work): comment on transitional provisions preserving the effect of the "old" reg.17: work undertaken on the advice of a doctor*

2.042   In *CIB/2679/2003*, Commissioner Fellner endorsed Commissioner Walker's view in *CIB/1749/1997* that the doctor's advice had to be given in advance of starting the work, but expressed no view on his additional requirement that it should later be shown that the work done had actually had the hoped-for effect (para.11). She also was of the opinion that the wording in "old" reg.17(1)(a)(i), "helps to improve, or to prevent or delay deterioration in, the disease or bodily or mental disablement which causes that person's incapacity for work", requires:

> "considerable specificity about the actual work to be undertaken and the favourable impact it might have, in any of the ways recited in (i), on the condition causing incapacity for work. This specificity is reflected in the form DL/S 603 which is issued to GPs and which asks what specific objectives the doctor expects the work to achieve for the

patient's future progress and whether it will help to improve, or prevent or delay the deterioration in the disease or disablement which causes the incapacity for work . . .

The wording of such forms is of course not legally binding, reflecting as it does only the government's view of the policy it is pursuing, a view which may judicially be held not justified by the wording of the regulations. But it can be an indicator where, as here, disputes arise about both the specificity and the timing of advice given. The wording of the questions to the GP also indicates that a future state of affairs is contemplated: what specific objectives does the GP 'expect' this work to achieve in relation to 'future' progress, 'will' the work help to improve, etc." (paras 9, 10).

She also noted that the definition of "doctor" in reg.2(1) meant that advice from the physiotherapist and, probably, the consultant clinical psychologist, did not suffice (para.7). Even if the latter's evidence could count, however, his general advice given five or six years earlier that the claimant should pursue activities she found pleasurable or rewarding (which at that time included, among other things, writing short stories) had neither been received by the claimant and, in any event, came too far before the start of the work in question (para.12).

In the Northern Ireland decision *C29/02–03*, Commissioner Brown considered a claimant, who had undertaken some work on the recommendation of his GP, which alleviated the depression caused by the drugs used to treat his rheumatoid arthritis and resulting immobility, the arthritis being one of the conditions causing incapacity for work. The work done was thus exempt work under the "old" reg.17(1)(a)(i).

p.723, *annotation to Incapacity for Work (General) Regulations 1995, reg.17 (exempt work) (work on the advice of a doctor)*

C/9/00–01(IB) has been reported as *R2/02(IB)*.   2.043

pp.734–737, *annotation to the Incapacity for Work (General) Regulations 1995, reg.24 (the personal capability assessment): dealing with the evidence, in particular with differing medical opinions and reports*

In *CIB/3074/2003* Commissioner Bano allowed the claimant's appeal 2.044
because the tribunal had dismissed the appeal "on the basis of a formulaic endorsement of the examining medical practitioner's report", rather than looking at it in the light of its nature and the evidence as a whole. He noted that in *CIB/15663/1996*, deputy Commissioner Fellner (as she then was):

"stated that a tribunal was entitled to give full weight to an examining medical practitioner's findings. A tribunal should of course give full weight to all the evidence, but may often be justified in regarding the clinical findings of an examining medical officer as reliable, although even clinical findings should not be regarded as conclusive and may in some cases be displaced by other evidence. However, the impact of any given degree of loss of function will vary from claimant to claimant. In some cases (such as incontinence) a clinical examination will often give very little indication of the extent of impairment of the activities which need to be considered in carrying out the personal capability assessment, although in such cases the examining medical practitioner will often be able to make an informed assessment of the degree of impairment on the basis of the claimant's medical history and other evidence of functional ability. The examining medical officer's choice of a descriptor will therefore generally require the exercise of judgment to a greater or lesser degree, and a tribunal may therefore not necessarily give the same weight to an examining medical officer's choice of descriptors as it does to clinical findings on examination" (para.13).

Commissioner Bano considered the EMP's report as perfunctory and as failing to address the crucial issues of impairment of physical activities caused by bowel incontinence and by backache (para.16). He awarded the claimant nine points for bowel incontinence under descriptor 13(e) (loses bowel control occasionally), with the result that the claimant with that additional score satisfied the personal capability assessment with a score of 16 points. See further update to pp.784–785, below.

p.745, *annotation to the Incapacity for Work (General) Regulations 1995, reg.27 (exceptional circumstances)*

2.045   In *CSIB/146/2004*, Commissioner May expressly disagreed with Commissioner Levenson's statement in *CIB/248/1997*, para.15, which is quoted in the annotation. Commissioner May stated that the tribunal:

> "applied regulation 27 without any indication by them that they were satisfied that the condition for its operation was met. It was not a matter of choice for the tribunal to determine whether to postpone consideration of regulation 27 until after considering the personal capability assessment as was suggested by Mr Commissioner Levenson. There is a sequence to the approach required encompassed within regulation 27. It is not open to the tribunal to make what it may consider to be a pragmatic adaptation of the legislation" (para.11).

pp.746–747, *annotation to the Incapacity for Work (General) Regulations 1995, reg.27 (exceptional circumstances): the old head (b) as preserved by* Howker *and* Moule: *assessing risk in relation to the kind of work for which the claimant would otherwise require to be available*

2.046   In *CSIB/33/2004*, Commissioner Parker expressly approved Commissioner Jacob's analysis in *CIB/26/2004* as making sense of a difficult regulation. She also gave some helpful approaches to resolving some of the problems created as a result of that analysis:

> "A claimant whose IB is refused may have claimed jobseeker's allowance (JSA) pending the IB appeal; alternatively, he or she may have claimed income support (IS), (despite a 'benefit penalty' unless certain circumstances are applicable), or have claimed no other benefit.
> If a claim for JSA has been made, a claimant must have suggested some employment which there is a reasonable prospect of securing

having regard to his or her skills, qualifications and experience. A JSA claimant may, however, place restrictions, if these are reasonable in the light of the claimant's physical or mental condition, irrespective of the effect these restrictions have on the reasonable prospect of obtaining work, provided there are none which cannot be so justified. It is a complex process.

In this kind of case, the task of the IB tribunal is to elicit the kind of work which the JobCentre has accepted as that for which the claimant must be both available and actively seeking, as set out in the 'Job-seeker's Agreement'. The claimant then has to satisfy the IB tribunal that even such work nevertheless raises the necessary 'substantial risk'. It is important to keep in mind that the question only arises following a determination that a claimant is not incapable of work in accordance with the PCA, nor does he or she fall under regulation 10 where their condition is expressly acknowledged as sufficiently severe.

So far as those who have not made a JSA claim are concerned, the tribunal (which through its chairman possesses the necessary expertise in the conditions of entitlement to JSA) will have to consider all the evidence and relevant law to determine the likely content of a job-seeker's agreement to which a claimant would be subject had a successful JSA claim been made and then ask if the type of job set out in the hypothetical agreement raises the specified risk. The problems are not insuperable but it does illustrate the difficult interface between the IB and JSA rules when applying regulation 27(b).

Finally, I judge that Mr Kinghorn is right to emphasise that the risk must arise from the broad results of a claimant being found capable of work and is not confined to the risks arising directly from the tasks within a claimant's job description. Thus, for example, if a claimant sustains the relevant risk because she has to get up quickly in the morning to go to work, rather than pace herself as would be the situation if no such necessity arose, this is a pertinent factor for consideration. Likewise, Mr Brodie accepted that any apprehension sustained by a claimant with mental disablement at the prospect of having to look for work, is pertinent. But there must be a causal link between being 'found capable of work' and an ensuing 'substantial risk to the mental or physical health of any person if [the claimant] were found capable of work'. If the situation of risk is exactly the same whether or not the claimant is exposed to the rigours of work, regulation 27(b) has no application" (paras 36–40).

p.748, *annotation to the Incapacity for Work (General) Regulations 1995, reg.27 (exceptional circumstances): insertion of new paragraph headed: "Para. (2)(b) Meaning of 'previously undiagnosed' "*

In *R1/04(IB)*, a decision by a Northern Ireland tribunal of Commissioners, it was held that "previously undiagnosed" refers to the diagnosis of a medical practitioner, so that once a condition is diagnosed by such a practitioner, it can no longer be argued that the condition was previously undiagnosed.   2.047

pp.749–750, *annotation to the Incapacity for Work (General) Regulations 1995, reg.28 (conditions for treating a person as incapable of work until the personal capability assessment is carried out)*

2.048   Useful clarification of the operation of reg.28 has been given by Commissioner Rowland in *CIB/3106/2003* and by Commissioner Howells in *CIB/3956/2003*. Where the six-month period mentioned has expired, there is no need to make a new claim to take advantage of the protection of the regulation. It should be considered by the decision-maker as a change of circumstances (*CIB/3106/2003*, para.5). Moreover, where on a claim for incapacity the decision-maker decides that the claimant cannot be treated as incapable under reg.28 pending assessment, the decision-maker must still arrange a personal capability assessment to determine *actual* incapacity. If the result of that assessment was incapacity for work, arrears of benefit will be payable from the date of claim. As explained in *R(IB) 1/01* and *R(IB) 2/01*, the purpose of reg.28 is simply to enable payment of benefit pending assessment and irrespective of the results of that assessment (*ibid.*, para.6). In contrast, where the period of six months since a previous determination has not expired, reg.28 can only come into play where one of the conditions in para. (2)(b)(i)–(iii) are met, for example, that the claimant is suffering from some fresh disease or disablement, or a significant worsening of an existing disease or disablement, since the date of that determination (the determination by the Secretary of State, not the date of a tribunal decision confirming it on appeal) (*CIB/3956/2003*). The opening words of reg.28(1) refer to the necessity to make a determination in respect of each day of claimed incapacity, and so the six-month period must thus be run back from each day of the current claim to see if on that day the claimant can benefit from the protection of the regulation. Where such days are not covered by that protection, the decision-maker must nonetheless consider actual incapacity in respect of those days, to be determined by carrying out a personal capability assessment and drawing the appropriate conclusions from it. Where a claim is made for a period that started within six months of a previous adverse determination, but is not decided until after the expiry of that six-month period, the further determination must take account of that expiry of the six-month period as a change of circumstances:

> "so that days of claimed incapacity within the period of the new claim supported by prescribed medical evidence and falling outside the six months are entitled to the protection of regulation 28(1) (even though earlier days were not) until such time as a personal capability assessment has actually been carried out or for some other reason that protection ceases to apply" (*ibid.*, para.8).

pp.757–758, *annotation to the Incapacity for Work (General) Regulations 1995, Sch: an important note on amendment and possible invalidity*

2.049   In *CIB/1239/2004*, Commissioner Henty followed *Howker* and Commissioner Jacobs in *CIB/884/2003* (to be reported as *R(IB) 3/04*) to hold invalid the 1996 amendments to Activity 3 (sitting in an upright chair with a back but no arms). See further, update to pp.776–777, below.

pp.776–777, *annotation to the Incapacity for Work (General) Regulations 1995, Sch: Activity 3 (sitting in an upright chair with a back but no arms)*

In *CIB/1239/2004*, Commissioner Henty followed *Howker* and Commissioner Jacobs in *CIB/884/2003* (to be reported as *R(IB) 3/04*) to hold invalid the 1996 amendments to Activity 3, thus striking out the added words "[because the degree of discomfort makes it impossible to continue sitting]". This made a difference because in his view those words had tangibly altered the meaning of the descriptor in question. The words struck out: 2.050

> "connote a high degree of discomfort which means that, albeit maybe only temporarily, the claimant *cannot* continue to sit. The words of the descriptor, without the offending words, in my view, connotes some lesser degree of discomfort which, while not making continued sitting actually impossible, necessarily means that the act of moving from the chair affords some relief. There is a difference between not being able to continue sitting comfortably and not being able to continue sitting because the discomfort makes it impossible.
>
> The tribunal should therefore have considered the descriptor without the offending words in brackets. That must have some effect on how long it takes a claimant to satisfy any relevant condition" (paras 6, 7, emphasis in original).

Looking at the evidence before the tribunal, he held that the claimant could sit for 1–2 hours, thus adding to his total a score of three points from descriptor 3(d), and bringing his score to 15 points so that he satisfied the personal capability assessment.

pp.780–781, *annotation to the Incapacity for Work (General) Regulations 1995, Sch: Activity 7 (manual dexterity): descriptors (b) and (f) [knobs on sink tap or cooker: the meaning of "or"]*

In a Northern Ireland decision, *R1/03(IB)*, Chief Commissioner Martin held the "or" was here to be read disjunctively so that the adjudicating authorities are concerned with the capacity, or lack thereof, of a claimant to turn a sink tap *or* control knobs of a cooker. The movements required to turn a sink tap rather than a cooker knob are not necessarily the same or similar, so that a claimant can have real difficulty with one rather than the other. Hence, if a claimant is not able to carry out either one or the other function he will satisfy the appropriate test and score the relevant score.   2.051

pp.784–785, *annotation to the Incapacity for Work (General) Regulations 1995, Sch: Activity 13 (bowel incontinence)*

In *CIB/3074/2003*, Commissioner Bano emphasised the need to look at the EMP's evidence in the light of all the evidence in the case (see update to pp.734–737, above) and to examine the claimant's questionnaire as a whole (including statements in the "additional information" section of the form), rather than relying exclusively on the boxes ticked or not ticked by the claimant. He applied this to the difficult area   2.052

of bowel incontinence attributable to "irritable bowel syndrome". He stated that such claims:

> "need to be treated with caution, and I must bear in mind that the claimant did not tick the boxes indicating problems controlling his bowels on either of the two incapacity benefit questionnaires which he completed. On the other hand, the claimant did give a detailed account in both questionnaires of 'accidents', and other circumstantial details indicating genuine loss of control of bowel function, rather than mere urgency of defecation. Since the claimant did tick the box indicating no problems controlling his bladder, I think it likely that the claimant did not tick the boxes relating to bowel control because he considered that he had given all the information which was needed in relation to control of his bowels in the 'additional information' section of the form. The diagnosis of irritable bowel syndrome has been corroborated by the claimant's general practitioner and the symptoms described by the claimant are entirely consistent with those which were described by the consultant physician who provided an expert report on the condition in *CIB/14322/1996*. I can find no reason to doubt the claimant's account and, on that basis, I am satisfied that the claimant does lose bowel control at least occasionally, attracting an award of 9 points in respect of descriptor 13(e). I can also see no reason to doubt that the claimant was correctly awarded 7 points in respect of mental descriptors. The claimant therefore scores 16 points on the personal capability assessment, and accordingly is to be regarded as incapable of work" (para.18).

pp.788–790, *annotation to the Incapacity for Work (General) Regulations 1995, Sch: Activity 13 (continence): descriptor (b) "no voluntary control over bladder"*

2.053   In *CIB/1005/2004*, Commissioner Mesher agreed with Commissioner May on there being a difference between "no voluntary control" and "loses control": the former imports no voluntary control at all, the latter imports some control that is lost.

Commenting on Commissioner Walker's starting point in *CSIB/ 38/1996* (quoted on p.788) and giving valuable guidance on pertinent questions, Commissioner Mesher thought that there is:

> "room in the concept of 'no voluntary control' for a person only to be able to resist, by the exercise of the will, the muscular reflex to empty the bladder for a very short time indeed. I consider that Mr Commissioner Walker's reference to *de minimis* was intended to cover time as well as the degree of leakage. But the time must be very short indeed, in the context of 'no voluntary control', and it must be remembered that cases like *CIB/14332/1996, CIB/1995/2002* and *CIB/2200/2003* were about when a person loses control of bowels or bladder. Moreover, too much must not be read into Mr Commissioner Walker's statement. He had set aside an appeal tribunal's decision that a claimant had no voluntary control over the bladder because there was not evidence to support that conclusion, merely evidence of frequency.

Then in paragraph 8 he was merely setting out, for the guidance of a new appeal tribunal, a starting point in the proper consideration of the descriptor, not an exhaustive set of conditions. There would not only have to be evidence of an inability to postpone by exercise of the will the operation of the muscular reflex, but that inability would have to exist at all times and on all occasions, subject to trivial exceptions, before it could be concluded that a person had 'no' voluntary control.

It follows from the above that the fact that a claimant, or even an EMP, ticks a box labelled 'occasionally loses control' is not inconsistent with the true situation being 'no voluntary control'. Such answers may be given on an assumption that only actual wetting or soiling counts for that purpose, whereas that is not the case. And if a person can only postpone the muscular reflex for a very short time, with occasional failures, that can be consistent with 'no voluntary control'. In the present case, the claimant's evidence to the effect that, if he needed a toilet, he had to go because he could not hold his water at all (if accepted) would go part of the way to establishing his case. But questions needed to be asked about just how quickly he needed to get to a toilet and about how often and in what circumstances he was able to do so without an accident. Those questions needed to include what happened during the night when the claimant woke needing to empty his bladder. Possibly questions should also have been asked about the claimant's ability to terminate the stream of urine by the exercise of will (another element of voluntary control), but there was evidence from the GP of a failure of voluntary control to that extent. And express consideration needed to be given to the consistency of the claimant's evidence as above with the normal effects of prostate problems and of hesitancy (see the GP's evidence that the claimant has to stand at the toilet for quite some time before urine started to flow), but that is a matter where medical expertise and experience would be needed for a proper evaluation to be made. Finally, the consistency with measures taken to mitigate the effects of the claimed absence of voluntary control was a relevant factor" (paras 13, 14).

p.797, *annotation to Incapacity of Work (General) Regulations 1995, Sch: Activity 16: daily living; descriptor (c): "is frequently distressed at some time of the day due to fluctuation of mood"*

The Northern Ireland decision *C/25/01002(IB)* has been reported as *R4/02(IB)*.   2.054

pp.818–819, *annotation to the Incapacity Benefit (Transitional) Regulations 1995, reg.17 (transitional awards of long-term incapacity benefit)*

Although this regulation means that an award of invalidity benefit has   2.055
effect as, and is to be treated as, an award of long-term incapacity benefit, it does not become incapacity benefit, and so, for the purposes of reg.6 of the Decisions and Appeals Regulations 1999 it does not rank as an incapacity benefit decision because it could not have been a

determination under Pt XIIA of the Social Security Contributions and Benefits Act 1992 since that did not come into force until April 1995. A decision in 1990 is not converted by reg.17 into an incapacity benefit decision "because it relates only to the continuing effect and not to a change into the new benefit" (*CSIB/510/2003*, para.10).

p.893, *annotation to the General Benefit Regulations 1982, reg.11(6)*

2.056   *CI/1293/2003* has been reported as *R(I) 4/04.*

pp.912–913, *annotation to Prescribed Diseases Regulations 1985, reg.6 (date of onset)*

2.057   With the support of the Secretary of State's representative, Commissioner Howell applied in *CI/3463/2003*, his decision in *CI/5270 & 5271/2002* that *Whalley* reasoning does not apply to decisions made under the Social Security Act 1998 processes. He could not better the summary of the position as stated in his submission by that representative:

> "The effects of finality for the purposes of section 17 of the SS Act 1998 was considered by the Commissioner in *CI/5270/02*. In that case it was held that following the introduction of DMA, decisions on diagnosis were not freestanding but were a question of fact embodied in a decision of the Secretary of State under section 8(1) of the Act on entitlement to benefit. In paragraph 17 the Commissioner stated '*In the absence of such express provision, an earlier finding made under the 1998 Act machinery on such a question cannot fall within the modified statutory form of the principle of* res judicata *which now applies to social security decisions under section 17*'.
>
> The Secretary of State accepts the reasoning in decision *CI/5270/02* and submits that provided no claim had been made under the previous legislation where section 60 of the SS Admin Act [1992] did provide for finality on the question of the date of onset, then that question [sc. the previous negative diagnosis] is a matter of fact and not final for the purposes of section 17 of the SS Act 1998."

p.913, *annotation to Prescribed Diseases Regulations 1985, reg.6 (date of onset)*

2.058   *CI/1605/2002* has been reported as *R(I) 2/04.*

p.961, *annotation to Prescribed Diseases Regulations 1985, Sch.1: PDA11 (Vibration white finger)*

2.059   *CI/4582/2002* has been reported as *R(I) 3/04.*

PART III

UPDATING MATERIAL
VOLUME II

INCOME SUPPORT, JOBSEEKER'S ALLOWANCE, STATE PENSION CREDIT AND THE SOCIAL FUND

pp.50–52, *annotation to Jobseekers Act 1995, s.2(1)(c) (the earnings condition)*

In *CJSA/3928 & 3931/2003*, Commissioner Howell applied this earn- **3.001**
ings condition, using the Computation of Earnings Regulations so as to
spread forward the payment received at the end of a month in respect of
a range of past work (the claimant's hours were irregular), thus ruling
out the particular weeks of claim because the earnings thus assessed were
in each week above the prescribed amount.

pp.124–125, *annotation to Jobseekers Act 1995, s.19(6)(c) (failure of
claimant without good cause to pursue a job vacancy notified to him)*

In *CJSA/2931/2003*, Commissioner Howell upheld a tribunal decision **3.002**
disqualifying the claimant for 18 weeks as fully justified on the facts. It
had thought suspect the claimant's credibility in claiming that he had
telephoned and been told that the vacancy was filled whereas in fact it
had remained open. The sanction imposed was well within the bounds of
reasonableness in a case where a long-term claimant is found to have
made no real effort to follow up a vacancy notified to him.

p.130, *annotation to Jobseekers Act 1995, s.19(9): National Minimum
Wage*

With effect from October 1, 2004, the National Minimum Wage **3.003**
Regulations 1999 (Amendment) (No.2) Regulations 2004 (SI
2004/1930) increased the minimum hourly rate of the national minimum wage from £4.50 to £4.85. They also increased the rate to be paid
to those (including workers aged between 18 and 21) who qualify for the
national minimum wage at a different rate, from £3.80 to £4.10. In
addition, the Regulations provide, for the first time, that workers aged
below 18 who have ceased to be of compulsory school age qualify for the
national minimum wage. The Regulations set an hourly rate of £3.00 for
such workers.

p.137, *annotation to Jobseekers Act, s.26*

The back-to-work bonus scheme was abolished on October 25, 2004. **3.004**
However, note reg.10 of the Social Security (Back to Work Bonus and
Lone Parent Run-on) (Amendment and Revocation) Regulations 2003
(SI 2003/1589) (see Pt I of this Supplement), which allows claims for the
bonus to be made within a transitional period.

p.155, *State Pension Credit Act 2002, Introduction and General Note*

Note that the House of Commons Work and Pensions Select Commit- **3.005**
tee is conducting an inquiry into the introduction of the new pension
credit. The Committee's report is expected to appear in 2005.

p.175, *State Pension Credit Act 2002, s.13 (transitional provisions)*

3.006   Note that the 12-month automatic backdating rule, which originally applied just in the first year of the new pension credit scheme, has now been made a permanent feature: Social Security (Claims and Payments) Regulations 1987 (SI 1987/1968), reg.19 and Sch.4, as amended by Social Security (Claims and Payments) Amendment (No.2) Regulations 2004 (SI 2004/1821), reg.2.

p.214, *Income Support (General) Regulations 1987, reg.2(1) (Definition of "ERA Payment")*

3.007   With effect from April 1, 2004, reg.2(2) of the Social Security (Miscellaneous Amendments) Regulations 2004 (SI 2004/565) deleted the definition of "ERA Payment" in reg.2(1).

p.217, *Income Support (General) Regulations 1987, reg.2(1) (Definition of "qualifying person")*

3.008   With effect from May 12, 2004, reg.2(a) of the Social Security (Miscellaneous Amendments) (No.2) Regulations 2004 (SI 2004/1141) amended the definition of "qualifying person" in reg.2(1) to read:

    " "qualifying person" means a person in respect of whom payment has been made from the Fund [, the Eileen Trust or the Skipton Fund];"

p.218, *Income Support (General) Regulations 1987: amendment of reg.2(1) (Definition of "self-employment route")*

3.009   With effect from May 4, 2004, reg.2 of the Social Security (Income-Related Benefits Self-Employment Route Amendment) Regulations 2004 (SI 2004/963) amended reg.2(1) by substituting a new definition of "self-employment route" to read:

    " "self-employment route" means assistance in pursuing self-employed earner's employment whilst participating in—

       (a) an employment zone programme; or
       (b) a programme provided or other arrangements made pursuant to section 2 of the Employment and Training Act 1973 (functions of the Secretary of State) or section 2 of the Enterprise and New Towns (Scotland) Act 1990 (functions in relation to training for employment etc.);".

p.219, *Income Support (General) Regulations 1987, reg.2(1) (Definition of "the Skipton Fund")*

3.010   With effect from May 12, 2004, reg.2(b) of the Social Security (Miscellaneous Amendments) (No.2) Regulations 2004 (SI 2004/1141) inserted after the definition of "the Macfarlane Trust" the following definition:

" "the Skipton Fund" means the ex-gratia payment scheme administered by the Skipton Fund Limited, incorporated on 25th March 2004, for the benefit of certain persons suffering from hepatitis C and other persons eligible for payment in accordance with the scheme's provisions;".

p.229, *annotation to Income Support (General) Regulations 1987, reg.2(1), definition of "self-employment route"*

The new form of the definition of *"self-employment route"* is intended to encompass assistance in pursuing self-employed earner's employment while participating in *any* programme provided or other arrangement made under s.2 of the Employment and Training Act 1973 or s.2 of the Enterprise and New Towns (Scotland) Act 1990. It also applies to such assistance while taking part in an employment zone programme (such programmes do not come under those provisions but s.60 of the Welfare Reform and Pensions Act 1999). A person who is receiving assistance under the self-employment route is not treated as in remunerative work (see the new sub-para.(dd) of reg.6(1) of the Income Support Regulations and the amended form of reg.53(bb) of the JSA Regulations). 3.011

pp.243–244, *Income Support (General) Regulations 1987: amendment of reg.4 (Temporary absence from Great Britain)*

With effect from October 4, 2004, reg.2 of the Social Security (Income Support and Jobseeker's Allowance) Amendment Regulations 2004 (SI 2004/1869) amended reg.4 by the insertion of a new para.(3A) as follows: 3.012

"(3A) A claimant's entitlement to income support shall continue during a period of temporary absence from Great Britain if—

(a) he satisfied the conditions of entitlement to income support immediately before the beginning of that period of temporary absence; and

(b) that period of temporary absence is for the purpose of the claimant receiving treatment at a hospital or other institution outside Great Britain where that treatment is being provided—

   (i) under section 3 of the National Health Service Act 1977 (services generally);

   (ii) pursuant to arrangements made under section 23 of that Act (voluntary organisations and other bodies); or

   (iii) pursuant to arrangements made under paragraph 13 of Sch.2 to the National Health Service and Community Care Act 1990 (National Health Service Trusts—specific powers)."

p.247, *annotation to Income Support (General) Regulations 1987, reg.4 (Temporary absence from Great Britain)*

At the end of the annotation, add: 3.013

Para. (3A)

From October 4, 2004 claimants who are temporarily absent from Great Britain in order to receive NHS treatment at a hospital (or similar institution) in another country, and who were entitled to IS immediately before their departure, continue to be so entitled during their absence.

p.258, *Income Support (General) Regulations 1987: amendment of reg. 6 (Persons not treated as engaged in remunerative work)*

3.014   With effect from October 25, 2004, reg.2(a) of the Social Security (Back to Work Bonus and Lone Parent Run-on) (Amendment and Revocation) Regulations 2003 (SI 2003/1589) amended reg.6 by revoking paras (2), (3) and (6)(b), the word "; or" after para.(6)(a) and the words "(2)(b) or" and "(3) or" in para.(7).

p.258, *Income Support (General) Regulations 1987: amendment of reg. 6(1) (Persons not treated as engaged in remunerative work)*

3.015   With effect from May 4, 2004, reg.3 of the Social Security (Income-Related Benefits Self-Employment Route Amendment) Regulations 2004 (SI 2004/963) amended reg.6(1) by inserting a new sub-para.(dd) as follows:

"(dd) he is receiving assistance under the self-employment route;".

p.261, *annotation to Income Support (General) Regulations 1987, reg. 6(1) (Persons not treated as engaged in remunerative work)*

3.016   Under para.(1)(dd) those receiving assistance under the self-employment route of the New Deal are treated as not being in remunerative work. See the annotation to the definition of "self-employment route" in reg.2(1) and the General Note to reg.39A at pp.229 and 362–363, respectively, of the main volume.

p.262, *annotation to Income Support (General) Regulations 1987: reg. 6(2) and (3): lone-parent run-on*

3.017   The "lone-parent run-on" previously established by these paragraphs was abolished on October 25, 2004.

p.262, *annotation to Income Support (General) Regulations 1987: reg. 6(5) to (8): mortgage interest run-on*

3.018   The "lone-parent run-on" previously established by paras (2) and (3), and previously referred to in para.(6)(b), was abolished on October 25, 2004. Paragraph (6)(b) was therefore revoked with effect from the same date, so that in all cases the mortgage interest run-on now lasts for the four-week period specified in para.(6)(a).

p.264, *Income Support (General) Regulations 1987, reg.12(2)*

With effect from October 4, 2004, reg.5(1)(a) of the Social Security **3.019**
(Miscellaneous Amendments) (No.3) Regulations 2004 (SI 2004/2308)
substituted the words "a higher national certificate" for the words "a
higher national diploma or higher national certificate of either the Business & Technology Education Council or the Scottish Vocational Education Council" in sub-para.(a).

Regulation 5(1)(b) of the same amending regulations substituted the
following sub-paragraph for sub-para.(b):

"(b)   any other course which is a course of a standard above
        advanced GNVQ or equivalent, including a course which is of
        a standard above a general certificate of education (advanced
        level) or a Scottish national qualification (higher or advanced
        higher)."

pp.288–290, *Income Support (General) Regulations 1987: amendment of*
reg.21 (Special cases)

With effect from May 1, 2004, reg.3 of the Social Security (Habitual **3.020**
Residence) Amendment Regulations 2004 (SI 2004/1232) amended
reg.21. The text of the amendments is set out on pp.1309–1310 in Pt VI
(Forthcoming Changes) of the main volume. The amendments are
subject to the transitional protection provided by reg.6 of SI 2004/1232
(see p.1311 of the main volume).

p.295, *Income Support (General) Regulations 1987: annotation to reg.21*
(Special Cases): definition of "maintenance undertaking"

In *CIS/426/2003* Mr Commissioner Turnbull refused to follow **3.021**
CIS/47/2002. He held that a document would not be a written undertaking unless it contains an agreement or promise by the sponsor to pay
the cost of maintaining and either to provide or to pay the cost of
providing accommodation for that person. The words "I am able and
willing to maintain and accommodate the applicant without recourse to
public funds and in suitable accommodation" which appeared in a
standard form of sponsorship declaration (N.B. not the RON 112 or
SET(F) forms) did not amount to such an agreement or promise but
only to a declaration of the facts that, at the time of the declaration, the
"sponsor's" circumstances were such that he was able to do so and that
his state of mind was that he was and would be willing to do so. An
assertion that an individual was able and willing to act in a particular way
fell well short of a promise that he would act in that way.

p.319, *Income Support (General) Regulations: annotation to reg.21ZB*
(Treatment of refugees)

In *CJSA/4843/2003* Deputy Commissioner Wikeley held that a refu- **3.022**
gee who fails to make a claim for income support within the 28-day
period prescribed by reg.21ZB(2) (and therefore does not qualify for

backdating to the date on which s/he applied for asylum) may nevertheless qualify for up to three months' backdating if s/he satisfies reg.19(4) and (5) of the Social Security (Claims and Payments) Regulations 1987 (see pp.425–438 of Vol.III of the main volume).

p.323, *annotation to Income Support (General) Regulations 1987, reg.23*

3.023   See *CH/3013/2003* in which the Commissioner states that resources provided by the use of an overdraft facility do not amount to income.

p.338, *annotation to Income Support (General) Regulations 1987, reg.31(1)*

3.024   In *CJSA/4261/2003* the claimant was a "core casual" dockworker who was laid off and claimed JSA the next day. His employers said that six days' holiday pay was due to him and a decision-maker therefore treated him as in remunerative work for that period. However, evidence was provided by his union which confirmed that as a core casual worker his employment was not terminated when he was laid off. He could chose, but was not obliged, to take his holiday when he was laid off. Furthermore, if he did not take his holiday when laid off (or by agreement at other times), he could not receive payment for any accrued holiday entitlement until more than four weeks after the termination or interruption of his employment. Thus the terms of his contract clearly showed that no holiday pay was due when he was laid off and he was entitled to JSA from the day he claimed, subject to the three waiting days rule.

p.351, *Income Support (General) Regulations 1987, reg.36(2)*

3.025   With effect from October 25, 2004, reg.2(b) of the Social Security (Back to Work Bonus and Lone Parent Run-on) (Amendment and Revocation) Regulations 2003 (SI 2003/1589) substituted the words "or 15A" for the words ", 15A or 15B".

p.351, *annotation to Income Support (General) Regulations 1987, reg.36(2)*

3.026   The reference to para.15B of Sch.8 has been removed as a consequence of the abolition of the "lone parent run-on" with effect from October 25, 2004 (see the amendments to reg.6 above).

p.357, *Income Support (General) Regulations 1987, reg.38(2)*

3.027   With effect from October 25, 2004, reg.2(c) of the Social Security (Back to Work Bonus and Lone Parent Run-on) (Amendment and Revocation) Regulations 2003 (SI 2003/1589) omitted the words "or 15B".

p.359, *annotation to Income Support (General) Regulations 1987,*
reg.38(2)

The reference to para.15B of Sch.8 has been removed as a con- 3.028
sequence of the abolition of the "lone parent run-on" with effect from
October 25, 2004 (see the amendments to reg.6 above).

p.367, *annotation to Income Support (General) Regulations 1987, reg.40*

See *CH/3013/2003* in which the Commissioner states that resources 3.029
provided by the use of an overdraft facility do not amount to income.

p.371, *annotation to Income Support (General) Regulations 1987, reg.41*

Paragraph (3) of reg.41 was omitted with effect from April 6, 2004 by 3.030
reg.2 of and para.9 of Sch.1 to the Social Security (Working Tax Credit
and Child Tax Credit) (Consequential Amendments) Regulations 2003
(SI 2003/455), except in "transitional cases" (*i.e.* those cases in which
the claimant is still receiving amounts for his children in his income
support—see further the note to reg.17 of the Income Support Regulations in the 2004 edition of Vol.II. It was intended that the phased
transfer to child tax credit of these cases would begin in October 2004
but this has now been deferred until 2005). For "transitional cases"
reg.41(3) continues in force (see the 2003 edition of Vol.II for this
provision). With effect from May 12, 2004, reg.5 of the Social Security
(Miscellaneous Amendments) (No.2) Regulations 2004 (SI 2004/1141)
substituted the words "section 12 of the Social Work (Scotland) Act
1968 or sections 29 or 30 of the Children (Scotland) Act 1995" for the
words "section 12, 24 or 26 of the Social Work (Scotland) Act 1968" in
reg.41(3). The effect of this amendment is simply to update the references to the Scottish legislation referred to in reg.41(3).

p.377, *Income Support (General) Regulations 1987, reg.42*

With effect from October 4, 2004, reg.5(2)(a) of the Social Security 3.031
(Miscellaneous Amendments) (No.3) Regulations 2004 (SI 2004/2308)
omitted the words ", but this sub-paragraph shall only apply in respect
of a claimant to the extent that he has been engaged in such work
experience during the period specified in paragraph (6B)" in para.
(6A)(c).
Regulation 5(2)(b) of the same amending regulations omitted paras
(6B) and (6C).

p.388, *annotation to Income Support (General) Regulations 1987,*
reg.42(6A)–(6C)

The amendments made with effect from October 4, 2004 remove the 3.032
limits on the exemption from the notional earnings rule for lone parents
who are on work experience while participating in the New Deal for
Lone Parents or a related pilot scheme. Previously the exemption only

lasted for up to 150 hours, or six months, work with the same employer but it now applies without limit.

p.402, *annotation to Income Support (General) Regulations 1987, reg. 48(9)*

3.033   On the meaning of "voluntary payment" see *CH/3013/2003*. The claimant had been unable to work following a stroke and had received irregular payments from a friend and his parents. The friend had written a letter which indicated that the payments from her were by way of a loan to be repaid at some unspecified date. However in the Commissioner's view the payments were made without any clear thought about their legal nature. The overall circumstances showed that no legally enforceable rights or obligations were created by the payments to the claimant and that she obtained nothing in return for the payments (see *R. v Doncaster BC Ex p. Boulton* [1992] 25 H.L.R. 195 referred to in the notes to para.15 of Sch.9 to the Income Support Regulations in the main volume). The payments were therefore voluntary payments within the meaning of reg.40(6) of the Housing Benefit Regulations (the equivalent of reg.48(9)). The payments from the claimant's parents, where the presumption of gift applied in the absence of evidence to the contrary, also fell within reg.40(6).

p.407, *Income Support (General) Regulations 1987, reg. 51(3A)(a)*

3.034   With effect from October 4, 2004, reg.3(1) and (2)(a) of the Social Security (Miscellaneous Amendments) (No.3) Regulations 2004 (SI 2004/2308) substituted the words ", the Independent Living Funds or the Skipton Fund" for the words "or the Independent Living Funds".

pp.447–449, *Income Support (General) Regulations 1987, reg. 61(1)*

3.035   With effect from September 1, 2004 (or if the student's period of study begins between August 1 and August 31, 2004, the first day of the period), reg.5(1)(a) of the Social Security (Students and Income-related Benefits) Amendment Regulations 2004 (SI 2004/1708) substituted the words "a Scottish national qualification (higher or advanced higher)" for the words "a Scottish certificate of education (higher level) or a Scottish certificate of sixth year studies" in the definition of "course of advanced education".

Regulation 5(1)(b) of the same amending regulations added the words "or any payment to which paragraph 11 of Schedule 9 or paragraph 63 of Schedule 10 applies" after the words "a payment from access funds" in the definition of "grant".

p.461, *Income Support (General) Regulations 1987, reg. 62*

3.036   With effect from September 1, 2004 (or if the student's period of study begins between August 1 and August 31, 2004, the first day of the period), reg.2(1) and (3)(c) of the Social Security (Students and Income-related Benefits) Amendment Regulations 2004 (SI 2004/1708) substituted the sum "£275" for the sum "£270" in para.(2A)(a).

Regulation 2(2) and (3)(c) of the same amending regulations substituted the sum "£343" for the sum "£335" in para.(2A)(b).

Regulation 3(3)(a) of the same amending regulations deleted the words "or child care costs" in para.(2)(i) and reg.3(3)(b) added the following new sub-paragraph after para.(2)(i): "(j) intended for the child care costs of a child dependant".

p.464, *annotation to Income Support (General) Regulations 1987, reg.62*

The amendments made to reg.62 with effect from April 6, 2004 by **3.037** reg.2 of and para.16 of Sch.1 to the Social Security (Working Tax Credit and Child Tax Credit) (Consequential Amendments) Regulations 2003 (SI 2003/455) (see the 2004 edition of Vol.II for these amendments) do not apply in "transitional cases" (*i.e.* those cases in which the claimant is still receiving amounts for his children in his income support—see further the note to reg.17 of the Income Support Regulations in the 2004 edition of Vol.II. It was intended that the phased transfer to child tax credit of these cases would begin in October 2004 but this has now been deferred until 2005). For "transitional cases" the unamended form of reg.62 continues in force (see the 2003 edition of Vol.II for this form of reg.62). Among the amendments made by the 2003 Regulations was the insertion of a new para.(2)(i) which provided for a general disregard of payments intended for the maintenance or child care costs of a child. This replaced most of the disregards for students with child care responsibilities previously contained in para.(2B), except that in sub-para.(b) which became the new (2B).

However, the insertion of the new para.(2)(j) with effect from September 1, 2004 (or if the student's period of study begins between August 1 and August 31, 2004, the first day of the period), which provides for a general disregard of payments intended for the child care costs of a child dependant, means that the disregards contained in sub-paras (c), (cc) and (d) of the unamended form of reg.62(2B) are no longer needed. These have therefore been omitted with effect from September 1, 2004 (or if the student's period of study begins between August 1 and August 31, 2004, the first day of the period) (see reg.3(5) and (6)(c) of the Social Security (Students and Income-related Benefits) Amendment Regulations 2004 (SI 2004/1708)).

p.470, *Income Support (General) Regulations 1987, reg.66A(5)*

With effect from September 1, 2004 (or if the student's period of **3.038** study begins between August 1 and August 31, 2004, the first day of the period), reg.2(1) and (3)(c) of the Social Security (Students and Income-related Benefits) Amendment Regulations 2004 (SI 2004/1708) substituted the sum "£275" for the sum "£270" in sub-para.(a).

Regulation 2(2) and (3)(c) of the same amending regulations substituted the sum "£343" for the sum "£335" in sub-para.(b).

p.503, *annotation to Income Support (General) Regulations 1987, Sch.IB, para.3*

3.039   In *CIS/866/2004* the appellant argued that she came within para.3(a) because her husband was unable to look after their child due to his alcohol problems. However the Commissioner holds that for para.3(a) to apply either the parent of the child who usually looked after the child or some other person who usually looked after the child had to be ill or temporarily absent. In his view it was only if read in this way that the use of the term "the parent" in para.3(a) rather than "a parent" made sense.

p.509, *annotation to Income Support (General) Regulations 1987, Sch.1B, paras 24 and 25*

3.040   See *CIS/1614/2004* which holds that there is no entitlement to income support under para.25 of Sch.1B in the period between the date of the decision that supersedes the award of benefit on the ground that the person is not incapable of work and the date of the appeal against that decision. On the Commissioner's reasoning the same would apply in relation to para.24. It is understood that the Department are considering introducing amendments to the Decisions and Appeals Regulations in order to deal with this gap.

p.515, *Income Support (General) Regulations 1987; amendment of Sch.2, para.12 (Additional condition for the Higher Pensioner and Disability Premiums)*

3.041   With effect from May 12, 2004, reg.6 of the Social Security (Miscellaneous Amendments) (No.2) Regulations 2004 (SI 2004/1141) amended para.12(1)(d)(i) of Sch.2 to read:

> "(i) but payment of that benefit has been suspended under the [Social Security (Attendance Allowance) Regulations 1991 or the Social Security (Disability Living Allowance) Regulations 1991] or otherwise abated as a consequence of the claimant or his partner becoming a patient within the meaning of regulation 21(3);".

p.516, *Income Support Regulations 1987: amendment of Sch.2, para.12 (Additional condition for the Higher Pensioner and Disability Premiums)*

3.042   With effect from October 25, 2004, reg.2(d) of the Social Security (Back to Work Bonus and Lone Parent Run-on) (Amendment and Revocation) Regulations 2003 (SI 2003/1589) amended reg.6 by revoking para.(7).

p.533, *Income Support (General) Regulations 1987, Sch.3, para.1(2)*

With effect from November 28, 2004, reg.2(2) of the Social Security   3.043
(Housing Costs Amendments) Regulations 2004 (SI 2004/2825) substituted the words "determined in accordance with" for the words "specified in" in the definition of "standard rate".

Regulation 2(5) of the same amending regulations substituted the
following head for head (a) in the definition of "existing housing
costs":

"(a)   which replaces an existing agreement, provided that the person
        liable to meet the housing costs—

        (i)   remains the same in both agreements, or
        (ii) where in either agreement more than one person is liable to
              meet the housing costs, the person is liable to meet the
              housing costs in both the existing agreement and the new
              agreement;".

p.541, *Income Support (General) Regulations 1987, Sch.3, para.10*

With effect from November 28, 2004, in the explanation of "B",   3.044
reg.2(3) of the Social Security (Housing Costs Amendments) Regulations 2004 (SI 2004/2825) substituted the words "applicable in respect
of that loan" for the words "specified in respect of that loan under
paragraph 12".

p.542, *Income Support (General) Regulations 1987, Sch.3, para.12*

With effect from September 19, 2004, reg.2 of the Income Support   3.045
(General) (Standard Interest Rate Amendment) (No.3) Regulations
2004 (SI 2004/2174) substituted the words "5.88 per cent" for the
words "5.59 per cent" in sub-para.(1)(a).

With effect from November 28, 2004, reg.2(4) of the Social Security
(Housing Costs Amendments) Regulations 2004 (SI 2004/2825) substituted the following sub-paragraphs for the sub-paragraphs in para.12:

"(1) The standard rate is the rate of interest applicable per annum to
a loan which qualifies under this Schedule.

(2) Subject to sub-paragraphs (3), (4) and (6), the standard rate
shall be 1.58 per cent. plus—

(a)   the rate announced from time to time by the Monetary Policy
       Committee of the Bank of England as the official dealing rate,
       being the rate at which the Bank is willing to enter into transac-
       tions for providing short term liquidity in the money markets,
       or
(b)   where an order under section 19 of the Bank of England Act
       1998 (reserve powers) is in force, any equivalent rate deter-
       mined by the Treasury under that section.

(3) The Secretary of State shall determine the date from which the
standard rate calculated in accordance with sub-paragraph (2) takes
effect.

(4) Where—

(a) the actual rate of interest charged on the loan which qualifies under this Schedule is less than 5 per cent. per annum on the day the housing costs first fall to be met, and

(b) that day occurs before 28th November 2004,

the standard rate shall be equal to that actual rate.

(5) Sub-paragraph (4) shall cease to apply in a particular case to any one or more loans which fall within that sub-paragraph on whichever of the following dates occurs first—

(a) the date on which the actual rate of interest charged on such a loan is 5 per cent. per annum or higher,

(b) the anniversary of the date on which the housing costs first fell to be met, or

(c) where a supersession decision based on a change of circumstances arising on or after 28th November 2004 is made under section 10 of the Social Security Act 1998 (decisions superseding earlier decisions), the date of the change of circumstances.

(6) Where sub-paragraph (4) does not apply to a loan which qualifies under this Schedule, the standard rate shall be 5.88 per cent. until the first date determined by the Secretary of State under sub-paragraph (3)."

p.554, *annotation to Income Support (General) Regulations 1987, Sch.3, para.1*

3.046   The changes made to the definition of "existing housing costs" by the substitution of head (a) with effect from November 28, 2004 are significant. For a remortgage which replaces an agreement entered into before October 2, 1995 to come within the definition of "existing housing costs" it is no longer necessary for it to be between the same parties and in respect of the same property. The new agreement can be with a different lender and/or in respect of a different property, provided that the amount borrowed does not increase. In addition, as long as at least one of the persons liable for the housing costs remains the same, the remortgage can include a change in borrower (*e.g.* a new partner).

On the change to the definition of "standard rate" see the note to para.12 of Sch.3 below.

p.560, *annotation to Income Support (General) Regulations 1987, Sch.3, para.3(11)*

3.047   *CH/1237/2004* concerned a claimant who was temporarily absent from her home through fear of violence. The Commissioner decides that the question of whether the absence is unlikely to exceed 52 weeks, or in exceptional circumstances unlikely to substantially exceed that period, in reg.5(8B)(d) of the Housing Benefit Regulations (the equivalent of para. 3(11)(d)) had to be assessed at the date the claimant left. Furthermore, whether she continued to be entitled to housing benefit had to be judged on a week-by-week basis. The claimant's belief was a factor in deciding, but was not determinative of, the question whether the absence was unlikely to be longer than 52 weeks.

See also *CH/4574/2003* which holds that reg.5(8B)(c)(i) of the Housing Benefit Regulations (the equivalent of para.3(11)(c)(i)) does treat a person required as a condition of bail to live at a specified address away from "home" differently from a person who is required to live in a bail hostel but concludes that the difference in treatment is within the margin of judgment that is allowed to the legislature and so there was no breach of the European Convention on Human Rights. Leave to appeal to the Court of Appeal was granted by the Commissioner on May 25, 2004. Note however that the regulations have been changed so that a person who is required as a condition of bail to live at an address away from "home" may qualify for housing costs/housing benefit but these amendments are not due to come into effect until April 4, 2005 (see the Social Security (Housing Benefit, Council Tax Benefit, State Pension Credit and Miscellaneous Amendments) Regulations 2004 (SI 2004/2327)).

pp.575–576, *annotation to Income Support (General) Regulations 1987, Sch.3, para.12*

The new para.12 provides for a change in the method of calculating 3.048 the standard rate. The new method will use the Bank of England Base Rate plus 1.58 per cent. Following a change in the Bank of England Base Rate the Secretary of State will determine the date from which the new standard rate will be applicable. According to a footnote in the amending regulations the date determined and the standard rate will be published on the DWP website at least seven days before the new standard rate becomes applicable. It is understood that a new standard rate of 6.33 per cent will apply from December 5, 2004.

The other change is the phased abolition of the "five per cent rule". This provided that the actual rate of interest would be paid if this was less than five per cent on the day housing costs were first payable. This rule no longer applies where housing costs first fall to be met on or after November 28, 2004 and will cease to apply to existing claims on the day the actual rate of interest charged reaches five per cent or more, the anniversary of the date on which housing costs first fell to be met, or whenever a change of circumstances occurs, whichever is the earlier.

p.616, *Income Support (General) Regulations 1987, Sch.8, para.15B*

With effect from October 25, 2004, by reg.2(d) of the Social Security 3.049 (Back to Work Bonus and Lone Parent Run-on) (Amendment and Revocation) Regulations 2003 (SI 2003/1589) para.15B was omitted.

p.620, *annotation to Income Support (General) Regulations 1987, Sch.8, para.15B*

Paragraph 15B (which provided for a disregard of any earnings related 3.050 to work done in the "lone parent run-on" period) has been omitted as a consequence of the abolition of the run-on with effect from October 25, 2004 (see the amendments to reg.6 above).

p.622, *Income Support (General) Regulations 1987, Sch.9, para.11*

3.051   With effect from September 1, 2004 (or if the student's period of study begins between August 1 and August 31, 2004, the first day of the period), reg.5(2) of the Social Security (Students and Income-related Benefits) Amendment Regulations 2004 (SI 2004/1708) substituted the following new paragraph for para.11:

"**11.**—(1) Any payment—

> (a) by way of an education maintenance allowance made pursuant to—
>
>> (i) regulations made under section 518 of the Education Act 1996;
>> (ii) regulations made under section 49 or 73(f) of the Education (Scotland) Act 1980;
>> (iii) directions made under sections 12(2)(c) and 21 of the Further and Higher Education (Scotland) Act 1992; or
>
> (b) corresponding to such an education maintenance allowance, made pursuant to—
>
>> (i) section 14 or section 181 of the Education Act 2002; or
>> (ii) regulations made under section 181 of that Act.

(2) Any payment, other than a payment to which sub-paragraph (1) applies, made pursuant to—

> (a) regulations made under section 518 of the Education Act 1996;
> (b) regulations made under section 49 of the Education (Scotland) Act 1980; or
> (c) directions made under sections 12(2)(c) and 21 of the Further and Higher Education (Scotland) Act 1992,

in respect of a course of study attended by a child or a young person or a person who is in receipt of an education maintenance allowance made pursuant to any provision specified in sub-paragraph (1)."

p.623, *Income Support (General) Regulations 1987, Sch.9, para.15(2)*

3.052   With effect from October 4, 2004, reg.2(1) and (2)(a) of the Social Security (Miscellaneous Amendments) (No.3) Regulations 2004 (SI 2004/2308) inserted the words "council tax, water charges," after the words "household fuel," and omitted the words ", or is used for any council tax or water charges for which that claimant or member is liable".

p.625, *Income Support (General) Regulations 1987, Sch.9, para.25(1)*

With effect from October 4, 2004, reg.4(3) and (4)(a) of the Social   3.053
Security (Miscellaneous Amendments) (No.3) Regulations 2004 (SI
2004/2308) added the following new head (e) after head (d):

"(e)   in accordance with regulations made pursuant to section 14F of
the Children Act 1989 (special guardianship support
services);".

p.626, *Income Support (General) Regulations 1987, Sch.9, para.26*

With effect from May 12, 2004, reg.4(1) and (2)(c) of the Social   3.054
Security (Miscellaneous Amendments) (No.2) Regulations 2004 (SI
2004/1141) substituted the words "section 26 of the Children (Scotland)
Act 1995" for the words "section 21 of the Social Work (Scotland) Act
1968".

p.626, *Income Support (General) Regulations 1987, Sch.9, para.28*

With effect from May 12, 2004, reg.4(3) and (4)(c) of the Social   3.055
Security (Miscellaneous Amendments) (No.2) Regulations 2004 (SI
2004/1141) substituted the words "section 12 of the Social Work (Scotland) Act 1968 or sections 29 or 30 of the Children (Scotland) Act
1995" for the words "section 12, 24 or 26 of the Social Work (Scotland)
Act 1968".

p.628, *Income Support (General) Regulations 1987, Sch.9, para.39(7)*

With effect from October 4, 2004, reg.3(3) and (4)(a) of the Social   3.056
Security (Miscellaneous Amendments) (No.3) Regulations 2004 (SI
2004/2308) substituted the words ", the Eileen Trust and the Skipton
Fund" for the words "and the Eileen Trust".

p.631, *Income Support (General) Regulations 1987, Sch.9, para.70*

With effect from October 25, 2004, by reg.2(d) of the Social Security   3.057
(Back to Work Bonus and Lone Parent Run-on) (Amendment and
Revocation) Regulations 2003 (SI 2003/1589) para.70 was omitted.

p.638, *annotation to Income Support (General) Regulations 1987, Sch.9,
para.11*

A national scheme for the payment of education maintenance allow-   3.058
ances (EMAs) has been introduced from the start of the 2004/5 aca-
demic year (this replaces the previous pilot project). EMAs are
means-tested payments to support young people who remain in non-
advanced education after the age of 16. Under the national scheme they
include weekly payments of £10, £20 or £30 (depending on income),
together with periodic bonuses. EMAs are fully disregarded when calculating entitlement to means-tested benefits. The new form of para.11 has

been introduced so that it reflects all the legislation under which EMAs are paid; sub-para.(2) also applies the disregard to payments (*e.g.* scholarships or expenses) which are paid in respect of courses of education to children, young persons or people in receipt of EMAs (this wording is necessary because in some cases an EMA can be paid to a person who does not come within the definition of "young person" because he is not under 19).

See the new form of para.63 of Sch.10 below for the disregard where the allowance counts as capital.

p.639, *annotation to Income Support (General) Regulations 1987, Sch.9, para.15*

3.059   Paragraph 15(2) has been amended to make clear that payments for council tax and water charges are subject to the £20 limit on the disregard. The Department considered that the previous wording allowed payments for council tax and water charges to be disregarded in full and this is not the policy intention.

On the meaning of "voluntary payment" see *CH/3013/2003*. The claimant had been unable to work following a stroke and had received irregular payments from a friend and his parents. The friend had written a letter which indicated that the payments from her were by way of a loan to be repaid at some unspecified date. However in the Commissioner's view the payments were made without any clear thought about their legal nature. The overall circumstances showed that no legally enforceable rights or obligations were created by the payments to the claimant and that she obtained nothing in return for the payments (see *R. v Doncaster BC Ex p. Boulton* [1992] 25 H.L.R. 195 referred to in the main volume). The payments were therefore voluntary payments within the meaning of reg.40(6) of the Housing Benefit Regulations (the equivalent of reg.48(9) of the Income Support Regulations). The payments from the claimant's parents, where the presumption of gift applied in the absence of evidence to the contrary, also fell within reg.40(6).

p.644, *annotation to Income Support (General) Regulations 1987, Sch.9, para.26*

3.060   The references to the relevant Scottish legislation have now been updated by this amendment.

p.645, *annotation to Income Support (General) Regulations 1987, Sch.9, para.28*

3.061   The references to the relevant Scottish legislation have now been updated by this amendment.

p.647, *annotation to Income Support (General) Regulations 1987, Sch.9, para.39*

3.062   With effect from October 4, 2004 the disregard of payments covered by sub-paras (2) to (6) of para.39 will also apply to such payments that derive from a payment made by the Skipton Fund. The Skipton Fund is government-funded and has been set up to make lump sum ex-gratia payments to people (or their dependants if the person died after August 29, 2003) who have contracted hepatitis C from NHS blood, blood products or tissue.

p.649, *annotation to Income Support (General) Regulations 1987, Sch.9, para.70*

Paragraph 70 (which provided for a disregard of any working tax credit   3.063 during the "lone parent run-on" period) has been omitted as a consequence of the abolition of the run-on with effect from October 25, 2004 (see the amendments to reg.6 above).

p.653, *Income Support (General) Regulations 1987, Sch.10, para.17*

With effect from May 12, 2004, reg.3(1) and (2)(c) of the Social   3.064 Security (Miscellaneous Amendments) (No.2) Regulations 2004 (SI 2004/1141) substituted the words "section 12 of the Social Work (Scotland) Act 1968 or sections 29 or 30 of the Children (Scotland) Act 1995" for the words "section 12, 24 or 26 of the Social Work (Scotland) Act 1968".

p.653, *Income Support (General) Regulations 1987, Sch.10, para.22*

With effect from May 12, 2004, reg.3(3) and (4)(c) of the Social   3.065 Security (Miscellaneous Amendments) (No.2) Regulations 2004 (SI 2004/1141) substituted the words ", the Independent Living Funds or the Skipton Fund" for the words "or the Independent Living Funds" in sub-para.(1).

Regulation 3(5) and (6)(c) of the same amending regulations substituted the words ", the Eileen Trust and the Skipton Fund" for the words "and the Eileen Trust" in sub-para.(7).

p.657, *Income Support (General) Regulations 1987, Sch.10, para.57*

With effect from October 25, 2004, by reg.2(d) of the Social Security   3.066 (Back to Work Bonus and Lone Parent Run-on) (Amendment and Revocation) Regulations 2003 (SI 2003/1589) para.57 was omitted.

p.657, *Income Support (General) Regulations 1987, Sch.10, para.63*

With effect from September 1, 2004 (or if the student's period of   3.067 study begins between August 1 and August 31, 2004, the first day of the period), reg.5(3) of the Social Security (Students and Income-related Benefits) Amendment Regulations 2004 (SI 2004/1708) substituted the following new paragraph for para.63:

"**63.**—(1) Any payment—

(a) by way of an education maintenance allowance made pursuant to—

(i) regulations made under section 518 of the Education Act 1996;

(ii) regulations made under section 49 or 73(f) of the Education (Scotland) Act 1980;

(iii) directions made under sections 12(2)(c) and 21 of the Further and Higher Education (Scotland) Act 1992; or

(b) corresponding to such an education maintenance allowance, made pursuant to—

(i) section 14 or section 181 of the Education Act 2002; or

(ii) regulations made under section 181 of that Act.

(2) Any payment, other than a payment to which sub-paragraph (1) applies, made pursuant to—

(a) regulations made under section 518 of the Education Act 1996;

(b) regulations made under section 49 of the Education (Scotland) Act 1980; or

(c) directions made under sections 12(2)(c) and 21 of the Further and Higher Education (Scotland) Act 1992,

in respect of a course of study attended by a child or a young person or a person who is in receipt of an education maintenance allowance made pursuant to any provision specified in sub-paragraph (1)."

p.658, *Income Support (General) Regulations 1987, Sch.10, para.68A*

3.068   With effect from October 4, 2004, reg.4(5) of the Social Security (Miscellaneous Amendments) (No.3) Regulations 2004 (SI 2004/2308) inserted a new para.68A after para.68:

"**68A.** Any payment made to the claimant in accordance with regulations made pursuant to section 14F of the Children Act 1989 (special guardianship support services)."

p.663, *annotation to Income Support (General) Regulations 1987, Sch.10, para.3*

3.069   *CIS/4269/2003* confirms that there is nothing in para.3 which says that the proceeds of sale must be of the property that was occupied immediately before the property which is to be purchased. The disregard in para.3 can still apply if a claimant who has a sum directly attributable to the proceeds of sale of home A is currently living in home B, providing that the condition that the sum is to be used to purchase home C within 26 weeks (or reasonable longer period) of the sale of home A is met.

p.671, *annotation to Income Support (General) Regulations 1987, Sch.10, para.17*

3.070   The references to the relevant Scottish legislation have now been updated by this amendment.

p.671, *annotation to Income Support (General) Regulations 1987, Sch.10, para.22*

The amendment made with effect from May 12, 2004 adds the 3.071
Skipton Fund to the list of funds to which the disregard in para.22
applies. The Skipton Fund has been set up to make lump sum ex-gratia
payments to people (or their dependants if the person died after August
29, 2003) who have contracted hepatitis C from NHS blood, blood
products or tissue.

p.675, *annotation to Income Support (General) Regulations 1987, Sch.10, para.57*

Paragraph 57 (which provided that any back to work bonus or child 3.072
maintenance bonus paid during the "lone parent run-on" period would
be ignored) has been omitted as a consequence of the abolition of the
run-on with effect from October 25, 2004 (see the amendments to reg.6
above).

p.676, *annotation to Income Support (General) Regulations 1987, Sch.10, para.63*

See the note to the new form of para.11 of Sch.9 to the Income 3.073
Support Regulations above. Note that the new form of para.63 provides
for an indefinite disregard of any part of the education maintenance
allowance that counts as capital.

p.705, *annotation to Social Security (Working Tax Credit and Child Tax Credit) (Consequential Amendments) Regulations 2003, reg.7*

In *CIS/995/2004* the Commissioner acknowledges that there were 3.074
several problems in working out the meaning of reg.7(1) but on the facts
of that case he saw no difficulty in interpreting reg.7(1) as deeming a
claimant's income to include the amount equivalent to that contained in
the operative award of child tax credit.

pp.731–759, *Social Security (Back to Work Bonus) (No.2) Regulations 1996*

With effect from October 25, 2004, reg.8 of the Social Security (Back 3.075
to Work Bonus and Lone Parent Run-on) (Amendment and Revocation)
Regulations 2003 (SI 2003/1589) revoked the Social Security (Back to
Work Bonus) (No.2) Regulations 1996. However, note the transitional
provisions in reg.10 (see Pt I of this Supplement). Claimants who have
served the 13-week waiting period on October 24, 2004 will be able to
claim the bonus if they satisfy the conditions of entitlement for a bonus
(including making a claim) during the period October 25, 2004 to
January 28, 2005 or if they satisfy the other conditions of entitlement
during that transitional period and make a claim after January 28, 2005
within the relevant time limit. But they will not be able to build up any

further bonus after October 24, 2004. See further the note to reg.10 of the Social Security (Back to Work Bonus and Lone Parent Run-on) (Amendment and Revocation) Regulations 2003 in Pt I.

p.779, *Children (Leaving Care) (Wales) Regulations 2001, reg.4*

3.076   With effect from July 23, 2004, reg.2(1) of the Children (Leaving Care) (Wales) (Amendment) Regulations (SI 2004/1732) inserted the words "Subject to paragraph (2A)" at the beginning of para.(2).

Regulation 2(2) of the same amending regulations inserted the following new para.(2A) after para.(2):

> "(2A) In calculating the period of 13 weeks referred to in sub-paragraph (2)(b), no account is to be taken of any period in which the child was looked after in a series of short-term placements none of which individually exceeds four weeks, where, at the end of each such placement, the child returned to the care of his parent, or a person who is not a parent but who has parental responsibility for him."

p.811, *Jobseeker's Allowance Regulations 1996, reg.1(3)*

3.077   With effect from September 1, 2004 (or if the student's period of study begins between August 1 and August 31, 2004, the first day of the period), reg.6(1) of the Social Security (Students and Income-related Benefits) Amendment Regulations 2004 (SI 2004/1708) substituted the words "a Scottish national qualification (higher or advanced higher)" for the words "a Scottish certificate of education (higher level) or a Scottish certificate of sixth year studies" in the definition of "course of advanced education".

p.817, *Jobseeker's Allowance Regulations 1996, reg.1(3) (interpretation): amendment of the definition of "qualifying person"*

3.078   With effect from May 12, 2004, reg.2(a) of the Social Security (Miscellaneous Amendments) (No.2) Regulations 2004 (SI 2004/1141) amended the definition of "qualifying person" to read as follows:

> " "qualifying person" means a person in respect of whom payment has been made from the Fund [, the Eileen Trust or the Skipton Fund];".

pp.818–819, *Jobseeker's Allowance Regulations 1996, reg.1(3) (interpretation): substitution of a new definition of "self-employment route"*

3.079   With effect from May 4, 2004, reg.2 of the Social Security (Income-Related Benefits Self-Employment Route Amendment) Regulations 2004 substituted a new definition of "self-employment route" to read as follows:

> " "self-employment route" means assistance in pursuing self-employed earner's employment whilst participating in—
>
>   (a) an employment zone programme; or

(b) a programme provided or other arrangements made pursuant to section 2 of the Employment and Training Act 1973 (functions of the Secretary of State) or section 2 of the Enterprise and New Towns (Scotland) Act 1990 (functions in relation to training for employment etc.);".

p.819, *Jobseeker's Allowance Regulations 1996, reg.1(3) (interpretation): insertion of a new definition*

With effect from May 12, 2004, reg.2(b) of the Social Security (Mis- **3.080**
cellaneous Amendments) (No.2) Regulations 2004 (SI 2004/1141) inserted after the definition of "single claimant" a new definition, reading as follows:

" "the Skipton Fund" means the ex-gratia payment scheme administered by the Skipton Fund Limited, incorporated on 25th March 2004, for the benefit of certain persons suffering from hepatitis C and other persons eligible for payment in accordance with the scheme's provisions;".

p.856, *Jobseeker's Allowance Regulations 1996, reg.14 (circumstances in which a person is to be treated as available): insertion in para.(1) of new sub-paragraphs*

With effect from October 4, 2004, reg.3(2)(a) of the Social Security **3.081**
(Income Support and Jobseeker's Allowance) Amendment Regulations 2004 (SI 2004/1869) inserted after sub-para.(l), a new sub-paragraph, reading as follows:

"(ll) if he is treated as capable of work in accordance with regulation 55A, for the period determined in accordance with that regulation;".

From the same date, reg.3(2)(b) of those Regulations inserted after sub-para.(p), a new sub-paragraph, reading as follows:

"(q) if he is temporarily absent from Great Britain in the circumstances prescribed in regulation 50(6AA) or, as the case may be, (6C)."

p.870, *Jobseeker's Allowance Regulations 1996, reg.18 (steps to be taken by persons actively seeking employment): substitution of a new para.(1)*

Regulation 2(2) of the Jobseeker's Allowance (Amendment) Regula- **3.082**
tions 2004 (SI 2004/1008) substituted a new para.(1), reading as follows:

"(1) For the purposes of section 7(1) (actively seeking employment) a person shall be expected to have to take more than two steps in any week unless taking one or two steps is all that is reasonable for that person to do in that week."

Regulation 1 of those Regulations has the effect that the substitution took effect for new claimants from April 19, 2004. For those entitled to a jobseeker's allowance, or who had earnings credited to them under reg.8A of the Credits Regulations, on that date, the substitution took effect on October 18, 2004.

p.872, *annotation to Jobseeker's Allowance Regulations 1996, reg.18 (steps to be taken by persons actively seeking employment): the effect of the new para.(1)*

3.083 The new form of para.(1) increased the minimum number of steps that a jobseeker must take to be actively seeking employment from at least two to at least three in a week, unless taking one or two steps is all that it is reasonable to do in that week. It became effective on April 19, 2004 for new claimants, but only took effect from October 18, 2004 for those who on April 19, 2004 were entitled to a Jobseeker's Allowance or who had earnings credited to them under reg.8A of the Credits Regulations (credits for unemployment). Concerns were expressed by the SSAC (see Cmd. 6145) about the lack of need for and the effect of the change at a time of national low unemployment, and against a background of manpower cuts at Jobcentres. Despite this, the change was made. The Secretary of State was of the view that tailored support was an important way to help people return to work but that, in addition to special provision, it was reasonable in a buoyant labour market to increase expectations of the claimant unemployed through measures designed to be adapted to the individual to increase prospects of getting a job more quickly. The positive effects of being in work outweighed any negative effects. Impact on staff resources would be small. General evidence showed that more contact and increased quality job-search, designed to keep people attached to the labour market were among the most successful and cost effective measures in helping people find work.

pp.876–877, *Jobseeker's Allowance Regulations 1996, reg.19 (circumstances in which a person is to be treated as actively seeking employment): insertion in para.(1) of new sub-paragraphs*

3.084 With effect from October 4, 2004, reg.3(3)(a) of the Social Security (Income Support and Jobseeker's Allowance) Amendment Regulations 2004 (SI 2004/1869) inserted after sub-para.(l), a new sub-paragraph, reading as follows:

"(ll) in any week during which he is for not less than 3 days treated as capable of work in accordance with regulation 55A;".

From the same date, reg.3(3)(b) of those Regulations inserted after sub-para.(t), a new sub-paragraph, reading as follows:

"(u) if he is temporarily absent from Great Britain in the circumstances prescribed in regulation 50(6AA) or, as the case may be
(6C)."

pp.906–907, *Jobseeker's Allowance Regulations 1996: amendment of*
reg.50 (Persons temporarily absent from Great Britain)

With effect from October 4, 2004, reg.3(4) of the Social Security   3.085
(Income Support and Jobseeker's Allowance) Amendment Regulations
2004 (SI 2004/1869) amended reg.50 by the insertion of a new para.
(6AA) as follows:

"(6AA) For the purposes of the Act a claimant shall be treated as being
in Great Britain during any period of temporary absence from Great
Britain if—

   (a) he was entitled to a jobseeker's allowance immediately before
       the beginning of that period of temporary absence; and
   (b) that period of temporary absence is for the purpose of the
       claimant receiving treatment at a hospital or other institution
       outside Great Britain where that treatment is being pro-
       vided—

      (i) under section 3 of the National Health Service Act 1977
          (services generally);
     (ii) pursuant to arrangements made under section 23 of that
          Act (voluntary organisations and other bodies); or
    (iii) pursuant to arrangements made under paragraph 13 of
          Schedule 2 to the National Health Service and Commu-
          nity Care Act 1990 (National Health Service Trusts—
          specific powers)."

and a new para.(6C) as follows:

"(6C) For the purposes of the Act a member of a joint-claim couple
("the first member") shall be treated as being in Great Britain during
any period of temporary absence if—

   (a) he and the other member of that couple were entitled to a joint-
       claim jobseeker's allowance immediately before the beginning
       of that period of temporary absence; and
   (b) that period of temporary absence is for the purpose of the first
       member receiving treatment at a hospital or other institution
       outside Great Britain where that treatment is being pro-
       vided—

      (i) under section 3 of the National Health Service Act 1977;
     (ii) pursuant to arrangements made under section 23 of that
          Act; or
    (iii) pursuant to arrangements made under paragraph 13 of
          Schedule 2 to the National Health Service and Commu-
          nity Care Act 1990."

p.912, *annotation to Jobseeker's Allowance Regulations 1996, reg.51 (Remunerative work)*

3.086   For an example of the application of the principles in *R(JSA) 5/03* (and, in particular, the treatment of paid public or extra-statutory holidays falling outside term-time) see the decision of Mr Commissioner Mesher in *CJSA/1638/2003.*

p.914, *Jobseeker's Allowance Regulations 1996: amendment of reg.53 (Persons not treated as engaged in remunerative work)*

3.087   With effect from May 4, 2004, reg.4 of the Social Security (Income-Related Benefits Self-Employment Route Amendment) Regulations 2004 (SI 2004/963) amended reg.53(bb) to read:

"(bb) he is receiving assistance [under the self-employment route];".

p.919, *Jobseeker's Allowance Regulations 1996, reg.55*

3.088   With effect from October 4, 2004, reg.3(5) of the Social Security (Income Support and Jobseeker's Allowance) Amendment Regulations 2004 (SI 2004/1869) added the following new para.(5) after para.(4):

"(5) The preceding provisions of this regulation shall not apply to a claimant who is temporarily absent from Great Britain in the circumstances prescribed by regulation 50(6AA) or, as the case may be, (6C)."

Regulation 3(6) of the same amending regulations inserted the following new reg.55A after reg.55:

"Periods of sickness and persons receiving treatment outside Great Britain

55A.—(1) A person—

(a) who has been awarded a jobseeker's allowance, a joint-claim jobseeker's allowance or is a person to whom any of the circumstances mentioned in section 19(5) or (6) or 20A(2) apply; and

(b) who is temporarily absent from Great Britain in the circumstances prescribed by regulation 50(6AA) or, as the case may be, (6C); and

(c) who proves to the satisfaction of the Secretary of State that he is unable to work on account of some specific disease or disablement; and

(d) but for his disease or disablement, would satisfy the requirements for entitlement to a jobseeker's allowance other than those specified in section 1(2)(a), (c) and (f) (available for and actively seeking employment and capable of work),

shall be treated during that period of temporary absence abroad as capable of work, except where that person has stated in writing before that period of temporary absence abroad begins that immediately before the beginning of the period of that temporary absence abroad he has claimed incapacity benefit, severe disablement allowance or income support.

(2) The evidence which is required for the purposes of paragraph (1)(c) is a declaration made by that person in writing, in a form approved for the purposes by the Secretary of State, that he will be unfit for work from a date or for a period specified in the declaration."

GENERAL NOTE

The purpose of this provision, together with the amendments that have been made to regs 14, 19, 50 and 55 (see above), is to enable entitlement to JSA to continue during any period that the claimant (including a member of a joint-claim couple) goes abroad temporarily for the purpose of receiving treatment funded by the NHS. Regulation 55A treats such a person as capable of work, provided that he supplies a written declaration on an approved form that he is unfit for work from a stated date or for a specified period and satisfies the conditions for an award of JSA (other than the requirements of being available for and capable of, and of actively seeking, work). However, he will not be treated as capable of work if he has stated in writing before the absence abroad begins that he has claimed incapacity benefit, severe disablement or income support. Thus a person in these circumstances can choose to remain in receipt of JSA or to claim benefit on the ground of incapacity for work if he wishes to do so.   3.089

p.949, *Jobseeker's Allowance Regulations 1996, amendment of reg. 72(6)(b) (good cause for the purposes of s. 19(5)(a) and (6)(c) and (d))*

Regulation 2(2) of the Jobseeker's Allowance (Amendment) Regulations 2004 (SI 2004/1008) amended subs.(6)(b) to read as follows: 3.090

"(b) the time it took, or would normally take, for the person to travel from his home to the place of the employment, or a place mentioned in the jobseeker's direction, and back to his home where that time was or is normally less than [,—

(i) during the first 13 weeks of entitlement to a jobseeker's allowance, one hour either way; and
(ii) in all other cases, one hour and thirty minutes either way,

by a route and means appropriate to his circumstances and to the employment, or to the carrying out of the jobseeker's direction, unless, in view of the health of the person or any caring responsibilities of his, that time was or is unreasonable.]"

Regulation 1 of those Regulations has the effect that the amendment took effect for new claimants from April 19, 2004. For those entitled to a jobseeker's allowance, or who had earnings credited to them under reg.8A of the Credits Regulations, on that date, the amendment took effect on October 18, 2004.

pp.951–954, *annotation to Jobseeker's Allowance Regulations 1996,*
reg. 72: "Good cause" for purposes of Jobseekers Act 1995,
s. 19(5)(a)—jobseeker's direction and s. 19(6)(c), (d)

3.091   The amended form of subs.(6)(b) [see update to p.949, above] pre-
cludes, like its predecessor, founding good cause on traveling time of less
than a certain length with respect to refusing or failing to carry out a
jobseeker's direction (Jobseekers Act 1995, s.19(5)(a)) or to apply for or
accept employment to which a jobseeker has been referred by an
employment officer (s.19(6)(c)) or which has been offered in a qualifying
former employment (s.19(6)(d)). Where the failure relates to the travelling time between the jobseeker's home and the place of employment or
the place mentioned in the jobseeker's direction, a jobseeker will not
generally have good cause if the time is less than one hour and thirty
minutes either way. During the first 13 weeks of entitlement to a jobseeker's allowance a jobseeker will not have good cause for such a refusal
or failure if the travelling time is less than one hour either way. Previously, in all cases, a jobseeker did not have good cause if the travelling
time was less than one hour either way.

The amendment took effect for new claimants from April 19, 2004.
For those entitled to a jobseeker's allowance, or who had earnings
credited to them under reg.8A of the Credits Regulations, on that date,
the amendment took effect on October 18, 2004.

For criticism by the SSAC and the governmental response, see update
to p.872, above.

p.963, *Jobseeker's Allowance Regulations 1996, amendment or*
reg. 75(1)(a)(iii)

3.092   With effect from April 26, 2004, reg.23 of the Social Security (Working Neighbourhoods) Regulations 2004 (SI 2004/959) amended
reg.75(1)(a)(iii) by inserting at the end, after, "Employment Zone Regulations 2000" the words "or the Social Security (Working Neighbourhoods) Regulations 2004".

pp.980–981, *Jobseeker's Allowance Regulations 1996: amendment of*
reg. 85 (Special cases)

3.093   With effect from May 1, 2004, reg.4 of the Social Security (Habitual
Residence) Amendment Regulations 2004 (SI 2004/1232) amended
reg.85. The text of the amendments is set out on p.1310 in Pt VI
(Forthcoming Changes) of the main volume. The amendments are
subject to the transitional protection provided by reg.6 of SI 2004/1232
(see p.1311 of the main volume).

p.1016, *annotation to Jobseeker's Allowance Regulations 1996, reg. 104*

3.094   Paragraph (3) of reg.104 was omitted with effect from April 6, 2004 by
reg.3 of and para.9 of Sch.2 to the Social Security (Working Tax Credit
and Child Tax Credit) (Consequential Amendments) Regulations 2003

(SI 2003/455), except in "transitional cases" (*i.e.* those cases in which the claimant is still receiving amounts for his children in his income-based JSA—see further the notes to reg.83 of the Jobseeker's Allowance Regulations and reg.17 of the Income Support Regulations in the 2004 edition of Vol.II. It was intended that the phased transfer to child tax credit would begin in October 2004 but this has been deferred until 2005). For "transitional cases" reg.104(3) continues in force (see the 2003 edition of Vol.II for this provision). With effect from May 12, 2004, reg.5 of the Social Security (Miscellaneous Amendments) (No.2) Regulations 2004 (SI 2004/1141) substituted the words "section 12 of the Social Work (Scotland) Act 1968 or sections 29 or 30 of the Children (Scotland) Act 1995" for the words "section 12, 24 or 26 of the Social Work (Scotland) Act 1968" in reg.104(3). The effect of this amendment is simply to update the references to the Scottish legislation referred to in reg.104(3).

p.1027, *Jobseeker's Allowance Regulations 1996, reg.113(3A)(a)*

With effect from October 4, 2004, reg.3(1) and (2)(d) of the Social **3.095** Security (Miscellaneous Amendments) (No.3) Regulations 2004 (SI 2004/2308) substituted the words ", the Independent Living Funds or the Skipton Fund" for the words "or the Independent Living Funds".

p.1044, *Jobseeker's Allowance Regulations 1996, reg.130*

With effect from September 1, 2004 (or if the student's period of **3.096** study begins between August 1 and August 31, 2004, the first day of the period), reg.6(2) of the Social Security (Students and Income-related Benefits) Amendment Regulations 2004 (SI 2004/1708) added the words "or any payment to which paragraph 12 of Schedule 7 or paragraph 52 of Schedule 8 applies" after the words "a payment from access funds" in the definition of "grant".

pp.1046–1047, *Jobseeker's Allowance Regulations 1996, reg.131*

With effect from September 1, 2004 (or if the student's period of **3.097** study begins between August 1 and August 31, 2004, the first day of the period), reg.2(1) and (3)(d) of the Social Security (Students and Income-related Benefits) Amendment Regulations 2004 (SI 2004/1708) substituted the sum "£275" for the sum "£270" in para.(3)(a).

Regulation 2(2) and (3)(d) of the same amending regulations substituted the sum "£343" for the sum "£335" in para.(3)(b).

Regulation 3(4)(a) of the same amending regulations omitted the words "or child care costs" in para.(2)(h) and reg.3(4)(b) added the following new sub-paragraph after para.(2)(h): "(i) intended for the child care costs of a child dependant".

p.1049, *annotation to Jobseeker's Allowance Regulations 1996, reg.131*

The amendments made to reg.131 with effect from April 6, 2004 by **3.098** reg.3 of and para.16 of Sch.2 to the Social Security (Working Tax Credit and Child Tax Credit) (Consequential Amendments) Regulations 2003 (SI 2003/455) (see the 2004 edition of Vol.II for these amendments) do not apply in "transitional cases" (*i.e.* those cases in which the claimant is still receiving amounts for his children in his income-based jobseeker's allowance—see further the notes to reg.83 of the Jobseeker's Allowance Regulations and reg.17 of the Income Support Regulations in the 2004 edition of Vol.II. It was intended that the phased transfer to child tax credit of these cases would begin in October 2004 but this has now been deferred until 2005). For "transitional cases" the unamended form of reg.131 continues in force (see the 2003 edition of Vol.II for this form of reg.131). Among the amendments made by the 2003 Regulations was the insertion of a new para.(2)(h) which provided for a general disregard of payments intended for the maintenance or child care costs of a child. This replaced most of the disregards for students with child care responsibilities previously contained in para.(3A), except that in sub-para.(b) which became the new (3A).

However, the insertion of the new para.(2)(i) with effect from September 1, 2004 (or if the student's period of study begins between August 1 and August 31, 2004, the first day of the period), which provides for a general disregard of payments intended for the child care costs of a child dependant, means that the disregards contained in sub-paras (c), (cc) and (d) of the unamended form of reg.131(3A) are no longer needed. These have therefore been omitted with effect from September 1, 2004 (or if the student's period of study begins between August 1 and August 31, 2004, the first day of the period) (see reg.3(5) and (6)(d) of the Social Security (Students and Income-related Benefits) Amendment Regulations 2004 (SI 2004/1708)).

p.1053, *Jobseeker's Allowance Regulations 1996, reg.136(5)*

3.099   With effect from September 1, 2004 (or if the student's period of study begins between August 1 and August 31, 2004, the first day of the period), reg.2(1) and (3)(d) of the Social Security (Students and Income-related Benefits) Amendment Regulations 2004 (SI 2004/1708) substituted the sum "£275" for the sum "£270" in sub-para.(a).

Regulation 2(2) and (3)(d) of the same amending regulations substituted the sum "£343" for the sum "£335" in sub-para.(b).

p.1109, *Jobseeker's Allowance Regulations 1996, Sch.2, para.1(2)*

3.100   With effect from November 28, 2004, reg.2(2) of the Social Security (Housing Costs Amendments) Regulations 2004 (SI 2004/2825) substituted the words ""determined in accordance with" for the words "specified in" in the definition of "standard rate".

Regulation 2(5) of the same amending regulations substituted the following head for head (a) in the definition of "existing housing costs":

"(a) which replaces an existing agreement, provided that the person liable to meet the housing costs—

(i) remains the same in both agreements, or

(ii) where in either agreement more than one person is liable to
meet the housing costs, the person is liable to meet the housing
costs in both the existing agreement and the new agreement;".

p.1117, *Jobseeker's Allowance Regulations 1996, Sch.2, para.9*

With effect from November 28, 2004, in the explanation of "B", 3.101
reg.2(3) of the Social Security (Housing Costs Amendments) Regulations 2004 (SI 2004/2825) substituted the words "applicable in respect
of that loan" for the words "specified in respect of that loan under
paragraph 11".

p.1118, *Jobseeker's Allowance Regulations 1996, Sch.2, para.11*

With effect from November 28, 2004, reg.2(4) of the Social Security 3.102
(Housing Costs Amendments) Regulations 2004 (SI 2004/2825) substituted the following sub-paragraphs for the sub-paragraphs in para.11:

"(1) The standard rate is the rate of interest applicable per annum to
a loan which qualifies under this Schedule.
(2) Subject to sub-paragraphs (3), (4) and (6), the standard rate
shall be 1.58 per cent. plus—

(a) the rate announced from time to time by the Monetary Policy
Committee of the Bank of England as the official dealing rate,
being the rate at which the Bank is willing to enter into transac-
tions for providing short term liquidity in the money markets,
or
(b) where an order under section 19 of the Bank of England Act
1998 (reserve powers) is in force, any equivalent rate determined by the Treasury under that section.

(3) The Secretary of State shall determine the date from which the
standard rate calculated in accordance with sub-paragraph (2) takes
effect.
(4) Where—

(a) the actual rate of interest charged on the loan which qualifies
under this Schedule is less than 5 per cent. per annum on the
day the housing costs first fall to be met, and
(b) that day occurs before 28th November 2004,

the standard rate shall be equal to that actual rate.
(5) Sub-paragraph (4) shall cease to apply in a particular case to any
one or more loans which fall within that sub-paragraph on whichever
of the following dates occurs first—

(a) the date on which the actual rate of interest charged on such a
loan is 5 per cent. per annum or higher,
(b) the anniversary of the date on which the housing costs first fell
to be met, or
(c) where a supersession decision based on a change of circumstances arising on or after 28th November 2004 is made under

section 10 of the Social Security Act 1998 (decisions super-seding earlier decisions), the date of the change of circum-stances.

(6) Where sub-paragraph (4) does not apply to a loan which quali-fies under this Schedule, the standard rate shall be 5.88 per cent. until the first date determined by the Secretary of State under sub-paragraph (3)."

p.1128, *annotation to Jobseeker's Allowance Regulations 1996, Sch.2*

3.103   On the amendments to the definitions in para.1(2) and to para.11, see the notes to para.1(2) and para.12 of Sch.3 to the Income Support Regulations above.

p.1147, *Jobseeker's Allowance Regulations 1996, Sch.7, para.12*

3.104   With effect from September 1, 2004 (or if the student's period of study begins between August 1 and August 31, 2004, the first day of the period), reg.6(3) of the Social Security (Students and Income-related Benefits) Amendment Regulations 2004 (SI 2004/1708) substituted the following new paragraph for para.12:

"**12.**—(1) Any payment—

(a) by way of an education maintenance allowance made pursuant to—

(i) regulations made under section 518 of the Education Act 1996;
(ii) regulations made under section 49 or 73(f) of the Educa-tion (Scotland) Act 1980;
(iii) directions made under sections 12(2)(c) and 21 of the Further and Higher Education (Scotland) Act 1992; or

(b) corresponding to such an education maintenance allowance, made pursuant to—

(i) section 14 or section 181 of the Education Act 2002; or
(ii) regulations made under section 181 of that Act.

(2) Any payment, other than a payment to which sub-paragraph (1) applies, made pursuant to—

(a) regulations made under section 518 of the Education Act 1996;
(b) regulations made under section 49 of the Education (Scotland) Act 1980; or
(c) directions made under sections 12(2)(c) and 21 of the Further and Higher Education (Scotland) Act 1992,

in respect of a course of study attended by a child or a young person or a person who is in receipt of an education maintenance allowance made pursuant to any provision specified in sub-paragraph (1)."

p.1148, *Jobseeker's Allowance Regulations 1996, Sch.7, para.15(2)*

With effect from October 4, 2004, reg.2(1) and (2)(b) of the Social Security (Miscellaneous Amendments) (No.3) Regulations 2004 (SI 2004/2308) inserted the words "council tax, water charges," after the words "household fuel," and omitted the words ", or is used for any council tax or water charges for which that claimant or member is liable". — 3.105

p.1150, *Jobseeker's Allowance Regulations 1996, Sch.7, para.26(1)*

With effect from October 4, 2004, reg.4(3) and (4)(b) of the Social Security (Miscellaneous Amendments) (No.3) Regulations 2004 (SI 2004/2308) added the following new head (e) after head (d): — 3.106

"(e) in accordance with regulations made pursuant to section 14F of the Children Act 1989 (special guardianship support services);".

p.1151, *Jobseeker's Allowance Regulations 1996, Sch.7, para.27*

With effect from May 12, 2004, reg.4(1) and (2)(d) of the Social Security (Miscellaneous Amendments) (No.2) Regulations 2004 (SI 2004/1141) substituted the words "section 26 of the Children (Scotland) Act 1995" for the words "section 21 of the Social Work (Scotland) Act 1968". — 3.107

p.1151, *Jobseeker's Allowance Regulations 1996, Sch.7, para.29*

With effect from May 12, 2004, reg.4(3) and (4)(d) of the Social Security (Miscellaneous Amendments) (No.2) Regulations 2004 (SI 2004/1141) substituted the words "section 12 of the Social Work (Scotland) Act 1968 or sections 29 or 30 of the Children (Scotland) Act 1995" for the words "section 12, 24 or 26 of the Social Work (Scotland) Act 1968". — 3.108

p.1153, *Jobseeker's Allowance Regulations 1996, Sch.7, para.41*

With effect from October 4, 2004, reg.3(5) of the Social Security (Miscellaneous Amendments) (No.3) Regulations 2004 (SI 2004/2308) added the following new sub-paragraph after sub-para.(6): — 3.109

"(7) For the purposes of paragraphs (2) to (6), any reference to the Trusts shall be construed as including a reference to the Skipton Fund."

p.1159, *annotation to Jobseeker's Allowance Regulations 1996, Sch.7*

On the new para.12, see the note to the new para.11 of Sch.9 to the Income Support Regulations above; and on the new sub-para.(7) of para.41, see the note to para.39(7) of Sch.9 above. — 3.110

pp.1161–1162, *Jobseeker's Allowance Regulations 1996, Sch.8, para.22*

3.111   With effect from May 12, 2004, reg.3(1) and (2)(d) of the Social Security (Miscellaneous Amendments) (No.2) Regulations 2004 (SI 2004/1141) substituted the words "section 12 of the Social Work (Scotland) Act 1968 or sections 29 or 30 of the Children (Scotland) Act 1995" for the words "section 12, 24 or 26 of the Social Work (Scotland) Act 1968".

p.1162, *Jobseeker's Allowance Regulations 1996, Sch.8, para.27(1)*

3.112   With effect from May 12, 2004, reg.3(7) and (8)(b) of the Social Security (Miscellaneous Amendments) (No.2) Regulations 2004 (SI 2004/1141) inserted the words ", the Skipton Fund" after the words "the Eileen Trust".

p.1164, *Jobseeker's Allowance Regulations 1996, Sch.8, para.52*

3.113   With effect from September 1, 2004 (or if the student's period of study begins between August 1 and August 31, 2004, the first day of the period), reg.6(4) of the Social Security (Students and Income-related Benefits) Amendment Regulations 2004 (SI 2004/1708) substituted the following new paragraph for para.52:

"**52.**—(1) Any payment—

(a) by way of an education maintenance allowance made pursuant to—

(i) regulations made under section 518 of the Education Act 1996;

(ii) regulations made under section 49 or 73(f) of the Education (Scotland) Act 1980;

(iii) directions made under sections 12(2)(c) and 21 of the Further and Higher Education (Scotland) Act 1992; or

(b) corresponding to such an education maintenance allowance, made pursuant to—

(i) section 14 or section 181 of the Education Act 2002; or

(ii) regulations made under section 181 of that Act.

(2) Any payment, other than a payment to which sub-paragraph (1) applies, made pursuant to—

(a) regulations made under section 518 of the Education Act 1996;

(b) regulations made under section 49 of the Education (Scotland) Act 1980; or

(c) directions made under sections 12(2)(c) and 21 of the Further and Higher Education (Scotland) Act 1992,

in respect of a course of study attended by a child or a young person or a person who is in receipt of an education maintenance allowance made pursuant to any provision specified in sub-paragraph (1)."

p.1166, *Jobseeker's Allowance Regulations 1996, Sch.8, para.61A*

With effect from October 4, 2004, reg.4(7) of the Social Security 3.114
(Miscellaneous Amendments) (No.3) Regulations 2004 (SI 2004/2308)
inserted a new para.61A after para.61:

"**61A.** Any payment made to the claimant in accordance with regulations made pursuant to section 14F of the Children Act 1989 (special
guardianship support services)."

p.1168, *annotation to Jobseeker's Allowance Regulations 1996, Sch.8*

On para.52, see the note to the new para.63 of Sch.10 to the Income 3.115
Support Regulations above.

p.1175, *State Pension Credit Regulations 2002: insertion of definition of*
"equity release scheme" into reg.1(2)

With effect from October 4, 2004, reg.7(2) of the Social Security 3.116
(Housing Benefit, Council Tax Benefit, State Pension Credit and Miscellaneous Amendments) Regulations 2004 (SI 2004/2327) inserted
after the definition of "Eileen Trust" the following definition:

" "equity release scheme" " means a loan—

    (a) made between a person ("the lender") and the claimant;
    (b) by means of which a sum of money is advanced by the lender to
        the claimant by way of payments at regular intervals; and
    (c) which is secured on a dwelling in which the claimant owns an
        estate or interest and which he occupies as his home;".

p.1177, *State Pension Credit Regulations 2002: amendment of definition of*
"qualifying person" in reg.1(2)

With effect from May 12, 2004, reg.2(a) of the Social Security (Mis- 3.117
cellaneous Amendments) (No.2) Regulations 2004 (SI 2004/1141)
amended the definition of "qualifying person" in reg.1(2) to read as
follows:

" "qualifying person" means a person in respect of whom payment has
been made from the Fund [, the Eileen Trust or the Skipton
Fund];".

p.1177, *State Pension Credit Regulations 2002: insertion of definition of*
"the Skipton Fund" into reg.1(2)

With effect from May 12, 2004, reg.2(b)(iv) of the Social Security 3.118
(Miscellaneous Amendments) (No.2) Regulations 2004 (SI 2004/1141)
inserted after the definition of "qualifying person" the following definition:

" "the Skipton Fund" means the ex-gratia payment scheme administered by the Skipton Fund Limited, incorporated on 25th March

2004, for the benefit of certain persons suffering from hepatitis C and other persons eligible for payment in accordance with the scheme's provisions;".

p.1178, *State Pension Credit Regulations 2002: amendment of reg.2 (persons not in Great Britain)*

3.119   With effect from May 1, 2004, reg.5(a) of the Social Security (Habitual Residence) Amendment Regulations 2004 (SI 2004/1232) inserted the words "—(1) Subject to paragraph (2)," at the beginning of reg.2.

p.1179, *State Pension Credit Regulations 2002: amendment of reg.2(a) (now reg.2(1)(a)) (persons not in Great Britain)*

3.120   With effect from May 1, 2004, reg.5(b) of the Social Security (Habitual Residence) Amendment Regulations 2004 (SI 2004/1232) added the following words after "No.73/148/EEC" in reg.2(a) (now reg.2(1)(a)):

"or a person who is an accession State worker requiring registration who is treated as a worker for the purpose of the definition of "qualified person" in regulation 5(1) of the Immigration (European Economic Area) Regulations 2000 pursuant to regulation 5 of the Accession (Immigration and Worker Registration) Regulations 2004."

p.1179, *State Pension Credit Regulations 2002: insertion of new reg.2(2) (persons not in Great Britain)*

3.121   With effect from May 1, 2004, reg.5(c) of the Social Security (Habitual Residence) Amendment Regulations 2004 (SI 2004/1232) inserted the following new paragraph:

"(2) For the purposes of treating a person as not in Great Britain in paragraph (1), no person shall be treated as habitually resident in the United Kingdom, the Channel Islands, the Isle of Man or the Republic of Ireland if he does not have a right to reside in the United Kingdom, the Channel Islands, the Isle of Man or the Republic of Ireland."

These amendments to reg.2 are subject to the saving provision in reg.6 of the Social Security (Habitual Residence) Amendment Regulations 2004 (SI 2004/1232).

p.1194, *State Pension Credit Regulations 2002: amendment of reg.15(5) (income for the purposes of the Act)*

3.122   With effect from October 4, 2004, reg.7(3) of the Social Security (Housing Benefit, Council Tax Benefit, State Pension Credit and Miscellaneous Amendments) Regulations 2004 (SI 2004/2327) inserted after para.(i) the following:

"(j) any payment made at regular intervals under an equity release scheme."

p.1196, *State Pension Credit Regulations 2002: amendment of reg.16 (retirement pension income)*

With effect from October 4, 2004, reg.7(4) of the Social Security 3.123
(Housing Benefit, Council Tax Benefit, State Pension Credit and Miscellaneous Amendments) Regulations 2004 (SI 2004/2327) inserted
after para.(l) the following:

> "(m) any payment made at regular intervals under an equity release
> scheme."

p.1218, *State Pension Credit Regulations 2002: amendment of Sch.II, para.1(2)(iii)(c) (housing costs: definition of "standard rate")*

With effect from November 28, 2004, reg.2(2) of the Social Security 3.124
(Housing Costs Amendments) Regulations 2004 (SI 2004/2825)
amended the definition of "standard rate" to read:

> " "standard rate" means the rate for the time being [determined in
> accordance with] paragraph 9."

p.1224, *State Pension Credit Regulations 2002: amendment of Sch.II, para.7(1) (housing costs: calculation for loans—explanation of "B")*

With effect from November 28, 2004, reg.2(3) of the Social Security 3.125
(Housing Costs Amendments) Regulations 2004 (SI 2004/2825)
amended the explanation of "B" to read: "B = the standard rate for the
time being [applicable in respect of that loan]."

p.1226, *State Pension Credit Regulations 2002: amendment of Sch.II, para.9 (housing costs: the standard rate)*

With effect from November 28, 2004, reg.2(4) of the Social Security 3.126
(Housing Costs Amendments) Regulations 2004 (SI 2004/2825) substituted a new para.9 to read:

> "(1) The standard rate is the rate of interest applicable per annum to
> a loan which qualifies under this Schedule.
>
> (2) Subject to sub-paragraphs (3), (4) and (6), the standard rate
> shall be 1.58 per cent. plus—
>
> (a) the rate announced from time to time by the Monetary Policy
>   Committee of the Bank of England as the official dealing rate,
>   being the rate at which the Bank is willing to enter into transac-
>   tions for providing short term liquidity in the money markets,
>   or
> (b) where an order under section 19 of the Bank of England Act
>   1998 (reserve powers) is in force, any equivalent rate deter-
>   mined by the Treasury under that section.

(3) The Secretary of State shall determine the date from which the standard rate calculated in accordance with sub-paragraph (2) takes effect.

(4) Where—

(a) the actual rate of interest charged on the loan which qualifies under this Schedule is less than 5 per cent. per annum on the day the housing costs first fall to be met, and

(b) that day occurs before 28th November 2004,

the standard rate shall be equal to that actual rate.

(5) Sub-paragraph (4) shall cease to apply in a particular case to any one or more loans which fall within that sub-paragraph on whichever of the following dates occurs first—

(a) the date on which the actual rate of interest charged on such a loan is 5 per cent. per annum or higher,

(b) the anniversary of the date on which the housing costs first fell to be met, or

(c) where a supersession decision based on a change of circumstances arising on or after 28th November 2004 is made under section 10 of the Social Security Act 1998 (decisions superseding earlier decisions), the date of the change of circumstances.

(6) Where sub-paragraph (4) does not apply to a loan which qualifies under this Schedule, the standard rate shall be 5.88 per cent. until the first date determined by the Secretary of State under sub-paragraph (3)."

p.1237, *State Pension Credit Regulations 2002: amendment of Sch.V, para.4(a) (capital disregarded for the purpose of calculating income—premises occupied by another)*

3.127   With effect from October 4, 2004, reg.7(6) of the Social Security (Housing Benefit, Council Tax Benefit, State Pension Credit and Miscellaneous Amendments) Regulations 2004 (SI 2004/2327) amended para.4(a) to read:

"(a) by a [person who is a close relative, grandparent, grandchild, uncle, aunt, nephew or niece of the claimant or of his partner] as his home where that person is either aged 60 or over or incapacitated;".

p.1239, *State Pension Credit Regulations 2002: amendment of Sch.V, para.15(1) (capital disregarded for the purpose of calculating income—payments from various Trusts)*

3.128   With effect from from May 12, 2004, reg.3(3) and 3(4)(d) of the Social Security (Miscellaneous Amendments) (No.2) Regulations 2004 (SI 2004/1141) substituted the words ", the Independent Living Funds or the Skipton Fund" for the words "or the Independent Living Funds" in Sch.V, para.15(1).

p.1240, *State Pension Credit Regulations 2002: amendment of Sch. V,*
para.15(7) (capital disregarded for the purpose of calculating
income—payments from various Trusts)

With effect from from May 12, 2004, reg.3(5) and 3(6)(d) of the   3.129
Social Security (Miscellaneous Amendments) (No.2) Regulations 2004
(SI 2004/1141) substituted the words ", the Eileen Trust and the
Skipton Fund" for the words "and the Eileen Trust" in Sch.V,
para.15(7).

p.1256, *Social Fund Cold Weather Payments Regulations 1988:*
amendment of reg.1A (Prescribed description of persons)

With effect from November 1, 2004, reg.2 of the Social Fund Cold   3.130
Weather Payments (General) Amendment Regulations 2004 (SI
2004/2600) amended reg.1A(1) to read:

"**1A.**—(1) Subject to paragraph (3), the description of persons prescribed as persons to whom a payment may be made out of the Social
Fund to meet expenses for heating under section 32(2A) of the Act is
claimants who have been awarded income support state pension credit
or income-based jobseeker's allowance in respect of at least one day
during the recorded or the forecasted period of cold weather specified
in regulation 2(1)(a) and either—

   (i) whose applicable amount includes one or more of the premi-
       ums specified in paragraphs 9 to 14 of Part III of Schedule 2 to
       the General Regulations; or

 (ia) whose applicable amount includes one or more of the premi-
       ums specified in paragraphs 10 to 16 of Part III of Sch.1 to the
       Jobseeker's Allowance Regulations 1996 ; or

 (ib) the person is entitled to state pension credit and is not resident
       in a care home; [or

 (ic) whose child tax credit includes an individual element referred
       to in regulation 7(4)(a), (b), (d) or (e) of the Child Tax Credit
       Regulations 2002; or]

 (ii) whose family includes a member aged less than 5."

pp.1260–1262, *Social Fund Cold Weather Payments Regulations 1988:*
substitution of Sch.1 (Identification of Stations and Postcode Districts)

With effect from November 1, 2004, reg.3 of the Social Fund Cold   3.131
Weather Payments (General) Amendment Regulations 2004 (SI
2004/2600) a new Sch.1 as follows:

SCHEDULE 1

(Regulation 2(1)(a) and (2))

3.132   IDENTIFICATION OF STATIONS AND POSTCODE DISTRICTS

Column (1)	Column (2)
Meteorological Office Station	*Postcode districts*
1. Aberporth	SA35–48, SA64–65. SY20, SY23–25.
2. Andrewsfield	AL1–10. CB10–11. CM1–9, CM11–24, CM77. CO9. RM14–20. SG1–2, SG9–14.
3. Aultbea	IV21–22, IV26, IV40, IV52–54
4. Aviemore	AB31, AB33–34, AB36–37. PH18–26.
5. Bedford	LU1–7. MK1–19, MK40–46. NN1–16, NN29. PE19. SG3–7, SG15–19.
6. Bingley	BB4, BB8–12, BB18. BD1–24. DE4, DE45. HD1–9. HX1–7. LS21, LS29. OL3, OL12–15. S32–33, S35–36. SK12, SK17, SK22–23. ST13. WF15–17.
7. Bishopton	G1–5, G11–15, G20–23, G31–34, G40–46, G51–53, G60–62, G64–69, G71–78, G81–84. KA1–26, KA28–30. ML1–5. PA1–27, PA30, PA32.
8. Boltshope Park	DH8–9. DL8, DL11–17. NE19, NE44, NE47–48.
9. Boscombe Down	BA12. RG28. SP1–5, SP7, SP9–11.
10. Boulmer	NE22, NE24, NE61–71. TD12, TD15.
11. Braemar	AB35.
12. Brize Norton	CV36. GL54–56. OX1–8, OX10–18, OX20, OX25–29, OX33, OX39, OX44, OX49. SN7.
13. Capel Curig	LL24–25, LL41.
14. Cardinham (Bodmin)	PL13–17, PL22–35. TR2, TR9.
15. Carlisle	CA1–11, CA16–17. LA6–10, LA22–23. NE49.
16. Cassley	IV27–28. KW11, KW13.
17. Charlwood	BN5–6, BN44. GU5–8, GU26–33, GU35. ME14–20. RH1–20. TN1–20, TN22, TN27.
18. Chivenor	EX22–23, EX31–34, EX39.
19. Coleshill	B1–21, B23–38, B40, B42–50, B60–80, B90–98. CV1–12, CV21–23, CV31–35, CV37, CV47. DY1–14. LE10. WS1–15. WV1–16.
20. Coltishall	NR1–35.
21. Crosby	BB1–3, BB5–7. CH1–8, CH41–49, CH60–66. FY1–8. L1–40. LL11–14. PR1–9, PR25–26. SY14. WA1–2, WA4–12. WN1–6, WN8.

Column (1)	Column (2)
Meteorological Office Station	*Postcode districts*
22. Culdrose	TR1, TR3–6, TR10–20, TR26–27.
23. Dundrennan	DG1–2, DG5–7, DG11–12, DG16.
24. Dunkeswell Aerodrome	DT6–8. EX1–15, EX24. TA21. TQ1–6, TQ9–14.
25. Dyce	AB10–16, AB21–25, AB30, AB32, AB39, AB41–43, AB51–54. DD8–11.
26. Edinburgh Gogarbank	EH1–42, EH47–49, EH51–55. FK1–21. G63. KY3, KY11–13. PH3–6. TD5, TD11, TD13–14.
27. Eskdalemuir	DG3–4, DG10, DG13–14. ML12. TD1–4, TD6–10.
28. Fylingdales	TS13. YO11–18, YO21–22, YO25.
29. Great Malvern	GL1–6, GL10–20, GL50–53. HR1–9. NP15, NP25. SY8. WR1–15.
30. Heathrow	BR1–8. CR0, CR2–8. DA1–2, DA4–8, DA14–18. E1–18. E1W. EC1–4. EN1–11. HA0–9. IG1–11. KT1–24. N1–22. NW1–11. RM1–13. SE1–28. SL0, SL3. SM1–7. SW1–20. TW1–20. UB1–10. W1–14. WC1–2. WD1–7, WD17–19, WD23–25.
31. Herstmonceux, West End	BN7–8, BN20–24, BN26–27. TN21, TN31–40.
32. High Wycombe	HP1–23, HP27. OX9. RG9. SL7–9.
33. Hurn (Bournemouth Airport)	BH1–25, BH31. DT1–2, DT11. SP6.
34. Isle of Portland	DT3–5.
35. Kinloss	AB38, AB44–45, AB55–56. IV1–3, IV5, IV7–20, IV30–32, IV36.
36. Kirkwall	KW15–17.
37. Lake Vyrnwy	LL20–21, LL23. SY10, SY15–17, SY19, SY21–22.
38. Lerwick	ZE1–3.
39. Leuchars	DD1–7. KY1–2, KY4–10, KY14–16. PH1–2, PH7, PH12–14.
40. Linton on Ouse	DL1–7, DL9–10. HG1–5. LS1–20, LS22–28. S21, S62–64, S70–75.TS1–12, TS14–26. WF1–17. YO1, YO7–8, YO10, YO19, YO23–24, YO26, YO30–32, YO41–43, YO51, YO60–62.
41. Liscombe	EX16–21, EX35–38. PL19–20. TA22, TA24.
42. Loch Glascarnoch	IV4, IV6, IV23–24, IV63.
43. Lusa	IV47–49, IV51, IV55–56.
44. Lyneham	BA1–3, BA11, BA13–15. GL7–9. RG17. SN1–6, SN8–16, SN25–26.

Column (1)	Column (2)
Meteorological Office Station	*Postcode districts*
45. Machrihanish	KA27. PA28–29, PA31, PA34, PA37, PA41–49, PA60–76. PH36, PH38–41.
46. Manston	CM0. CT1–21. DA3, DA9–13. ME1–13. SS0–17. TN23–26, TN28–30.
47. Marham	IP24–28. PE12–14, PE30–38.
48. Newcastle	DH1–7. NE1–13, NE15–18, NE20–21, NE23, NE25–43, NE45–46. SR1–8. TS27–29.
49. Nottingham	CV13. DE1–3, DE5–7, DE11–15, DE21–24, DE55–56, DE65, DE72–75. LE1–9, LE11–14, LE16–19, LE65, LE67. NG1–22, NG25, NG31–34. S1–14, S17–18, S20, S25–26, S40–45, S60–61, S65–66, S80–81. ST10, ST14.
50. Pembrey Sands	SA1–8, SA10–18, SA31–34, SA61–63, SA66–73.
51. Plymouth	PL1–12, PL18, PL21. TQ7–8.
52. Rhyl	LL15–19, LL22, LL26–32.
53. St. Athan	BS1–11, BS13–16, BS20–24, BS29–32, BS34–37, BS39–41, BS48–49. CF3, CF5, CF10–11, CF14–15, CF23–24, CF31–36, CF61–64, CF71–72. NP10, NP16, NP18–20, NP26.
54. St. Catherine's Point	PO30, PO38–41.
55. St. Mawgan	TR7–8.
56. Salsburgh	EH43–46. ML6–11.
57. Scilly, St. Mary's	TR21–25.
58. Sennybridge	CF37–48, CF81–83. LD1–8. NP4, NP7–8, NP11–13, NP22–24, NP44. SA9, SA19–20. SY7, SY9, SY18.
59. Shawbury	ST1–9, ST11–12, ST15–21. SY1–6, SY11–13. TF1–13.
60. South Farnborough	GU1–4, GU9–25, GU46–47, GU52. RG1–2, RG4–8, RG10, RG12, RG14, RG18–27, RG29–31, RG40–42, RG45. SL1–2, SL4–6.
61. Stornoway Airport	HS1–9.
62. Thorney Island	BN1–3, BN9–18, BN25, BN41–43, BN45. GU34. PO1–22, PO31–37. SO14–24, SO30–32, SO40–43, SO45, SO50–53.
63. Tiree	IV41–46. PA77–78. PH42–44.

Column (1)	Column (2)
Meteorological Office Station	*Postcode districts*
64. Tulloch Bridge	PA33, PA35–36, PS38, PA40. PH8–11, PH15–17, PH30–35, PH37, PH49–50.
65. Valley	LL33–40, LL42–49, LL51–78.
66. Waddington	DN1–22, DN31–41. HU1–20. LN1–13. NG23–24. PE10–11, PE20–25.
67. Walney Island	CA12–15, CA18–28. LA1–5, LA11–21.
68. Wattisham	CB9. CO1–8, CO10–16. IP1–23, IP29–33.
69. West Freugh	DG8–9.
70. Wick Airpot	IV25. KW1–3, KW5–10, KW12, KW14.
71. Wittering	CB1–8. LE15. NN17–18. PE1–9, PE15–17, PE26–29. SG8.
72. Woodford	BL0–9. CW1–12. M1–9, M11–35, M38, M40–41, M43–46, M50, M90. OL1–2, OL4–11, OL16. SK1–11, SK13–16. WA3, WA13–16. WN7.
73. Yeovilton	BA4–10, BA16, BA20–22. BS25–28. DT9–10. SP8. TA1–20, TA23.

p.1264, *Social Fund Winter Fuel Payments Regulations 2000: insertion of definition of "state pension credit" into reg.1(2) (Citation commencement and interpretation)*

With effect from September 20, 2004, reg.2(a) of the Social Fund **3.133** Winter Fuel Payment (Amendment) Regulations 2004 (SI 2004/2154) inserted after the definition of "residential accommodation" the following definition:

" "state pension credit" has the meaning assigned to it by section 1 of the State Pension Credit Act 2002;".

p.1264, *annotation to the Social Fund Winter Fuel Payment Regulations 2000*

See also ss.1–6 of the Age-Related Payments Act 2004 in Pt I of this **3.134** Supplement.

p.1265, *Social Fund Winter Fuel Payments Regulations 2000: amendment of reg.2 (Social fund winter fuel payments)*

With effect from September 20, 2004, reg.2(b) of the Social Fund **3.135** Winter Fuel Payment (Amendment) Regulations 2004 (SI 2004/2154) amended reg.2(1)(b)(ii) to read:

"(ii) £100 if [state pension credit] or an income-based jobseeker's allowance has not been, nor falls to be, paid to him in respect of the qualifying week and he is—

(aa) in that week living with a person to whom a payment under these Regulations has been, or falls to be, made in respect of the winter following the qualifying week; or
(bb) in residential care."

p.1267, *Social Fund Winter Fuel Payments Regulations 2000: amendment of reg.3 (Persons not entitled to a social fund winter fuel payment)*

3.136   With effect from September 20, 2004, reg.2(c) of the Social Fund Winter Fuel Payment (Amendment) Regulations 2004 (SI 2004/2154) amended reg.3(1)(a) to read:

"**3.**—(1) Regulation 2 shall not apply in respect of a person who—

(a) is in the qualifying week—

(i) a partner of, and living with, a person aged 60 or over in the qualifying week to whom [state pension credit] or an income-based jobseeker's allowance has been, or falls to be, paid in respect of the qualifying week;
(ii) receiving free in-patient treatment and has been receiving free in-patient treatment for more than 52 weeks; or
(iii) detained in custody under a sentence imposed by a court; or".

p.1268, *Social Fund Winter Fuel Payments Regulations 2000: amendment of reg.4 (Making a winter fuel payment without a claim)*

3.137   With effect from September 20, 2004, reg.2(d) of the Social Fund Winter Fuel Payment (Amendment) Regulations 2004 (SI 2004/2154) amended reg.4(2) to read:

"(2) Where a person becomes entitled to income support [or state pension credit] in respect of the qualifying week by virtue of a decision made after that week that section 115 of the Immigration and Asylum Act 1999 (exclusions) ceases to apply to him the Secretary of State shall make a winter fuel payment to that person under regulation 2 in respect of the winter following the qualifying week."

p.1268, *Social Fund Winter Fuel Payment Regulations: annotation to reg.3 (time limit for claiming)*

3.138   In *CIS/2337/2004*, Mr Commissioner Jacobs held that the time limit in reg.3(1)(b) does not infringe claimants' rights under Art.1 of the First Protocol to the European Convention on Human Rights even when a payment has been made without a claim in respect of previous years. Winter fuel payments are not a contributory benefit and the time limit

114

did not deprive claimants of any rights but merely defined the scope of those rights.

p.1278, *annotation to Social Fund Maternity and Funeral Expenses Regulations 1987, reg.5 (Entitlement to a sure start maternity grant)*

In *CIS/1965/2003*, Mr Commissioner Williams held that *CIS/ 13389/1996* (which had decided that a parental responsibility agreement under s.4 of the Children Act 1989 did not amount to adoption within reg.5(1)(b)(ii)) remained good law after the coming into force of the Human Rights Act 1998 and the Adoption and Children Act 2002. The same was true of a residence order under s.8 of the 1989 Act. Article 26 of the UN Convention on the Rights of the Child did not alter that conclusion. A decision of Mr Commissioner Williams is under appeal to the Court of Appeal. **3.139**

p.1282, *Social Fund Maternity and Funeral Expenses Regulations 1987: amendment of reg.7 (Entitlement)*

In respect of deaths occurring on or after October 25, 2004, reg.3(2) of the Social Fund Maternity and Funeral Expenses (General) Amendment Regulations 2004 (SI 2004/2536) amended reg.7(4) to read: **3.140**

"(4) Paragraph (3) shall not apply to disentitle the responsible person from a funeral payment where the immediate family member to whom that paragraph applies is—

(za) a person who has not attained the age of 18;

(a) a person who has attained the age of 18 but not the age of 19 and who is attending a full-time course of advanced education as defined in regulation 61 of the Income Support Regulations or, as the case may be, a person aged 19 or over but under pensionable age who is attending a full-time course of study at an educational establishment;

(aa) a person in receipt of asylum support under section 95 of the Immigration and Asylum Act 1999;

(b) a member of, and fully maintained by, a religious order;

(c) being detained in a prison, remand centre or youth custody institution and either that immediate family member or his partner had been awarded a benefit to which paragraph (1)(a) refers immediately before that immediate family member was so detained; [. . .]

(d) a person who is regarded as receiving free in-patient treatment within the meaning of the Social Security (Hospital In-Patients) Regulations 1975 or, as the case may be, the Social Security (Hospital In-Patients) Regulations (Northern Ireland) 1975 and either that immediate family member or his partner had been awarded a benefit to which paragraph (1)(a) refers immediately before that immediate family member was first regarded as receiving such treatment[; or

(e) a person ordinarily resident outside the United Kingdom.]"

p.1283, *Social Fund Maternity and Funeral Expenses Regulations 1987: amendment of reg.7 (Entitlement)*

3.141   In respect of deaths occurring on or after October 25, 2004, reg.3(3) of the Social Fund Maternity and Funeral Expenses (General) Amendment Regulations 2004 (SI 2004/2536) substituted a new para.(7) as follows:

"(7) Paragraph (6) shall not apply where the close relative who was in closer contact with the deceased than the responsible person or, as the case may be, was in equally close contact with the deceased—

(a) was under the age of 18 at the date of death and was the only close relative (apart from any other person who was under the age of 18 at that date) to whom either sub-paragraph (a) or (b) of paragraph (6) applies; or

(b) is a person ordinarily resident outside the United Kingdom."

pp.1285–1287, *Social Fund Maternity and Funeral Expenses Regulations 1987: annotation to reg.7(1)(b): requirement that the funeral take place in the United Kingdom—Human Rights Act*

3.142   In *CIS/1870/2003, CIS/2302/2003, CIS/2305/2003* and *CIS/2624/2003*, Mr Commissioner Howell Q.C. held that reg.7(1)(b) did not infringe the claimants rights under Arts 8 and 14 (taken together) of the European Convention on Human Rights. For a discussion of the Commissioner's approach see pp.165–166 of this supplement.

pp.1288–1289, *annotation to Social Fund Maternity and Funeral Expenses Regulations 1987, reg.5 (Entitlement to funeral payments): estrangement*

3.143   In *CIS/1228/2004*, Ms Commissioner Fellner held "that registering a death is [not] enough *in itself* to show that the person who does so *cannot* have been estranged from the deceased" (original emphasis).

pp.1291–1292, *Social Fund Maternity and Funeral Expenses Regulations 1987: annotation to reg.7(4) (Entitlement)*

3.144   The observation on p.1292 of the main volume (para.5.61) that "the 'immediate family test' will make it difficult to claim a funeral payment where a parent, son or daughter of the deceased is living outside the UK, as they will not be entitled to a UK means-tested benefit" is no longer apposite where the deceased died on or after October 25, 2004. From that date, the new para.(4)(e) means that an "immediate family member" who is ordinarily resident outside the UK is excluded from consideration when applying the condition of disentitlement in para.(3). From the same date, a close relative who is ordinarily resident outside the UK is excluded from the "closer contact" test in para.(6) (see para.5.62 of the main volume).

116

p.1294, *Social Fund Maternity and Funeral Expenses Regulations 1987: amendment of reg.7A (Amount of funeral payment)*

In respect of deaths occurring on or after October 25, 2004, reg.3(3)   **3.145**
of the Social Fund Maternity and Funeral Expenses (General) Amendment Regulations 2004 (SI 2004/2536) amended reg.(7)(2)(a)(ii) to
read:

> "(ii) the fees levied in respect of a burial by the authority or person
> responsible for the provision and maintenance of cemeteries for
> the area where the burial takes place [, or the fees levied by a
> private grave-digger,] in so far as it is necessary to incur those
> fees;".

p.1296, *Social Fund Maternity and Funeral Expenses Regulations 1987: annotation to reg.7A(2)(g): other funeral expenses*

In *CIS/1345/2004*, Mr Commissioner Williams held that "suitable   **3.146**
funeral attire" might amount to a funeral expense within sub-para.(g).
The test was not, as had been suggested by the Secretary of State,
whether the expense was "wholly exclusively and necessarily required for
the funeral". There was no basis in law for restricting the scope of the
paragraph beyond the words actually used in the sub-paragraph. The
only tests for applying reg.7A(2)(g) were:

> "(i)   Were the expenses in fact funeral expenses that took into account
>   any relevant discounts?
> (ii)   If so, were the expenses met by the claimant or partner (or will
>   they be)?
> (iii) If so, were they of a nature covered by any of the provisions in
>   regulation 7A(2)(a) to (f)?
> (iv)   If not, do they exceed the set sum?
> If they do not, they are allowable."

In *CIS/1924/2004*, Ms Commissioner Fellner held that flowers were
capable of amounting to a funeral expense within the sub-paragraph but
that obituary notices and the cost of a memorial stone and flower
container were not.

p.1298, *Social Fund Maternity and Funeral Expenses Regulations 1987: amendment of reg.8 (Deductions from an award of a funeral payment)*

With effect from May 12, 2004, reg.8 of the Social Security (Miscella-   **3.147**
neous Amendments) (No.2) Regulations 2004 (SI 2004/1141) amended
reg.8(2) to read:

> "(2) The amount of any payment made under the Macfarlane Trust,
> the Macfarlane (Special Payment) Trust, the Macfarlane (Special
> Payments) (No. 2) Trust, the Fund [, the Eileen Trust or the Skipton
> Fund] or under a trust established out of funds provided by the
> Secretary of State in respect of persons who suffered, or who are
> suffering, from variant Creutzfeldt-Jakob disease for the benefit of

117

persons eligible for payments in accordance with its provisions shall be disregarded from any deduction made under this regulation and for the purpose of this paragraph, 'the Macfarlane Trust', 'the Macfarlane (Special Payments) Trust', 'the Macfarlane (Special Payments) (No.2) Trust', 'the Fund' [, 'the Eileen Trust' and 'the Skipton Fund'] shall have the same meaning as in regulation 2(1) of the Income Support Regulations."

PART IV

UPDATING MATERIAL
VOLUME III

ADMINISTRATION, ADJUDICATION AND
THE EUROPEAN DIMENSION

pp.38–40, *annotations to Social Security Administration Act 1992, s.5: regulations about claims and payments for benefit*

An argument was put in *CDLA/2751/2003, CDLA/3567/2003* and   **4.001**
CDLA/3752/2003 concerning the relationship of reg.13C of the Claims and Payments Regulations (further claim for and award of disability living allowance—the provision which permits a continuation claim for a disability living allowance to be made during the last six months of the current award) with s.5. The Tribunal of Commissioners responded:

"Although at first sight regulation 13C(2)(b) may appear to provide a power to make an award, that is not so. Regulation 13C can best be understood by looking at the enabling provisions in section 5 of the 1992 Act. Section 5(1)(c) authorises the making of a regulation that permits a claim to be made in advance. Section 5(1)(d) authorises the making of a regulation that permits an award on such a claim to be made subject to a condition. It does not authorise the making of a regulation that permits an award to be made in advance because it is unnecessary to do so. The power to make an award follows from the duty to determine a claim, imposed on the Secretary of State by sections 1 and 8(1) of the 1998 Act. One can see that regulation 13C(1) is made under section 5(1)(c), regulation 13C(2)(a) is made under section 5(1)(b), regulation 13C(2)(b) is made under section 5(1)(d) and regulation 13C(3) is made under section 5(1)(e). Thus, what regulation 13C(2)(b) permits is not the making of an award in the light of the prospective claim but the imposition of a condition on the award that is required to be made by the 1998 Act. The word 'accordingly' [in reg.13C(2)(b)] therefore means no more than 'on that claim' and its only significance is that it links paragraph (2)(b) with paragraphs (1) and (2)(a) so that, in conformity with the enabling provision (giving effect to the word 'such' in both places where it occurs in section 5(1)(d)), the condition may be imposed only on an award made on a renewal claim made in advance and treated as made on the renewal date" (para.16).

pp.54–88, *annotations to s.71: overpayments—general*

The requirement for revision

The technical requirements in terms of decision making in over-   **4.002**
payments cases continue to cause difficulties. In *CIS/3228/2003* the Commissioner re-affirms the requirement in s.71(5A) that an amount is not recoverable under s.71 unless there has been a revision under s.9 of the Social Security Act 1998 or a supersession under s.10 of that Act. Revision decisions take effect as from the date of the decision revised in the absence of a specific provision in regulations to the contrary. Supersession decisions take effect from the date of the supersession decision. Generally revision decisions will be needed in overpayment cases in order to ensure that there is a decision covering the whole of the overpayment period. Furthermore, where the overpayment period covers a period in which several benefit decisions have been made, they must all

be revised. It will be for the Department to show this as a precondition of recovery of overpaid benefit. The Commissioner says:

> "Proof of a supersession or revision decision complying with section 71(5A) of the Administration Act is not a question of 'constructing a narrative', as the Secretary of State has submitted, but of establishing that the necessary decision was actually taken by a decision maker, or by a computer in accordance with the procedure now authorised by section 2(1) of the Social Security Act 1998" (para.24).

In *CIS/0170/2003* a different Commissioner took the same view, noting further that there could not be a supersession decision based upon change of circumstances where the claimant's circumstances had not changed. It is not a change of circumstances where something new which has been in existence for a long time comes to the notice of the Secretary of State. In this decision, the Commissioner warns tribunals against being too ready to substitute revision decisions for faulty supersession decisions. In many cases, there will be insufficient evidence (especially where one or both parties is not present) and the tribunal must take care not simply to "construct a narrative" to borrow a phrase from *CIS/3228/2003*. Furthermore, where computer printouts are provided under the Generalised Matching Service, these must be accompanied by full explanations of the significance of the various codes used. Otherwise there is a real risk of making findings of fact which no reasonable tribunal could make.

Misrepresentation

4.003   In *CTC/4025/2003*, the Commissioner considered an appeal by a claimant against whom a decision seeking to recover overpaid tax credits had been made. The claimant had responded to a question on the claim form "Do you have a partner with whom you normally live?" in the negative. At the time a marriage of very short duration was in difficulties and the claimant and her husband were living apart. However, the effect of reg.9(1) of the Family Credit (General) Regulations was that the husband and wife were to be treated as members of the same household for the purposes of claims to Working Families Tax Credit. The Commissioner rejects the argument originally put to the tribunal (and which the Secretary of State conceded in the submission to the Commissioner involved "quite a leap") that because the regulations treated the claimant and the husband as members of the same household, she must have misrepresented the facts by saying that she was not living with a partner. The overpayments were not recoverable from her.

The appeal in *CFC/2766/2003* concerned entitlement to working families tax credit. Shortly before the claim was made, the claimant disposed of significant amounts of capital. When the claim was made, the claimant correctly reported capital of no more than £2,500. When the capital disposal came to light, the Department sought recovery of an overpayment of the tax credit on the grounds that the claimant had misrepresented the position in relation to their capital. But the claimant had not done so. There was no question asking about capital they once had but no longer have. For this decision's approach to failure to disclose see below.

CSIS/0345/2004 concerned a claimant who had misrepresented her income. When the claimant claimed income support, she had not disclosed sick pay received from her employer under income protection insurance offered by the employer. She claimed not to have done so on the basis of advice from an officer of the Department to the effect that such income was not relevant to entitlement to income support. The Commissioner notes that, where recovery of overpayments is sought on the grounds of misrepresentation, the reason for the misrepresentation is irrelevant. The sole issue was, accordingly, whether (assuming that the tribunal accepted that there had been the course of dealing put forward by the claimant) the representation on the claim form could be regarded as qualified by the earlier disclosure of receipt of the sick pay when the enquiry was made. The Commissioner said:

" . . . even if . . . the disclosure was clearly made in terms of 'sick pay', the connection between such a prior general enquiry and the later determination made on the claim once the form was actually submitted, was much too remote for there to be any reasonable expectation that a link would be made and the disclosure taken into account. The concept of a prior disclosure qualifying a later written representation, so that the latter is no longer to be regarded as an incorrect one, must be restricted to very special circumstances; otherwise, the rationale behind recoverability based even on *innocent* misrepresentation, that it was positive and deliberate action upon which a decision maker must be entitled to rely, would be subverted" (para.29).

Failure to disclose

The most significant development in the law on recovery of overpayments is the dramatic decision of the Tribunal of Commissioners in *CIS/4348/2003* of October 12, 2004. This decision overturns some leading authorities of long standing in ruling, in essence, that there is no qualification in relation to failure to disclose that the disclosure must in all the circumstances be reasonably expected. However, the detail is rather more complex than this simple statement suggests. Permission to appeal has been granted by the Tribunal of Commissioners on the application of the claimant. The facts in the appeal before the Tribunal of Commissioners can be simply stated. The claimant has a learning disability. She was a lone parent in receipt of income support and received an allowance for her children. When they were taken into care, she did not disclose this fact despite clear indications in documentation she received from the Department that this was a specific change of circumstances that required disclosure. The tribunal had accepted that she would not have understood the meaning of what was written in the order book, and presumably also in other written communications from the Department. The issue was whether the mental capacity of the claimant was such as to prevent the Secretary of State from seeking recovery of the overpayment of income support (para.8).

4.004

The Tribunal of Commissioners begins by examining the relevant principles before considering the conflicting Commissioners' decision. The following matters were accepted as common ground:

(a) there can be a wholly innocent failure to disclose, exemplified by those who do not disclose some material fact because they do not appreciate that it is a material fact;

(b) a person cannot fail to disclose for the purposes of s.71 a matter unless it is known to them. Whether a matter is known to someone is determined by applying a subjective test;

(c) a material fact for the purposes of s.71 is a fact which is objectively material to the decision to award benefit;

(d) failure to disclose is not the same as mere non-disclosure. "It imports a breach of some obligation to disclose" (para.13).

Where the obligation to disclose comes from was more contentious. The Tribunal of Commissioners reject the importing of insurance law obligations; these flow from a common law duty, whereas in the social security context, there are "specific duties of disclosure set out in a statutory scheme in respect of benefits" (para.15). The Tribunal of Commissioners expresses some difficulty with the concept of breach of a "moral" obligation to disclose (to which reference is made in *R(SB) 21/82*) and could not envisage a case where it would be necessary to rely on a moral duty as distinction from a legal duty to disclose. However, the appeal before them turned on the nature of the legal duty to disclose and the Tribunal of Commissioners does not consider the issue further.

The duty to disclose is not found in s.71; that section presupposes a duty but does not impose it (para.20). The duty is to be found in reg.32 of the Claims and Payments Regulations. The Tribunal of Commissioners was concerned with the version of this regulation in force prior to its amendment by SI 2003/1050, but does not regard the amendment made by the 2003 amending regulations as affecting the substance of the provisions. The reasoning adopted is expressly stated to apply to the current version of reg.32.

4.005 Regulation 32 contains two duties. The first duty required a claimant to furnish information on request material to any decision relating to entitlement to or payment of benefit (this is contained in reg.32(1) and (1A) of the current version). The second duty required a claimant to notify a change of circumstances affecting the continuance of entitlement to benefit (this is contained in reg.32(1B) of the current version). The two duties are "entirely distinct" (para.30).

The first duty is not qualified in any way, but the second duty is. It requires notification of changes of circumstances as soon as reasonably practicable which claimants might reasonably be expected to know might affect the continuance of entitlement to benefit or the payment of benefit. The Tribunal of Commissioners expressly reject the argument that the words qualifying the second duty also inform the first duty.

Some of the s.71 case law is relevant to the proper construction of reg.32. First, one cannot fail to furnish information or notify a change of circumstances unless the information or change of circumstances is known (para.32(a)). Secondly, where information is requested by the

Secretary of State under the first duty, any view the claimant might have as to the relevance of the information to benefit entitlement does not arise.

In the context of meeting the obligation set out in the first duty, no question arises concerning the mental capacity of the person required to furnish the information. It is not open to claimants to argue that they were unable to respond to an unambiguous request because, as a result of mental incapacity, they did not understand the request (para.34). The consequences of failing to disclose information in breach of the first duty in reg.32 are to be found in s.71:

> "That provides simply that, where there was a breach of the obligation to disclose any material fact under regulation 32(1), whether fraudulent or innocent, then the Secretary of State shall be entitled to recover any overpayment that results" (para.36).

The Tribunal of Commissioners then considers whether, on basic principles, s.71 can be said to import a notion that disclosure is only required where it can reasonably be expected of the claimant:

> " . . . even had we been persuaded that the duty to disclose sufficient to enable recovery of overpayments arose from section 71 itself, we would not have been persuaded that the duty was restricted to circumstances in which the claimant could reasonably have been expected to disclose it. That construction is simply impermissible in context. We would have held that in respect of any duty arising under section 71—as with the duty actually arising under regulation 32(1)—the subjective opinion or appreciation of the claimant as to materiality has no part to play in the scope of the duty" (para.42).

The Tribunal of Commissioners then turns to the well-established line of authority which had adopted the approach that the test did involve consideration of whether disclosure was reasonably to be expected of the claimant. The leading authority is, of course, *R(SB) 21/82*, which has been cited in many Commissioners' decisions including three decisions of Tribunals of Commissioners: *R(SB) 15/87*; *CG/4494/1999*; and *R(IS) 5/03*. The Tribunal of Commissioners conclude that successive decisions of Commissioners have been misled by the importation into s.71 of qualifying words from the then-equivalent of the second duty in reg.32 in *R(SB) 21/82*. The Tribunal of Commissioners says that: "On the most generous view, the words do not represent a possible construction of section 71" (para.52). The Tribunal of Commissioners further concludes that the issue has "never been the subject of any analysis or full argument" (para.58). The Tribunal of Commissioners concludes:

> "59. We do not resile from the fact that, in adopting the proper construction of the relevant statutory provisions, we are changing the direction of the law by abandoning a supposed but erroneous requirement in respect of recovery cases to which regular reference has been made over the years. However, having the law properly applied cannot of itself be unfairly prejudicial, even if that law is adverse to the interests of a particular person. We do not see any way in which claimants could be unfairly prejudiced by the benefit system adopting

4.006

the proper construction of these statutory provisions now. They cannot for example possibly have organised their affairs on the basis that *R(SB) 21/82* is good law, with the result that they would suffer a detriment if the position were changed now. There seems to us to be no reason to perpetuate error now by slavish adherence to previous decisions.

60. For these reasons, insofar as previous decisions of Commissioners (including Tribunals of Commissioners) are inconsistent with the reasoning of this decision, they must be treated as wrongly decided."

4.007   The Tribunal of Commissioner refer specifically to *R(A) 1/95*. The Tribunal agrees that mental capacity is relevant to the whether the claimant knew of the matter not disclosed, and that mental capacity is not relevant to the issue of whether there was a failure to disclose. However, they disapprove of the reasoning in para.6 of this decision, partly because they cannot deduce any proper explanation of the passage from *R(SB) 21/82* to which the Commissioner makes reference, and partly because it relies upon an insurance analogy which the Tribunal of Commissioners does not consider to be helpful in this context of recovery of overpayments.

The Tribunal of Commissioners goes on to consider what protection there is for claimants whose capacity may affect their ability to handle their affairs. Two protections are identified. First, there is the possibility that an appointee is appointed to act on their behalf. The Tribunal of Commissioners notes that, where no appointment has been made, "the higher courts have in the past taken a fairly robust approach to submission based on a lack of capacity" (para.64). Secondly, there is the possibility that the Secretary of State will exercise the discretion not to recover the overpayment in the particular circumstances of any given case, though the Tribunal comments that it is not "aware of any published guidelines on the exercise of this discretion" (para.65).

The decision is bound to reverberate through the system for some time. It is certain to generate appeals to the Commissioner on its application in the variety of circumstances in which overpayments of benefit arise. The following points should be borne in mind in applying the decision:

(1) this decision should be the starting point in any overpayment case involving a failure to disclose;
(2) the decision does not equate the words "failed to disclose" with "did not disclose". There must still be some breach of duty;
(3) the legal duty can be found in reg.32 of the Claims and Payments Regulations;
(4) where the first duty in reg.32 is in issue, it follows that the adjudicating authorities will need to identify with some clarity where the requirement to furnish information came from. In the case before the Commissioners, this was straightforward. The information provided to the claimant in connection with her claim required her to notify the Secretary of State if her children ceased

to live with her or were taken into care. It is submitted that it will not be enough to convert the first duty into some general duty to furnish information to the Secretary of State. There are bound to be cases where the requirement to furnish information is rather less clear cut, and will need to be explored with some care;

(5) if the case falls within the second duty, then there is a requirement that the change of circumstances is one which claimants might reasonably be expected to know is one which might affect the continuance of entitlement or the payment of benefit. There will also be a temporal question to consider: whether the claimant notified the Secretary of State of the change as soon as reasonably practicable.

CFC/2766/2003 was decided after *CIS/4348/2003*, and concerned a **4.008** situation where it was alleged that the claimant had failed to disclose spending of capital prior to her first claim for benefit. As noted above, her answers on the claim form did not constitute misrepresentations as she was only asked what her current level of capital was. Moreover, on the face of it neither of the duties under reg.32(1) discussed in *CIS/4348/2003* would apply as the loss of the capital was not a change in circumstances since the claim had been made nor had the claimant been asked by the Secretary of State to provide information about changes in her capital prior to the date of claim. This may have provided the basis for Commissioner Howell distinguishing *CIS/4348/2003*, but his comments perhaps suggest a deeper unease with the correctness of that decision. On the issue of failure to disclose, he directed the new tribunal in the following terms:

> "it is not of course necessary for the Board to prove that the failure of disclosure was other than innocent, and I further direct the tribunal that, as is well settled law, the principal question is whether disclosure was reasonably to be expected of the claimant in all the circumstances. That long established principle as laid down and confirmed by two Commissioners of unquestionable learning and experience, Mr I Edwards-Jones QC and Mr J S Watson QC, in the (reported) cases *R(SB) 21/82* and *R(SB) 28/83*, has since been followed and applied as good law and practical sense on countless occasions by Commissioners and tribunals over the last 20 years and more, and should at least for the present continue to be applied in the context of facts such as these, notwithstanding the doubts voiced in quite a different context by a recent tribunal of Commissioners in case *CIS/4348/2003*".

A different Commissioner has also commented on the ambit of *CIS/4348/2003* in *CDLA/1823/2004*. The Commissioner indicates that the Tribunal of Commissioners was dealing with cases where disclosure had not been made despite being required by clear and unambiguous instructions. In many cases, the situation will not be as clear cut. In such cases, the Commissioner considers that whether there has been a failure to disclose "must inevitably be determined by considering whether the Secretary of State could reasonably have expected the claimant to disclose or notify that fact" (para.9). A tribunal would need to consider whether a reasonable claimant would have construed any instruction to report changes in circumstances or some other instruction. In the case before him, there was no evidence as to the instructions given to the claimant.

The amount of the overpayment which is recoverable

4.009 For a case on the proper application of reg.13 of the Payments on account Regulations, see updated annotations to that regulation.

pp.91–94, *annotations to Social Security Administration Act 1992, s.74: income support and other payments*

4.010 *CIS/3378/2003* is now reported as *R(IS) 14/04*.

pp.137–138, *annotations to Social Security Administration Act 1992, s.179: reciprocal agreements with countries outside the United Kingdom*

4.011 For a discussion on how s.179 acts to modify other social security provisions, see *CIB/3645/2002*.

p.200, *annotation to Social Security Act 1998, s.8*

4.012 The provisions of Ch.II of Pt I of the 1998 Act are applied to decisions under ss.2 and 3 of the Age-Related Payments Act 2004, not by virtue of regulations made under this subsection but by s.5(5) of the 2004 Act.

p.200, *annotation to Social Security Act 1998, s.8(1)*

4.013 Where another body has made a decision on a question relevant to a claim for benefit, it is not necessary for the Secretary of State to decide the issue from scratch as though the other decision did not exist, provided the other body made a considered decision on the point. He is entitled, in the absence of anything to compel a contrary conclusion, to regard the existence of that decision as satisfactory evidence (*R(H) 9/04*). Obviously, though, he must consider any contrary submission made by the claimant before deciding whether to accept or reject that evidence.

pp.201–202, *annotation to Social Security Act 1998, s.8(2)*

4.013.1 Where the Secretary of State takes the view that a claimant is not habitually resident in the UK at the date of his decision on the ground that, although the claimant has an intention to reside in the UK for a prolonged period, a sufficient period of residence has not yet elapsed, the Secretary of State is entitled to make an advance award from the date on which habitual residence is likely to be established on the assumption that there will be no change in the claimant's circumstances (*CIS/ 3280/2003*).

p.205 *annotation to Social Security Act 1998, s.9(5)*

The approach taken in *R(IS) 15/04* has been approved by the Court of Appeal in *Beltekian v Westminster City Council* [2004] EWCA Civ 1784. 4.013.2

[THE NEXT PARAGRAPH IS 4.014.]

p.211, *annotation to Social Security Act 1998, s.12*

Section 12 is applied to decisions of the Secretary of State under the Social Security (Quarterly Work-focused Interviews for Certain Lone Parents) Regulations 2004 (SI 2004/2244) (see reg.9) and under the Age-Related Payments Act 2004 (see s.5(5)). 4.014

pp.213–219, *annotation to Social Security Act 1998, s.12(2)*

Kerr v Department for Social Development [2004] UKHL 23; [2004] 1 W.L.R. 1372 (mentioned in the main work) has now been also reported as an appendix to *R1/04(SF)*. *CIS/1459/03* (also mentioned in the main work) has been reported as *R(IS) 17/04*. The approach taken in *R(IS) 15/04* (mentioned in the main work) has been approved by the Court of Appeal in *Beltekian v Westminster City Council* [2004] EWCA Civ 1784. 4.015

In *CCS/3757/2004*, the Commissioner points out that a failure to provide evidence does not necessarily justify the drawing of an adverse inference against the person who should have provided the evidence. All the circumstances and the other evidence that is available must be considered. It may be particularly relevant to consider whether the failure to produce evidence might have been due to it being unfavourable to the party concerned. In many cases, a failure to produce evidence merely justifies a conclusion that there is no, or no adequate, evidence on a particular point, which will then fall to be determined against the person who bears the "burden of collective ignorance" (see *Kerr* as explained in the annotation in the main work). That is not quite the same as drawing an adverse inference, which involves making a positive finding against the party concerned. However, the effect will be much the same in many cases and, where it is not, it will often be appropriate to draw an adverse inference, which *Kerr* makes clear is permissible. Thus, for instance, a claimant's failure to produce evidence of the amount of her income following a clear request may well justify a positive finding that she receives income at a level that makes her ineligible for benefit (*R(H) 3/05*). *CCS/3757/2004*, however, emphasises the need to consider any other evidence in the case before going so far as to draw an adverse inference. Note, also, that providing evidence late is unlikely to justify the drawing of an adverse inference, unless it justifies ignoring the evidence altogether (see the supplemental annotation to p.622, below).

Tribunals are not bound by the common law rules of evidence and so a tribunal erred in refusing to allow a disability consultant to give evidence of his opinion. However, it does not follow that those rules of evidence have no relevance at all. Tribunals have no power to override any privilege of a witness not to give evidence, such as the privilege attaching to solicitor-client communications and the privilege against self-incrimination. Furthermore, the common law rules of evidence may be relevant in the evaluation of evidence because the considerations which have led to the evidence being inadmissible often mean that it has little weight. Thus, there might have been good reasons for treating a disability consultant's evidence with caution, but it was wrong to refuse to consider it at all (*CDLA/2014/2004*). In *CCS/3749/2003*, it was held that a tribunal should refuse to consider any information about proceedings relating to children where the court was sitting in private (because use of the information by a party is potentially a contempt of court) but is entitled to hear evidence about ancillary relief proceedings that have taken in place in private.

In *R(DLA) 3/99*, the Commissioner held that it was wrong for a tribunal to accept evidence of an examining medical practitioner on the basis that it must normally prevail over other evidence, even though in practice, once a proper weighing exercise had been carried out without giving an examining medical practitioner's evidence any special weight, the examining medical practitioner's evidence might be accepted in the majority of cases. In *CIB/3074/2003*, the Commissioner suggested that a distinction could be drawn in some cases between the weight to be given to clinical findings of an examining medical officer and the weight to be given to his or her assessment as to the claimant's capabilities in the light of those findings.

"13. In *CIB/15663/1996*, deputy Commissioner Fellner (as she then was) stated that a tribunal was entitled to give full weight to an examining medical officer's findings. A tribunal should of course give full weight to all the evidence, but may often be justified in regarding clinical findings of an examining medical officer as reliable, although even clinical findings should not be regarded as conclusive and may in some cases be displaced by other evidence. However, the impact of any given degree of loss of function will vary from claimant to claimant. In some cases (such as incontinence) a clinical examination will often give very little indication of the extent of impairment of the activities which need to be considered in carrying out the personal capability assessment, although in such cases the examining medical practitioner will often be able to make an informed assessment of the degree of impairment on the basis of the claimant's medical history and other evidence of functional ability. The examining medical officer's choice of a descriptor will therefore generally require the exercise of judgment to a greater or lesser degree, and a tribunal may therefore not necessarily give the same weight to an examining medical officer's choice of descriptors as it does to clinical findings on examination."

p.221, *annotation to Social Security Act 1998, s.12(8)(a)*

The approach taken in *R(IS) 15/04* has been approved by the Court of   4.015.1
Appeal in *Beltekian v Westminster City Council* [2004] EWCA Civ 1784.

pp.222–225, *annotation to Social Security Act 1998, s.12(8)(b)*

Where a tribunal takes the view that a claimant was not habitually   4.015.2
resident in the UK at the date of the Secretary of State's decision on the ground that, although the claimant had an intention to reside in the UK for a prolonged period, a sufficient period of residence had not elapsed by that date, the tribunal is entitled to make an award from the later date on which habitual residence was, or is likely to be, established on the basis of the claimant's circumstances at the date of the Secretary of State's decision (*CIS/3280/2003*).

[THE NEXT PARAGRAPH IS 4.016.]

p.226, *annotation to Social Security Act 1998, s.13(1)*

A decision may be set aside under s.13 only if the legally qualified   4.016
panel member could have granted leave to appeal. If the application is too late or there is no statement of reasons (see the annotation to reg.58(1) of the Social Security and Child Support (Decisions and Appeals) Regulations 1999 in the main work), the tribunal's decision cannot be set aside. Therefore, where the Secretary of State sought a statement of reasons within the prescribed time but the request was not acted upon immediately and the chairman was later unable to provide a statement of reasons, the setting aside of the tribunal's decision under reg.13(2) was invalid and so was the subsequent decision of another tribunal (*CDLA/1685/2004*). The Commissioner allowed the claimant's appeal against the second decision but suggested that the Secretary of State should apply to a Commissioner for leave to appeal against the first decision, as a Commissioner's power to grant leave to appeal is wider than a chairman's (see p.656 of the main work).

pp.231–237, *annotation to Social Security Act 1998, s.14(1)*

The Home Secretary has been given leave to appeal to the House of   4.017
Lords against the decision in *E v Secretary of State for the Home Department* [2004] EWCA Civ 49; [2004] 2 W.L.R. 1351 (mentioned in the main work). *Stansby v Datapulse plc* [2003] EWCA Civ 1951 (mentioned in the main work) has been reported at [2004] I.C.R. 523.

The Secretary of State's appeal against *CSDLA/444/2002* (mentioned in the main work) has been dismissed by the Court of Session (*Secretary of State for Work and Pensions v Cunningham* 2004 S.L.T. 1007 (also reported as *R(DLA) 7/04*)). The reference in *CSDLA/444/2002* to *CIS/ 343/1994* should have been to *CS/343/1994*.

pp.239–240, *annotation to Social Security Act 1998, s.14(10)*

4.018   *Mooney v Social Security Commissioner* (reported as *R(DLA) 5/04*) has now also been reported as *Mooney v Secretary of State for Work and Pensions* 2004 S.L.T. 1141.

The Lands Tribunal hears appeals from valuation tribunals and so is, to some extent, in a position analogous to that of a Commissioner. In *R. (Sinclair Gardens Investments (Kensington) Limited) v Lands Tribunal* [2004] EWHC 1910 (Admin), Sullivan J. applied *R. (Sivasubramaniam) v Wandsworth County Court (Lord Chancellor's Department intervening)* [2003] EWCA Civ 1738; [2003] 1 W.L.R. 475 (mentioned in the main work) and held that judicial review of a decision of the Lands Tribunal to refuse leave to appeal from a valuation tribunal should be granted only in an exceptional case. In *Gibson v Secretary of State for Work and Pensions* [2004] EWHC 561 (Admin) and *R. (Thomas) v Benefits Agency* [2004] EWHC 1352 (Admin) (both of which cases, despite their titles, involved applications for leave to apply for judicial review of Commissioners' refusals of leave to appeal from tribunals), Richards J. suggested that the *Sivasubramaniam* approach might also apply to judicial review of a Commissioner's decision, although he did consider the applications on a broader basis before dismissing them. However, the approach taken in *Sinclair Gardens* may not be applicable in respect of Commissioners because the relevant right of appeal to the Lands Tribunal, like the right of appeal to a circuit judge in *Sivasubramaniam*, was not restricted to points of law, whereas the right of appeal to a Commissioner is. It may therefore be that the approach taken by the Court of Appeal in *Cooke v Secretary of State for Social Security* [2001] EWCA Civ 734 (reported as *R(DLA) 6/01*) (mentioned in the main work) to appeals from Commissioners—"clear error of law"—would be a more appropriate approach to judicial review of Commissioners' decisions than the stricter approach taken in *Sivasubramaniam*—"exceptional circumstances". In the past, it has been said that, in order to show the Administrative Court (or, in Scotland, the Court of Session) that a Commissioner has erred in refusing leave to appeal from a tribunal, it is likely to be necessary to show either (a) that the Commissioner's reasons were improper or insufficient, or (b) that the tribunal clearly erred in law—or at least that there was a substantial argument to that effect—and that the error might have had some effect on the outcome of the case before the tribunal (*R. v Secretary of State for Social Services Ex p. Connolly* [1986] 1 W.L.R. 421, 432). The effect of applying *Cooke* would be that the Administrative Court or Court of Session would have to be satisfied that the tribunal actually had clearly erred in law and that the error might have affected the outcome of the case.

pp.364–367, *Claims and Payments Regulations 1987, reg.3: claims not required for entitlement to benefit in certain cases*

With effect from October 25, 2004, reg.5 of the Social Security (Back to Work Bonus and Lone Parent Run-on) (Amendment and Revocation) Regulations 2003 (SI 2003/1589) amend reg.3 as follows: **4.019**
(a) in para.(h)(i) the words "6(2) or" are omitted;
(b) in para.(h)(iii) the words "regulation 6(3) or, as the case may be," are omitted.

pp.367–377, *annotation to Claims and Payments Regulations 1987, reg.4: making a claim for benefit*

CIS/0540/2002 is now reported as *R(IS) 6/04.* The appeal to the Court   **4.020**
of Appeal to which reference is made in the main work was not pursued.

Para. (6)

In *CIB/2805/2003* the Deputy Commissioner rules that, having regard   **4.021**
to s.7 of the Interpretation Act 1978, the onus is on the Secretary of State to prove that a letter arrives at a date later than the date it should have been received in the ordinary course of post. This would involve producing some evidence of practice in the Department about date stamping incoming post. This was particularly important in this case since the letter in issue had been posted during the Easter holiday period.
In such cases, the use of reg.19(7)(c), which deals with adverse postal conditions may be relevant: see annotations to that provision.

Para. (7)

CP/3447/2003 concerned a claim for an adult dependency increase to   **4.022**
a retirement pension for the claimant's wife. The claimant had made his claim for retirement pension at the proper time in advance of his 65th birthday indicating on the claim form that he wished to claim the increase for his wife. Adult dependency increase is, by virtue of reg.2(3) of the Claims and Payments Regulations, treated as a separate benefit requiring a separate claim. The Department failed to pick up the statement in the retirement pension claim form and did not send the claimant a further form to complete. In the following year, the claimant wrote to ask whether he was getting the increase after a query on his tax return. The required form was then issued to him. He completed it and it was clear that he should have been receiving the increase all along. The Secretary of State refused to pay it back to the start of the retirement pension on the grounds that the claim was received following the enquiry and could only be backdated three months from that date. By the time the appeal came before the tribunal, the Secretary of State accepted that the decision was wrong. The issue turned on the proper interpretation of reg.4(7). In particular, what was the date on which the claim was made "in the first instance" in this case. Was it the date on which the claimant wrote his letter asking about his entitlement to the increase of his wife,

or was it the indication in his original claim form for retirement pension indicating that he wanted the increase for his wife?

The Commissioner concluded:

"In those circumstances, given that (a) a claim in writing for the increase is now accepted as having been made in the first instance by the claimant in early 1999 as part of the original claim for his pension, and (b) the Secretary of State did in fact exercise his powers in regulation 4(7) to supply the claimant with the approved form which was returned duly completed well within the month stipulated, the conditions under which the Secretary of State is bound to treat the claim as if it had been duly made 'in the first instance' are in my judgment satisfied in reference to the *original* date of claim in 1999, not just the enquiry letter the following year. Since the requirement to treat the claim as duly made 'in the first instance' is mandatory once the conditions are met, there is no further exercise of discretionary or administrative judgment for the Secretary of State to make under regulation 4(7) before the effect in terms of entitlement to benefit can be properly determined. Although it was only in response to the further enquiry that the form was eventually supplied the Secretary of State could not in my judgment possibly rely on that as an argument for saying that the existence of the first claim should be ignored, when the failure to supply the form in the first instance was admittedly an administrative error by his own local officials and should never have happened at all" (para.15).

The Commissioner does, however, note that in so finding in the particular circumstances of this case, he is not to be taken as pronouncing as a matter of general principle that ticking boxes on a form in the expectation of receiving a further form ought in every case to constitute making a claim in writing for the benefit in question (para.14).

Para. (7A)

4.023 There are special rules in reg.4 where the benefit claimed is income support. In *CIS/3173/2003*, the claimant had contacted an office of the Department with a view to making a claim for income support on October 14, 2002, and she had subsequently completed an income support claim form on October 24, 2002, but did not include payslips with that form. These were required since she declared that she was doing "therapeutic work" (actually work accepted as permitted for the purposes of incapacity benefit). The Department contacted the claimant on December 18, 2002 regarding the missing payslips. These were provided on December 19, 2002. The decision maker awarded income support only from December 19, 2002. The tribunal upheld that decision. The Commissioner also concludes that there was no entitlement until December 19, 2002. He concludes that the claim form sent in without the accompanying payslips was a defective claim under sub-para.(7A) with the consequences stated there, but that reg.6(1A) makes provision only for one month's leeway in providing the information or evidence required to cure the defect. More than one month had passed here, and accordingly no claim which complied with the requirement of reg.4(1A) was made until December 19, 2002. It did not matter that the Department had not requested the payslips earlier. The Commissioner has granted leave to appeal in this case.

pp.380–381, *Claims and Payments Regulations 1987, reg.4F: making a claim after attaining the qualifying age: date of claim*

With effect from October 6, 2004, reg.8 of the Social Security (Housing Benefit, Council Tax Benefit, State Pension Credit and Miscellaneous Amendments) Regulations 2004 (SI 2004/2327) amends reg.4F as follows: 4.024
   (a) by substituting for the word "claimant" where it first appears, the words "person wishing to make a claim"; and
   (b) by inserting after the word "informs" in sub-para.(a), the words "(by whatever means)".

pp.382–402, *annotation to Claims and Payments Regulations 1987, reg.6: date of claim*

Para. (1)

Note also *CIS/4901/2002* relating to arrangements between the Department and the Post Office for the handling of mail, which is reported in detail at para.2.126 of Vol.III.   4.025

Para. (1A)

CIS/58/2003 is now reported as *R(IS) 3/04*.   4.026
With effect from September 27, 2004, reg.2 of the Social Security (Retirement Pensions) Amendment Regulations 2004 (SI 2004/2283) adds new paras (31) and (32) to reg.6 as follows:

"(31) Subject to paragraph (32), where—

   (a) a person—
      (i) has attained pensionable age, but for the time being makes no claim for a Category A retirement pension; or
      (ii) has attained pensionable age and has a spouse who has attained pensionable age, but for the time being makes no claim for a Category B retirement pension;
   (b) in accordance with regulation 50A of the Social Security (Contributions) Regulations 2001, (Class 3 contributions: tax years 1996–97 to 2001–02) the Commissioners of Inland Revenue subsequently accept Class 3 contributions paid after the due date by the person or, in the case of a Category B retirement pension, the spouse;
   (c) in accordance with regulation 6A of the Social Security (Crediting and Treatment of Contributions, and National Insurance Numbers) Regulations 2001 the contributions are treated as paid on a date earlier than the date on which they were paid; and
   (d) the person claims a Category A or, as the case may be, a Category B retirement pension,

the claim shall be treated as made on—

    (i) 1st October 1998; or
    (ii) the date on which the person attained pensionable age in the case of a Category A retirement pension, or, in the case of a Category B retirement pension, the date on which the person's spouse attained pensionable age,

whichever is later.

(32) Paragraph (31) shall not apply where—

    (a) the person's entitlement to a Category A or B retirement pension has been deferred by virtue of section 55(2)(a) of the Contributions and Benefits Act (increase of retirement pension where entitlement is deferred); or
    (b) the person's nominal entitlement to a Category A or B retirement pension is deferred in pursuance of section 36(4) and (7) of the National Insurance Act 1965 (increase of graduated retirement benefit where entitlement is deferred),

nor where sub-paragraph (a) and (b) both apply."

GENERAL NOTE

4.027   These provisions "get around" the 12-month limitation on back-dating set out in s.1(2) of the Administration Act in relation to claims for retirement pension. They enable claimants to go back as far as October 1, 1998 in certain circumstances. The Explanatory Memorandum to the regulations indicates that the intended beneficiaries of the provisions are those who did not receive notice that their contribution records were deficient for the tax years 1996/97 to 2002/03 because the annual Deficiency Notice procedure which identifies such cases and advises customers of the need to consider making voluntary contributions to make good the shortfall did not take place in those years.

pp.402–404, *annotations to Claims and Payments Regulations 1987, reg.6A: claims by persons subject to work-focused interviews*

4.028   With effect from April 26, 2004, reg.22 of the Social Security (Working Neighbourhoods) Regulations 2004 (SI 2004/959) amends para.(5) to read as follows:

"In regulation 4 and this regulation, "work-focused interview" means an interview which [. . .] [is conducted for such purposes connected with employment or training as are specified under section 2A of the Social Security Administration Act 1992.]"

pp.404–407, *annotations to reg.7: evidence and information*

4.029   The decision of the House of Lords in *Kerr v Department for Social Development* [2004] UKHL 23; [2004] 1 W.L.R. 1372 (appendix to *R1/04(SF)*) was handed down on May 6, 2004. The discussion in the House of Lords broadened from the considerations which had taken place in the courts below. The comments, in particular of Baroness Hale, on the decision-making process are discussed in para.1.371.1 of Vol.III. The House of Lords dismissed the appeal. In their opinions, no mention is made of *R(IS) 4/93* which had been disapproved in the reasons of the Court of Appeal. Notwithstanding the absence of any comment, its authority must be considerably weakened by the dismissal of the appeal. However, it is suggested that it will still provide some useful guidance in those cases where, despite the best endeavours of the adjudicating authorities to collect all the evidence needed to determine a claim for benefit, they remain short of evidence on key matters. For a discussion of the similar provisions in relation to the adjudication of housing benefit and council tax benefit claims see the decision of the Tribunal of Commissioners in *CH/3600/2003* and others.

pp.414–416, *annotations to Claims and Payments Regulations 1987, reg.13C: further claim for and award of disability living allowance*

The decision of the Tribunal of Commissioners in *CIB/4751/2002, CDLA/4753/2002, CDLA/4939/2002* and *CDLA/5141/2002* is reported as *R(IB) 2/04.* **4.030**

pp.417–419, *annotations to Claims and Payments Regulations 1987, reg.15: advance notice of retirement and claim for and award of pension*

In *CP/3017/2004* the Commissioner held, applying *CDLA/2751/2003* **4.031** by analogy, that there is a power to disallow an advance claim made under reg.15(1) for an increase of retirement pension for a wife up to four months before a claimant might become entitled to the pension (para.7). However, the Commissioner considers:

" . . . in some cases where there was likely to be a significant change of circumstances before the start date of the period covered by a claim, it might well be good practice to defer making a decision until it was known whether that change had actually materialised. It seems to me that the present case is one where that course should have been taken. It was plain from the evidence provided that the claimant's wife's earnings fluctuated a great deal from one pay period to another. And the nature of the case is different from that of a person suffering some potentially disabling or incapacitating condition, where in most cases there can be a sensible prediction about how the condition might progress in the future. It was simply unknown on 3 March 2004 what the claimant's wife's earnings might be in the week prior to 31 May 2004. Quite apart from the doubts that I explain below about the averaging process carried out by the officer, it would have been better to have waited until close to 28 May 2004 and then considered the current evidence about the wife's earnings. I do not think that there would have been any difficulty in making an advance decision on the claimant's own retirement pension entitlement, but deferring the decision on the increase. However, that did not happen."

pp.425–438, *Claims and Payments Regulations 1987, reg.19: time for claiming benefit*

4.032   With effect from October 6, 2004, reg.2(a) of the Social Security (Claims and Payments) Amendment (No.2) Regulations 2004 (SI 2004/1821) amends reg.19(4) by omitting sub-para.(ff). This had been inserted by SI 2002/3019 but the provision was inadvertently omitted from Vol.III. It added State pension credit to the list in reg.19(4).

Paras (4) and (5)

4.033   In *R(IS) 16/04,* the reported decision in *CIS/4862/2003,* the Commissioner follows the approach adopted in *CIS/849/1998* and *CJSA/ 3994/1998* (the correctness of which was conceded by the Secretary of State) to the effect that a claim can be taken as including a claim for a period starting with the earliest date which would make the claim in time.

Note too that *R(IS) 3/01* holds that the maximum period of extension should be calculated backwards from the date of actual claim, not forwards from the first day of the period expressly claimed for.

In *R(IS) 16/04,* the reported decision in *CIS/4862/2003,* the Commissioner rules that the question of reasonableness under reg.19(4)(b) and 19(6)(b) can only be asked in relation to each particular period of claim, and not the totality of any delay. The Commissioner gives as an example the position of a claimant who delays making a claim for income support for several months, but who then makes a claim. Just after he posts the claim form, there is a strike by postal workers which holds up delivery of the claim for some weeks. The fact that the claimant could have claimed earlier than he did should not defeat his reliance on adverse postal conditions in relation to the claim he actually made.

Paras (6) and (7)

4.034   In *R(IS) 16/04,* the reported decision in *CIS/4862/2003,* the Commissioner accepts that delays in post arriving over the Christmas period constitute adverse postal conditions within para.(7)(c).

Para. (8)

4.035   Paragraph 8 should read:

"(8) This regulation shall not have effect with respect to a claim to which [[4] regulation 21ZB] of the Income Support (General) Regulations 1987 (treatment of refugees applies.]"

CJSA/4383/2003 concerns the relationship of the 28 day time limit for claiming income support by asylum seekers who have received notification that they have been accepted as having refugee status under reg.21ZB(2) of the Income Support General Regulations. Provided income support is claimed within this time limit, the award can be backdated to the date of the asylum application. Because of delays

inherent in the determination of such claims, this can be a very substantial period. In the appeal before the Commissioner, the issue arose as
to whether a person within the ambit of reg.21ZB(2) lost all ability to use
the provisions of reg.19(4) and (5) to seek backdating of a claim for
income support. The Secretary of State had argued that the reg.19(8)
had this effect. The Commissioner disagreed for the following reasons:

"17. . . . In my view this is to misunderstand the legislative framework.
The starting point is section 1 of the Social Security Administration
Act 1992, which (in virtually all cases) requires a claim to be made as
a precondition of entitlement to benefit. Section 5 of the 1992 Act
then grants the Secretary of State various regulation-making powers in
relation to claims. In the exercise of these powers, the Social Security
(Claims and Payments) Regulations 1987 have been made. Regulation
19(1) of, and Schedule 4 to, those Regulations sets out the basic rules
for claiming various benefits and the time limits that apply. Thus the
general rule is that claims for income support or jobseeker's allowance
must be made on 'the first day of the period in respect of which the
claim is made'. Regulation 19(4) and (5) then provide, by way of
exception to this general principle, that the prescribed period for
claiming these benefits can be extended for up to three months if
'good cause', as defined by the Regulations, can be established.

18. However, regulation 19(4) is expressly stated to be subject to
regulation 19(8). The purpose of regulation 19(8) is to provide that
those claimants who can avail themselves of regulation 21ZB are not
to be caught by the standard limit of three months on backdating
entitlement to income support. A successful applicant for asylum, who
claims arrears of income support within 28 days of receiving the Home
Office's notification, is a person who makes 'a claim to which regulation 21ZB [. . .] of the Income Support (General) Regulations 1987
(treatment of refugees) applies'. In that situation regulation 19(8) then
provides that 'this regulation' (i.e. the normal three month rule) 'shall
not have effect'. In other words, the claim for arrears of benefit, if
made within the 28 day time limit, may be backdated by many more
than three months and indeed right back to the date of the asylum
application. This is supported by regulation 6(4D) of the 1987 Regulations, which deems the claim so made to have been made actually
at the much earlier date when asylum was applied for—see the obiter
opinion of Mrs Deputy Commissioner Rowley in *CIS/579/2004* (at
paragraph. 43.4).

19. In my view, therefore, there are not two entirely separate and
mutually exclusive regimes, which appears to be the Secretary of
State's contention. The correct position in law is that a person in the
claimant's situation may be able to make a claim for backdated benefit
in accordance with regulation 19(4) and (5). Just because he is a
successful applicant for asylum does not take him out of that regime.
However, if he had made his claim within 28 days of the Home Office
letter, he might have his entitlement to benefit backdated to the date
of his original application for asylum, by virtue of regulation 21ZB,
regardless of the normal three month rule in regulation 19(4)."

pp.448–452, *annotations to Claims and Payments Regulations 1987, reg.30: payments on death*

4.036 *R(IS) 3/04* (discussed at para.2.69 of Vol.III) discusses aspects of reg.30 at paras 14–17 of the decision. The Commissioner notes that reg.30(5) is the only provision permitting claims to be made in respect of deceased persons, and reg.30(5) expressly does not apply to income support.

pp.453–456, *Claims and Payments Regulations 1987, reg.32: information to be given and changes to be notified*

4.037 See the discussion of the very important decision of the Tribunal of Commissioners in *CIS/4348/2003* discussed in the updated annotations to s.71 of the Administration Act.

pp.477–479, *Claims and Payments Regulations 1987, Sch.4: prescribed time for claiming benefit*

4.038 With effect from October 6, 2004, reg.2(a) of the Social Security (Claims and Payments) Amendment (No.2) Regulations 2004 (SI 2004/1821) adds a new para.12 to the Schedule as follows:

"12. State pension credit. As regards any day on which, apart from satisfying the condition of making a claim, the claimant is entitled to benefit, that day and the period of 12 months immediately following it."

Sometimes there is a need to be very precise about dates. *CIB/2805/2003* was just such a case. The Deputy Commissioner notes that the formulation used in relation to incapacity benefit (and, it should be noted, in relation to several other benefits) is to specify the time limit by reference to the day of claim and a period of three months immediately following it. The Deputy Commissioner rules that this means that the claimant gets the day of claim and a full three months immediately following the date in respect of which the claim is made. This gave the claimant two more days than the Secretary of State had calculated.

pp.497–503, *annotations to Claims and Payments Regulations 1987, Sch.9A: deductions of mortgage interest from benefit and payment to qualifying lenders*

4.039 With effect from November 28, 2004, reg.3(b) of the Social Security (Housing Costs Amendments) Regulations 2004 (SI 2004/2825) substitutes the words "determined in accordance with" for the words "specified in" in para.11(2)(a)(i).

p.532, *annotation to Commissioners' Procedure Regulations 1999, reg.23*

4.040 *R. (Thompson) v Law Society* [2004] EWCA Civ 167 (mentioned in the main work) has now been reported at [2004] 1 W.L.R. 2522. The House of Lords has refused leave to appeal [2004] 1 W.L.R. 2854.

p.547, *Decisions and Appeals Regulations 1999, reg.1(3)*

So that it will no longer be necessary to amend these regulations every   4.041
time a new set of regulations makes provision for work-focused interviews, the definition of "work-focused interview" is substituted by
reg.24(2) of the Social Security (Working Neighbourhoods) Regulations
2004 (SI 2004/959), with effect from April 26, 2004. Now:

> " "work focused-interview" means an interview in which a person is
> required to take part in accordance with regulations made under
> section 2A or 2AA of the Administration Act;".

pp.550–551, *annotation to Decisions and Appeals Regulations 1999, reg.2*

A fax is received for the purposes of reg.2(a) when it is successfully   4.042
transmitted to, and received by, a fax machine, irrespective of when it is
actually collected from the fax machine (*R(DLA) 3/05*). Furthermore,
the faxed request for a statement of reasons in that case was received by
the clerk to the appeal tribunal when received at the tribunal venue, even
though the clerk did not visit that venue until some days later. It would
have been different if the venue had been a casual venue, such as local
authority premises. Here, it was a dedicated venue and the fax number
had been given to representatives precisely to enable them to communicate with the clerk. There was nothing in any document issued with the
decision notice to indicate that the request for a statement of reasons had
to be addressed to a different place.

In *CG/2973/2004*, the Commissioner applied *CIB/303/1999* (mentioned in the main work) in holding there to have been a breach of the
rules of natural justice where a tribunal had not received medical evidence sent by the claimant in support of an application for a postpone-
ment. The tribunal's decision was therefore erroneous in point of law,
notwithstanding reg.2(a). Having set aside the tribunal's decision, the
Commissioner considered the main issue in the case, which was whether
the claimant had made a claim for benefit on a certain date. A claim is
generally effective only when received. The position is therefore similar
to that under reg.2(a), relating to documents to be sent to a clerk to a
tribunal. The Commissioner accepted that the claimant had posted a
claim form but found that it was more likely to have been lost in the post
before it reached the building where it was to be opened than lost in that
building or subsequently. Strictly speaking, it was therefore unnecessary
for him to consider whether, the claimant having succeeded in showing
that the form had been posted, the burden of proving that the letter was
lost after arrival at that building rested on her or whether the burden of
proving that it was lost before then rested on the Secretary of State.
However, having heard full legal argument, he said that the burden
would have lain on the claimant to prove delivery so that, if it had been
impossible to say where the letter was more likely to have been lost, the
claimant would still have failed. He preferred *CIS/306/2003* to *CSIS/
48/1992* and *CIS/759/1992*.

p.557, *annotation to Decisions and Appeals Regulations 1999, reg.3(5)*

4.042.1   The approach taken in *R(IS) 15/04* has been approved by the Court of Appeal in *Beltekian v Westminster City Council* [2004] EWCA Civ 1784.

The burden of proving that there was an "official error", as that term is defined in reg.1(3), lies on the claimant where it is he who is applying for revision, but it is for the Secretary of State to produce evidence of the supersession or revision that is in issue before the tribunal *(CH/3439/2004)*.

[THE NEXT PARAGRAPH IS 4.043.]

p.560, *annotation to Decisions and Appeals Regulations 1999, reg.4*

4.043   It was held in *R(TC) 1/05* that a tribunal did not have jurisdiction to consider whether the Inland Revenue ought, under reg.4, to have extended the time for applying for revision. In that case, the relevant decision was made on April 22, 2002, the claimant sought reconsideration on November 11, 2002 and the Inland Revenue refused to extend the time for applying for revision and therefore refused to revise the decision on November 25, 2002. The claimant appealed. There is no right of appeal against a revision or refusal to revise and so the appeal had to be treated as an appeal against the decision of April 22, 2002. The time for appealing against a decision is not extended under reg.31 when the application for revision is made late and time is not extended under reg.4. In those circumstances (and subject to the possibility that the decision of April 22, 2002 had not been sent to the claimant), the appeal should have been treated as having been late and therefore invalid, unless a legally qualified panel member extended, under reg.32, the time for appealing. On the facts of *R(TC) 1/05*, it made no difference whether the time for applying for revision was extended under reg.4 or whether the time for appealing was extended under reg.31, but the Commissioner pointed out that the test for extending the time for applying for revision is now different from that for extending the time for appealing. He also pointed out that the thirteen-month absolute time limit for appeals (see reg.32(1)) means that in some cases an appeal could be valid only if the time for applying for revision had been extended. It seems regrettable that a tribunal should not have the power to determine whether the Secretary of State ought to have extended time under reg.4, especially as the exercise the Secretary of State is required to perform is not all that simple and a considerable amount of money may turn on it.

p.560, *Decisions and Appeals Regulations 1999, reg.5*

4.044   Under the Social Security (Retirement Pensions) Amendment Regulations 2004 (SI 2004/2283) and with effect from September 27, 2004, reg.5 becomes reg.5(1) and a new para.(2) is added:

"(2) Where—

(a) a person attains pensionable age, claims a retirement pension after the prescribed time for claiming and the Secretary of State decides ("the original decision") that he is not entitled because—

    (i) in the case of a Category A retirement pension, the person has not satisfied the contribution conditions; or

    (ii) in the case of a Category B retirement pension, the person's spouse has not satisfied the contribution conditions;

(b) in accordance with regulation 50A of the Social Security (Contributions) Regulations 2001(Class 3 contributions: tax years 1996–97 to 2001–02) the Board subsequently accepts Class 3 contributions paid after the due date by the claimant or, as the case may be, the spouse;

(c) in accordance with regulation 6A of the Social Security (Crediting and Treatment of Contributions, and National Insurance Numbers) Regulations 2001 the contributions are treated as paid on a date earlier than the date on which they were paid; and

(d) the Secretary of State revises the original decision in accordance with regulation 11A(4)(a),

the revised decision shall take effect from—

    (i) 1st October 1998; or

    (ii) the date on which the claimant attained pensionable age in the case of a Category A pension, or, in the case of a Category B pension, the date on which the claimant's spouse attained pensionable age, whichever is later."

This is linked to the introduction of reg.6(31) and (32) of the Social Security (Claims and Payments) Regulations 1987 (see above). Both amendments are necessary to deal with a problem caused by the failure from 1996 to 2003 to inform contributors of deficiencies in their contribution records so that they could pay voluntary Class 3 contributions to make up the deficit. By reg.50A of the Social Security (Contributions) Regulations 2001, claimants are being allowed to pay their contributions very late. The amendment to reg.6 of the 1987 Regulations enables a late claim based on those contributions to be made and this amendment allows an earlier decision disallowing a claim to be revised with effect from October 1, 1998 or the date the claimant or, where appropriate, the claimant's spouse reached pensionable age. Without these amendments, the new claim or the revision might be effective from a much later date and that might be unfair because, having discovered about the deficiency, the claimant might have delayed claiming on what was then a correct understanding that there was nothing that could be done about it.

p.562, *Decisions and Appeals Regulations 1999, reg.6(2)(h)(ii)*

By reg.24(3) of the Social Security (Working Neighbourhoods) Regulations 2004 (SI 2004/959) and with effect from April 26, 2004, the   4.045

words from "under the Social Security (Jobcentre Plus Interviews for Partners) Regulations 2003 . . . " to the end of the subparagraph are replaced by:

"in accordance with regulations made under section 2AA of the Administration Act, ceased to be a partner for the purposes of those regulations or is no longer a partner to whom the requirement to take part in a work-focused interview under those regulations applies".

pp.567–568, *annotation to Decisions and Appeals Regulations 1999, reg.6(2)(a)(i)*

4.046 A number of cases have shown that, in incapacity for work cases, superseding a decision under reg.6(2)(a)(i) on the ground of change of circumstances, rather than superseding it under reg.6(2)(g), does not always produce a decision that is effective from the date of the change of circumstances rather than the date of supersession (see the supplemental annotation to reg.7, below).

pp.569–570, *annotation to Decisions and Appeals Regulations 1999, reg.6(2)(g)*

4.047 In *CIB/451/2004*, the claimant had twice been referred for medical examinations after being awarded incapacity benefit. On the first occasion he satisfied the personal capability assessment and on the second occasion he did not. Following the second examination, the Secretary of State issued a decision purporting to supersede the original award. The Commissioner declined to rule on a submission that there should have been a supersession decision after the first medical examination because the grounds for supersession under reg.6(2)(g) are such that it made no difference whether there should already have been a supersession of the original award or even whether there had been a supersession of that award. On any view, there must have been a decision that could properly be superseded under reg.6(2)(g) and it was unnecessary further to identify the decision.

In *R(IB) 1/05*, the Commissioner accepted that a decision treating a person as incapable of work under reg.28 of the Social Security (Incapacity for Work) (General) Regulations 1995 is an "incapacity determination" as that term is defined in reg.7A, but that made no difference to his decision.

The burden of proving grounds for supersession lies on the person seeking supersession so that, where a claimant has been entitled to incapacity benefit, it is for the Secretary of State to justify terminating the award by superseding it under reg.6(2)(g). However, it is pointed out in *CIB/1509/2004* that the burden of proof must be considered in two stages. For reg.6(2)(g) to apply at all, the Secretary of State must have received the necessary medical evidence following an appropriate medical examination. On an appeal to a tribunal, it is plainly for the Secretary of State to produce that evidence but he almost invariably does so and therefore that is not usually a live issue. The second stage is considering whether the claimant still satisfies the conditions for entitlement to benefit and so continues to be entitled to benefit notwithstanding that the requirements of reg.6(2)(g) are met. The Commissioner referred to *Kerr v Department for Social Development* [2004] UKHL 23; [2004] 1 W.L.R. 1372 (also reported as an appendix to *R1/04(SF)* (see the annotation to s.12 of the Social Security Act 1998 in the main work), where Baroness Hale talked of "a co-operative process of investigation" (para.[62]) and said that "it will rarely be necessary to resort to concepts taken from adversarial litigation such as the burden of proof" (para.[63]). A tribunal must have regard to all the evidence produced in the investigation and decide the case on the balance of probabilities. The Commissioner followed *CIS/427/1991* in holding that the burden of proof is relevant only (a) if there is no relevant evidence on an issue (despite an adequate investigation) or (b) if the evidence on the issue is so evenly balanced that it is impossible to determine where the balance of probabilities lies. The Commissioner held that, when superseding a decision on his own initiative, the burden of proof lies on the Secretary of State at both stages so that, in the few cases when it is relevant at the second stage, the case should be decided in favour of the claimant.

p.577, *Decisions and Appeals Regulations 1999, reg.7(25)(b)*

With effect from April 26, 2004, reg.24(4) of the Social Security 4.048 (Working Neighbourhoods) Regulations 2004 (SI 2004/959) makes two amendments to reg.7(25)(b). For the words "under the Social Security (Jobcentre Plus Interviews for Partners) Regulations 2003", there are substituted the words "in accordance with regulations made under section 2AA of the Administration Act" and, in head (i), the words in parenthasis are replaced by "(meaning the person who has been awarded benefit within section 2AA(2) of the Administration Act at a higher rate referable to that partner)".

pp.581–582, *annotation to Decisions and Appeals Regulations 1999, reg.7(2)*

On a claim where the claimant relies on his of her incapacity for work, 4.049 the claimant is usually treated under reg.28 of the Social Security (Incapacity for Work) (General) Regulations 1995 as incapable of work pending a personal capability assessment, provided he or she submits medical certificates. In *R(IB) 1/05*, the claimant submitted only one medical certificate and was not covered by a certificate from August 18, 2002. The Secretary of State therefore had to determine whether the claimant was incapable of work, which he did on May 9, 2003, following a medical examination. The Commissioner accepted that the lack of a medical certificate was a change of circumstances justifying supersession under reg.6(2)(a)(i), rather than reg.6(2)(g). However, as none of the provisions of reg.7 applied, the supersession could still have effect only from the date of decision, *i.e.* May 9, 2003, by virtue of s.10(5) of the Social Security Act 1998. Regulation 7(2)(c)(iii) did not apply because carrying out the personal capability assessment itself involved an incapacity determination and reg.7(2)(c)(ii) did not apply because there had

145

been no failure to notify a change of circumstances. That decision was distinguished in *CSIB/570/2004*, where the claimant failed to attend a medical examination without good cause. The Commissioner relied on reg.8(2) of the Social Security (Incapacity for Work) (General) Regulations 1995, which required that the claimant "shall be treated as capable of work" from the day after the failure to attend the examination. However, the Commissioner did not explain how that approach could be reconciled with s.10(5) of the 1998 Act, given the terms of reg.7. The answer may be that reg.7(2)(c)(iii) applied, because there had been no incapacity determination, although that again raises the question as to the meaning of "incapacity determination" and whether the interpretation accepted in *R(IB) 1/05* (that treating a person as satisfying the personal capability assessment under reg.28 of the Social Security (Incapacity for Work) (General) Regulations 1995 involves an "incapacity determination") is correct.

Another defect in the drafting of reg.7(2) has been revealed in *CIB/763/2004*, where the Commissioner was obliged to hold that a decision superseding an award of incapacity benefit on the ground that the claimant had been working was effective only from the date of decision and not from the date 20 months earlier when she had started work. An award of incapacity benefit had been superseded but the claimant had successfully appealed. She had returned to work while the appeal was pending. In those circumstances, reg.7(2)(c)(iii) did not apply, because the exception does not refer only to cases where the change of circumstances relates to the claimant's medical condition. There had clearly been an incapacity determination that had been reversed on appeal. The Commissioner held that reg.7(2)(c)(ii) also did not apply because there was no failure to disclose the return to work, given that the change of circumstances occurred at a time when it had been decided that she was not entitled to benefit and the Secretary of State had been informed of the change before any payment was made following the successful appeal against the incapacity determination. The result in this case would not be absurd if payment had been made to the claimant after she had disclosed her work because the overpayment would not be recoverable from her under s.71 of the Social Security Administration Act 1992 anyway. However, it is unfortunate that the Secretary of State should be required to make a payment to a person who plainly did not satisfy the conditions of entitlement, merely because he is unable to make a valid retrospective decision as to entitlement.

The question whether a claimant has "failed to notify" a change of circumstances for the purposes of reg.7(2)(c)(ii) was held in *CDLA/1823/2004*, to be similar to the familiar question whether a person has "failed to disclose" a change of circumstances for the purposes of s.71 of the Social Security Administration Act 1992 (see the main work at p.54). The Commissioner noted that the phrase "regulations under the Administration Act" refers to reg.32 of the Social Security (Claims and Payments) Regulations 1987 (see the main work at p.453) which was considered in some detail in the context of s.71 by a Tribunal of Commissioners in *CIS/4348/2003* (see the supplemental annotation to s.71, above). He suggested that there will be a failure to notify a change of circumstances if there is a breach of clear and unambiguous instructions, as was the position in *CIS/4348/2003*, but that otherwise the issue is likely to be whether the Secretary of State could reasonably have expected the claimant to notify him of the material fact. Determining the question whether reg.7(2)(c)(ii) applies may, therefore, require some evidence as to the instructions given to the claimant.

pp.610–611, *annotation to Decisions and Appeals Regulations, reg.31(2)*

The approach taken in *R(IS) 15/04* has been approved by the Court of Appeal in *Beltekian v Westminster City Council* [2004] EWCA Civ 1784.   4.049.1

[THE NEXT PARAGRAPH IS 4.050.]

pp.612–613, *annotation to Decisions and Appeals Regulations 1999, reg.32*

The absolute time limit prohibiting the bringing of appeals more than a year late is not incompatible with the European Convention on Human Rights (*Denson v Secretary of State for Work and Pensions* [2004] EWCA Civ 462 (also reported as *R(CS) 4/04*). Nonetheless, it can work injustice, particularly in a case where an unrepresented claimant has been challenging the wrong decision and nobody tells him or her until it is too late which decision it is that must be challenged if he or she is to succeed in obtaining the benefit sought.   4.050

In *R(TC) 1/05*, there was no evidence that anyone had considered whether there were grounds for admitting a late appeal, perhaps because the appeal had been proceeding on the basis that it was an in-time appeal against a supersession decision whereas, on a proper analysis, the supersession had been a refusal to revise so that the appeal was against an earlier decision and the circumstances were such that time had not been extended by virtue of reg.31(2). There was also a suggestion that notice of the original decision had not been sent to the claimant so that the appeal was not late at all. The Commissioner considered that the tribunal's brief reasons suggested that if the chairman had considered whether to extend the time for appealing, he would have refused. However, the Commissioner held the decision was invalid because, if the appeal had been late and there was no extension of time, the tribunal had had no jurisdiction to hear the appeal. The claimant was entitled to have the question of an extension of time properly considered. Had the chairman clearly refused an extension of time, the Commissioner said that it appeared that he would have had no jurisdiction to consider an appeal against that refusal, notwithstanding that there appeared to be no clear finding that notice of the decision under appeal to the tribunal had ever been issued. However, it is suggested that, if the tribunal had declined jurisdiction on the ground that time had not been extended, the refusal to accept jurisdiction would have been appealable and a failure to record a finding as to whether notice of the original decision had been issued might have led to the appeal being allowed. In an ordinary case, of course, the question of extending time is considered by a legally qualified panel member before the case is listed for hearing by a tribunal and, in many cases, a tribunal cannot be composed only of a legally qualified panel member.

The Commissioner also pointed out that, whereas under reg.32(2) the Secretary of State or Inland Revenue can consider whether the conditions in reg.32(4)(b) to (8) are satisfied, only a legally qualified panel member can consider whether the condition in reg.32(4)(a) is satisfied. Regulation 32(4)(a) bestows a fairly broad discretion on a legally qualified panel member to grant an extension of time and makes it unnecessary for him or her to consider the narrow conditions of reg.32(4)(b) to (8) in a meritorious case.

p.620, *annotation to Decisions and Appeals Regulations 1999, reg.36(6)*

4.051   The Secretary of State's appeal against *CSDLA/444/2002* (mentioned in the main work) has been dismissed by the Court of Session (*Secretary of State for Work and Pensions v Cunningham* 2004 S.L.T. 1007 (also reported as *R(DLA) 7/04)*).

p.622, *annotation to Decisions and Appeals Regulations 1999, reg.38*

4.051.1   Where a claimant has failed to produce evidence within the time allowed in a direction but produces it at a hearing before a tribunal, the tribunal may be entitled to refuse to admit the evidence. However, it must act proportionately, having regard to the purposes for which the time limit was placed in the direction and the prejudice caused by the failure to comply with it (*CIB/4253/2004*). Where the evidence can easily be absorbed at the hearing by the tribunal and any other party, it is unlikely to be appropriate to refuse to admit it. A failure to comply at all with a direction to produce evidence does not always justify the drawing of an adverse inference, although it may well do so (*CCS/3757/2004*, and see the supplemental annotation to s.12 of the Social Security Act 1998, above).

[THE NEXT PARAGRAPH IS 4.052.]

pp.624–625, *annotation to Decisions and Appeals Regulations 1999, reg.39*

4.052   In Northern Ireland, the Appeals Service had adopted a practice of not offering a claimant a hearing where the claimant had indicated in his or her letter of appeal that a hearing was not wanted. In *R3/04(IB)*, a Commissioner held there to have been a clear breach of reg.39(1) and that the claimant could not be taken to have waived his right to an oral hearing when the standard leaflet issued to appellants told him that he would be given a further opportunity of making a decision when he had seen the Department's submission.

Note that draft regulations propose that new paras (1) to (4) should be substituted for the old (see Pt VI of this supplement—"Forthcoming changes").

p.630, *Decisions and Appeals Regulations 1999, reg.46*

Note that from December 21, 2004 amendments will, in conjunction   4.053
with amendments to reg.39, reverse *CIS/4351/2001* (mentioned in the
main work), abolish the concept of a "misconceived appeal" and delete
reg.46(4) (see Pt VI of this supplement—"Forthcoming changes").

pp.638–639, *annotation to Decisions and Appeals Regulations 1999,*
reg.51

The power conferred under reg.51(4) to adjourn proceedings must   4.054
not be used arbitrarily or capriciously and, in particular, must not be
used in order to defeat the general purpose of the legislation, but otherwise there is a complete discretion so long as it is exercised judicially
(*CIS/2292/2000*, citing *Jacobs v Norsalta Ltd* [1977] I.C.R. 189). Nonetheless, in *CIS/2292/2000*, a tribunal erred in rejecting an application for
an adjournment made by the representative of a claimant who was in
prison, in circumstances where the claimant's oral evidence had an
important part to play.

In *CSDLA/90/1998* (mentioned in the main work), the Commissioner
held that, when representation is undertaken by a local authority, the
claimant is entitled to be fully represented by the authority until disposal
of the appeal and the local authority must, if necessary, arrange representation through their legal department in order to avoid a postpone-
ment or an adjournment of a hearing. In *CIB/1009/2004*, a
Commissioner disagreed with that approach and said that a local authority was entitled to limit the power of representatives to call upon other
resources of the authority when a particular representative was unavail-
able due to illness. However, he went on to say that a representative
should make reasonable efforts to secure alternative representation, even
if that meant cancelling some other appointments, and that that implied
that a request for an adjournment due to the non-availability of a
representative should contain a clear indication that consideration had
been given to the possibility of someone else representing the claimant.
In the absence of such an explanation, the tribunal might be entitled to
infer that reasonable efforts had not been made to find alternative
representation. However, a failure by a representing authority to make
reasonable efforts to secure alternative representation should not have
led to a refusal of an adjournment, when further efforts might not have
made any difference, the claimant himself was blameless, a lot of money
was at stake and the case was not straightforward so that an experienced
representative might have assisted the tribunal to reach a conclusion
favourable to the claimant.

In both *CIB/1009/2004* and *CIB/2058/2004*, Commissioners have
emphasised that the inquisitorial approach of tribunals is not a complete
substitute for representation and have cited *R. v Social Security Commissioner Ex p. Bibi* (unreported, May 23, 2000) in which Collins J. said that,
although there is no absolute right to representation, there is an absolute
right to be dealt with fairly and that it was hardly unreasonable for a
person to wish to be represented by the particular solicitor with whom

149

she had been dealing. Therefore, a claimant's desire to be represented, or to be represented by a particular person, is a factor that ought to be given proper weight in considering whether or not to grant an adjournment. As to the balancing exercise itself, in *CIB/1009/2004* the Commissioner said:

> "13. A tribunal will always require to be persuaded that an adjournment is necessary—because there is always a potential disadvantage in adjourning a case—but the arguments against an adjournment in tribunal proceedings in a social security case may not be quite the same as those applicable in adversarial proceedings in the courts. In particular, the interests of the parties are not usually as closely balanced. In an ordinary social security case, where the Secretary of State does not provide a representative or have witnesses in attendance, there is very little disadvantage to the Secretary of State in granting the claimant an adjournment. It is usually the claimant himself who suffers the principal disadvantage of delay. If the claimant judges that disadvantage to be less than the disadvantage of proceeding without representation, a tribunal should not too readily substitute its own judgment on the relative weight of those two factors. The main consideration for the tribunal will therefore be whether the adjournment can be justified in the light of the substantial cost of a further hearing and the delay in the determination of another case whose place the adjourned hearing will take. Thus the interests of taxpayers and claimants in general need to be balanced against the interests of the particular appellant.
>
> 14. If the claimant is to blame for the need to request an adjournment, his interests are likely to be given correspondingly less weight. A claimant's interests may also be given less weight where his representative's fault has led to the request for an adjournment. By agreeing to act for a claimant, a representative takes some responsibility for the case and tribunals are entitled to exert pressure on representatives to behave properly. However, in an environment where most representatives are not qualified lawyers and where most claimants are not paying for the services of their representatives, some care must be taken not to cause injustice to a claimant by visiting upon him the sins of his representative. The tribunal's response must be proportionate, having regard to the consequences for the claimant of possibly losing his appeal."

4.055　In *Evans v Secretary of State for Social Security* (reported as *R(I) 5/94*), a medical appeal tribunal disagreed with the opinions of two consultants. The Court of Appeal held that, where a tribunal proposed to put a different interpretation on the same clinical findings from that put by another expert, "fairness points to the need for an adjournment so that, where possible, the tribunal's provisional view can be brought to the attention of the claimant's own advisers". A similar approach has been taken by Park J. when hearing an appeal from a Pensions Appeal Tribunal (*Butterfield v Secretary of State for Defence* [2002] EWHC 2247 (Admin)). He said that, when a medically qualified member of a tribunal is the only person present with specialist medical knowledge and he perceives a possible medical objection to the claimant's case that has not been pointed out before, he must draw it to the claimant's attention and it may be necessary to offer the claimant an adjournment so that he has a realistic opportunity to consider the point "however inconvenient and irksome that may be". This makes clear what was probably meant in *Evans*. There need not always be an adjournment but the tribunal's provisional view should be put to the claimant and the claimant should expressly be *offered* an adjournment.

Where there is an adjournment after some evidence has been heard and only one member of the new tribunal was present at the hearing before the adjournment, there is a risk of subconscious impressions gained by that member being carried over from one hearing to the other or of that member remembering evidence from the first hearing that has not been recorded in the record of proceedings. Therefore, having regard to *R(U) 3/88* (mentioned in the main work) a decision was set aside where the chairman, but not the other two members, had heard a substantial amount of evidence before an adjournment (*CDLA/ 2429/2004*).

pp.641–647, *annotation to Decisions and Appeals Regulations 1999, reg.33(4)*

In *English v Emery Rheimbold & Strick Ltd* [2002] EWCA Civ 605;   4.056
[2002] 1 W.L.R. 377 (mentioned in the main work), the Court of Appeal suggested that there were cases in which, where the Court considered a lower court's reasons for its decision to be inadequate, it would be appropriate for the Court to adjourn to ask for the reasons to be supplemented by the lower court. That practice has been adopted by the Employment Appeal Tribunal in relation to appeals from employment tribunals (*Burns v Royal Mail Group plc (formerly Consignia plc)* [2004] I.C.R. 1103) but not by the Administrative Court in relation to statutory appeals against special educational needs and disability tribunals (*VK v Norfolk County Council* [2004] EWHC 2921 (Admin)). In the latter case, Stanley Burnton J. distinguished *English* on the ground that there was a permission requirement and so the appellate court could invite the lower court to provide further reasons at the permission stage and he distinguished *Burns* on the ground that reasons did not have to be given at the same time as the decision. On that analysis, it might be thought that Commissioners would, where appropriate, invite tribunals to provide further reasons, but that is not the usual practice. One significant difference between proceedings before tribunals in social security cases and proceedings in the county court or employment appeal tribunal is that the former rarely last for more than an hour or so, whereas proceedings in courts or employment tribunals may last for several days. In those circumstances, requiring a tribunal to supplement its reasons, which in *English* itself was not regarded as very satisfactory but merely a lesser evil than expensive appellate proceedings, may not be significantly quicker or cheaper than considering an appeal on the papers and remitting the case for a complete rehearing, particularly as any supplemented reasons might themselves be challenged.

pp.646–647, *annotation to Decisions and Appeals Regulations 1999, reg.53*

4.056.1   *C38/03–04(DLA)* (mentioned in the main work) has been reported as *R2/04(DLA)*.

The decision in the *South Bucks* case (also mentioned in the main work) has now been reported as *South Bucks DC v Porter (No.2)* [2004] UKHL 33; [2004] 1 W.L.R. 1953. *Kwamin v Abbey National PLC* (also mentioned in the main work) has been reported at [2004] I.C.R. 841.

[THE NEXT PARAGRAPH IS 4.057.]

p.650, *annotation to Decisions and Appeals Regulations 1999, reg.55*

4.057   *Erratum:* The reference to *CIS/343/1994* should be to *CS/343/1994*.

pp.653–654, *annotation to Decisions and Appeals Regulations 1999, reg.57(1)*

4.057.1   In *CG/2937/2004*, the Commissioner held a tribunal decision to be erroneous in point of law because medical evidence sent by the claimant in support of an application for an adjournment had not been received by the tribunal. He also held that the fact that the claimant had unsuccessfully tried to have the decision set aside on the same ground did not prevent her from taking the point on appeal to a Commissioner. He observed that the chairman who had refused to set the decision aside had done so on the basis that her presence could not have made any difference to the outcome of her hearing. The case is therefore distinguishable from *CSDLA/303/1998* (mentioned in the main work). The fact that the applicant's presence would not have made any difference is a matter that can legitimately be taken into account when considering whether "it appears just to set the decision aside" and it would also be relevant to the question whether there had been a breach of the rules of natural justice, but the Commissioner disagreed with the chairman's view of the possible importance of the claimant's evidence.

[THE NEXT PARAGRAPH IS 4.058.]

pp.663–664, *annotation to Decisions and Appeals Regulations 1999, Sch.2*

4.058   In *R(H) 3/05*, counsel for one of the claimants acknowledged that the reasoning in *R(IS) 6/04* had been overtaken by that in *Runa Begum v Tower Hamlets London Borough Council (First Secretary of State intervening)* [2003] UKHL 5; [2003] 2 A.C. 430 in which it was held that there was no breach of Art.6 of the European Convention on Human Rights where an appeal from a local authority's decision in respect of their duties to homeless people lay only on a point of law. One possible inference to be drawn from the House of Lords' decision is that the possibility of judicial review of the unappealable decisions listed in Sch.2

is an adequate alternative remedy under the Convention. However, counsel submitted that the House of Lords' conclusion that there was no unfairness in not having an appeal on a point of fact was reached against the background of a system of internal review by a different officer of appropriate seniority whereas, in housing benefit and council tax cases, such system of internal review as there had formerly been had been replaced by an appeal to a tribunal, which is the procedure available in other social security cases. In the absence of such a sophisticated system of review, he argued, there had to be a right of appeal on questions of fact. It was unnecessary for the Tribunal of Commissioners to express a view on that argument and they did not do so.

The claimant has been given leave to appeal to the Court of Appeal against *CIB/3645/2002* (mentioned in the main work).

Note that from December 21, 2004 amendments will be made to para.5(a) to (e) so as to permit appeals against decisions that claims are defective (see Pt VI of this supplement—"Forthcoming changes").

p.684, *General Benefit Regulations, reg.16: earnings level for the purposes of unemployability supplement under s.58 of the Act*

With effect from October 1, 2004, reg.2 of the Social Security (Inca-pacity) (Miscellaneous Amendments) Regulations 2004 (SI 2004/2301) substitutes for the amount of £3,744 in reg.16 the amount of £4,056. **4.059**

pp.709–711, *Jobcentre Plus Interviews Regulations 2002, reg.2: interpretation and application*

With effect from April 26, 2004, reg.26(2) of the Social Security (Working Neighbourhoods) Regulations 2004 (SI 2004/959) inserts in reg.2, after the words "Except in a case where regulation 16(2) applies," the words "or where a person is subject to provisions within the Social Security (Working Neighbourhoods) Regulations 2004 by virtue of reg-ulation 2(3) of those Regulations,". **4.060**

pp.711–713, *Jobcentre Plus Interviews Regulations 2002, reg.4: continuing entitlement to a specified benefit dependent upon interview*

With effect from April 26, 2004, reg.26(3) of the Social Security (Working Neighbourhoods) Regulations 2004 (SI 2004/959) substi-tutes, in para.(1)(a), for the words "paragraph (3)", the words "either paragraph (3) or (3A)". **4.061**

The same provision amends paragraph (2) to read as follows:

"(2) This paragraph applies in the case of a person who has taken part in an interview under regulation 3 or who would have taken part in such an interview [. . .] [but for the requirement—

  (i) being waived in accordance with regulation 6;

  (ii) being deferred in accordance with regulation 7; or

(iii) not arising because the person was at the time of the claim for the specified benefit subject to provisions within the Social Security (Working Neighbourhoods) Regulations 2004 by virtue of regulation 2(3) of those Regulations]."

The same provision amends para.(3) by inserting the words "Except where paragraph (3A) applies," at the beginning of the paragraph, and adds para.(3A) as follows:

"(3A) Where a lone parent to whom paragraph (1)(a) applies was not required to take part in an interview under regulation 3 or under this regulation because at the time the requirement would have arisen he was subject to provisions within the Social Security (Working Neighbourhoods) Regulations 2004 by virtue of regulation 2(3) of those Regulations, the lone parent shall be required to take part in an interview—

(a) after the expiry of six months, and
(b) after the expiry of one year, and
(c) at intervals of one year thereafter,

from the date on which he took part in, or was treated as having taken part in, an interview as a condition of his claim for income support, except that a requirement to take part in an interview shall not arise by virtue of sub-paragraphs (a), (b) or (c) if the period specified in those provisions has already expired when the lone parent becomes subject to these Regulations."

p.718, *Jobcentre Plus Interviews Regulations 2002, reg.16: revocations and transitional provisions*

4.062   With effect from April 26, 2004, reg.26(4) of the Social Security (Working Neighbourhoods) Regulations 2004 (SI 2004/959) inserts in para.(2) after the words "(except for regulations 3 and 11(2)(a) and (b)" the words:

"and except where a person who is a relevant person for the purpose of the 2001 Regulations becomes subject to provisions within the Social Security (Working Neighbourhoods) Regulations 2004 by virtue of regulation 2(3) of those Regulations."

pp.719–720, *Jobcentre Plus Interviews for Partners Regulations 2002, reg.2: interpretation and application*

4.063   With effect from April 26, 2004, reg.27(2) of the Social Security (Working Neighbourhoods) Regulations 2004 (SI 2004/959) inserts the following words at the beginning of the regulation, "Except in a case where a partner is subject to provisions within the Social Security (Working Neighbourhoods) Regulations 2004 by virtue of regulation 2(3) of those Regulations."

pp.768–770, *annotation to Payments on Account, etc. Regulations 1988, reg.13: sums to be deducted in calculating recoverable amounts*

CSIS/0355/2004 gives guidance on the significance of the Public 4.064 Records Act 1958 to the retention of documents by the Department, and the onus of proof where a claimant asserts that there has been an underpayment of benefit in the past which reduces the amount of a recoverable overpayment. The overpayment at issue in this case had arisen as a result of admitted false statements made by the claimant which resulted in the award of income support. The point of contention was whether the claimant could offset the substantial overpayment by underpayments of benefit in circumstances where many of the relevant documents had long since been destroyed by the Department under its document retention policy.

The requirements of the Public Records Act 1958 were seen as something of a red herring, and the Commissioner has little time for them, noting: "It is difficult to believe that these elaborate procedures [in the 1958 Act] were ever intended to apply to social security claim forms." In fairness, the claimant's representative had abandoned this point in arguing the case before the Commissioner.

The onus of proof in cases such as this was a rather more substantial point, particularly in the light of the House of Lords in *Kerr v Department for Social Development* [2004] UKHL 23 (see para.1.371.1 of Vol.III). The Commissioner sees no real difference in the views expressed by Lady Hale in *Kerr* and the long-established wisdom that:

"if a particular matter relates to the qualifying conditions of entitlement it is a claimant who must bear the consequences of ignorance; however, if what is in issue constitute an exception to such conditions, then the Department bears the burden of establishing that factor which operates to disentitled the claimant" (para.43).

The issue which arises under reg.13 is distinct from the recovery of the overpayment; it is not necessarily related to the period which is covered by the s.71 revision or supersession nor to the same benefit the subject of recovery. The Commissioner concludes:

"If, as is trite law, one who submits an initial claim for benefit has the burden of showing that its qualifying conditions are met, it can hardly be the case that one who must pay benefit back because it has been demonstrated that she should never have had it, has an easier task in establishing a similar entitlement to offset against the proven debt. In my judgement, nothing in principle or on account of the statutory language or from the structure of the overpayment scheme or to further its consistency can justify such a departure from what is usual and right" (para.47).

p.796, *Recovery of Benefits Regulations 1996, reg.2(2)*

With effect from May 12, 2004, reg.7 of the Social Security (Miscella- 4.065 neous Amendments) (No.2) Regulations 2004 (SI 2004/1141) adds a subpara.(j) to reg.2(2):

"(j) any payment made from the Skipton Fund, the ex-gratia payment scheme administered by the Skipton Fund Limited, incorporated on 25th March 2004, for the benefit of certain persons suffering from hepatitis C and other persons eligible for payments in accordance with the scheme's provisions."

p.808, *Work-focused Interview Regulations 2000, reg.4: circumstances where requirement to take part in an interview does not apply*

4.066   With effect from April 26, 2004, reg.25(3) of the Social Security (Working Neighbourhoods) Regulations 2004 (SI 2004/959) adds the following words at the end of reg.4(d): "or the Social Security (Working Neighbourhoods) Regulations 2004."

With effect from September 30, 2004, reg.10(2) of the Social Security (Quarterly Work-focused Interviews for Certain Lone Parents) Regulations 2004 (SI 2004/2244) amends reg.4(d) to read as follows:

"[¹ (d) is—
   (i) required to take part in an interview; or
   (ii) not required to take part in an interview by virtue of—
      (aa) a waiver of the requirement; or
      (bb) a deferment of an interview
[under the Social Security (Work-focused Interviews) Regulations 2000, the Social Security (Jobcentre Plus Interviews) Regulations 2001, the Social Security (Jobcentre Plus Interviews) Regulations 2002, the Social Security (Working Neighbourhoods) Regulations 2004 or the Social Security (Quarterly Work-focused Interviews for certain Lone Parents) Regulations 2004.]]"

pp.809–810, *Work-focused Interview Regulations 2000, reg.7: consequences of failure to take part in an interview*

4.067   With effect from April 26, 2004, reg.25(4) of the Social Security (Working Neighbourhoods) Regulations 2004 (SI 2004/959) inserts in para.(3)(b) after the words "regulation 2(1)(b)" the words "or (c)".

p.821, *Child Benefit and Guardians Allowance (Administration) Regulations 2003, reg.7: evidence and information*

4.068   With effect from May 1, 2004, a new para.(3) is added to reg.7 by the Child Benefit and Guardian's Allowance (Administration) (Amendment) Regulations 2004, as follows:

"(3) If a person is required, by virtue of paragraph (1) to furnish a certificate of a child's birth or adoption, the certificate so produced must be either an original certificate or a copy authenticated in such manners as would render it admissible in proceedings in any court in the jurisdiction in which the copy was made."

GENERAL NOTE

This provision would appear to reflect the rather more legalistic approach the   4.069
Board of Inland Revenue adopt to some issues, since the Department for Work
and Pensions never seem to have felt the need for such a provision.

pp.948–954, *annotations to European Communities Act 1972, s.2: general
implementation of the treaties*

On July 19, 2002 the UK Government and the European Commission   4.070
reached agreement acknowledging that winter fuel payments constitute
old-age benefits within Art.4 of Regulation 1408/71 and so were export-
able to other Member States, provided that the claimant had obtained an
entitlement to such payments in the UK.

In *CIS/0488/2004* the Deputy Commissioner held that the Community law doctrine on the effective enjoyment of Community rights
required the Secretary of State to allow a reasonable time after the
agreement for those claimants who were beneficiaries of the agreement
to claim winter fuel payments for the winters of 2000/01 and 2001/02
notwithstanding that the statutory time for claiming had expired respectively on March 30, 2001 and March 30, 2002.

In *CIS/1491/2004* the Commissioner had to consider whether there
was an entitlement to winter fuel payments by a person born in 1928
whose residence in Great Britain had ended before the introduction of
winter fuel payments. The Commissioner concluded that the payments
are not a supplement to retirement pension, but are a separate and free-
standing form of old age benefit. It was not accordingly contrary to
Community law to condition entitlement to such a benefit on residence
in Great Britain. Since the claimant could not secure entitlement to a
winter fuel payment, it followed that he could not export that to which
he was not entitled. Article 10 only permits the export of a benefit to
another Member State after entitlement to it has been acquired. That
was not the case here.

pp.960–965, *annotations to Art.39 EC Treaty*

In *Secretary of State for the Home Department v Limbuela, Tesema and*   4.071
Adam [2004] EWCA Civ 540, the Court of Appeal ruled that the refusal
to provide State support for three asylum seekers who had not applied
for asylum within three days of their arrival in the UK under s.55 of the
Nationality, Immigration and Asylum Act 2002 engaged their Convention rights under Art.3. The case is discussed in detail in the annotations
to Art.3 ECHR below. For a discussion of the potential impact of the
new rules on A8 nationals and some issues relating to their compatibility
with Community law, see *R. (on the application of H and D) v Secretary
of State for Work and Pensions* [2004] EWHC 1097 Admin. This is the
decision of Collins J. on the application for judicial review of the new
regulations. Collin J. dismissed the application in so far as it related to
compatibility with Community law since he regarded the matter as
covered by the derogation from the full application of the provisions on
the free movement of workers. Collins J. refers to what was at the time

the pending appeal in *Limbuela* as possibly being determinative of the human rights arguments raised in the application.

pp.976–978, *annotations to Art.7, Council regulation (EEC) No.1612/68*

4.072   The latest judgment in the line of citizenship cases is that in the *Trojani* case: Case C-456-02 *Trojani,* Judgment of September 7, 2004. Trojani was a single man of French nationality. He clearly fell on hard times. He was living in a Salvation Army hostel in Belgium under an arrangement where he undertook various jobs for the hostel as part of a personal rehabilitation scheme, in exchange for which he received board and lodging and an allowance of €25.00 per week. He claimed the minimex (the minimum subsistence allowance in Belgium). His claim was refused on the grounds that he was not a Belgian national. Trojani brought proceedings before the Labour Court in Brussels to challenge this refusal. That Court referred questions to the Court of Justice. The Court advised that Trojani did not appear to be a worker because of the nature of his commitment to the hostel where he lived. The second one essentially concerned the possible entitlement of Trojani to the minimex as a person exercising his right to reside in Belgium as a citizen of the EU. The Advocate General concluded that it was open to Belgium to deny Trojani a right of residence because he did not have the means to support himself. The Court was a little more circumspect. Referring to the ruling in the *Baumbast* case, the Court indicates that it would not be disproportionate to deny Trojani a right of residence on the basis that he did not have the means to be self-sufficient. In other words, he had no *Community* right to reside. But the Court went on to note that he may have a right to reside under *national law,* since he had been issued with a residence permit under national law by the municipal authorities in Brussels. The Court made three points (at paras 41–6 of its judgment):

(1)   social assistance falls within the scope of the EC Treaty;
(2)   a citizen of the Union who is not economically active may rely on the prohibition of discrimination on grounds of nationality where he has been "lawfully resident" in the host Member State "for a certain time or possesses a residence permit" (para.43);
(3)   restricting entitlement to social assistance to the nationals of the host Member State constitutes discrimination on grounds of nationality contrary to Art.12 EC. It would follow that, if the national court concludes that Trojani was "lawfully resident" in Belgium under *national law,* then the prohibition of discrimination in Community law would be engaged, and the restriction of entitlement to the minimex to Belgian nationals in the circumstances of this case would breach the equality provisions of the EC Treaty.

Note the comments on the compatibility of certain provisions in s.2 of the Child Trust Fund Act 2004 with the requirements of Art.7(2) noted in the update to Vol.IV.

pp.978–979, *annotations to Art.42*

It is *CIS/825/2001* not *CIS/852/2001*. Leave to appeal in this case has 4.073
been granted by the Court of Appeal in May 2004 under the name
Secretary of State for Work and Pensions v Bobezes. The appeal was heard
by the Court of Appeal on December 14 and 15, 2004.

p.1087, *annotations to Art.2, Association Council Decision No.3/80*

GENERAL NOTE

Case C-275/02 *Ayaz v Land Baden-Württemberg,* Judgment of September 30, 4.074
2004, concerned the interpretation of the term "members of the family" of a
Turkish worker under Art.7 of Decision 1/80, but the decision of the Court of
Justice would apply equally to the interpretation of Art.2 of Decision 3/80. The
Court ruled that a stepson who is under the age of 21 years or is a dependant of
a Turkish worker duly registered as belonging to the labour force of a Member
State is a member of the family of that worker provided that he has been duly
authorised to join that worker in the host Member State.

pp.1087–1088, *annotations to Art.3, Association Council Decision
No.3/80: equality of treatment*

Case C-373/02 *Öztürk v Pesionsversicherungsanstalt der Arbeiter,* Judg- 4.075
ment of April 28, 2004, concerned a Turkish national who had worked
in Germany and Austria. He became entitled to an early old-age pension
in Germany, but was refused a similar pension in Austria since he had
not received unemployment benefit in Austria (although he had done so
in Germany). The Court of Justice of the European Communities ruled
that the requirement of equal treatment in Art.3 meant that the Austrian
authorities had acted unlawfully in not considering his receipt of unemployment benefit in Germany as meeting the particular requirement for
entitlement to the pension in Austria.

pp.1100–1102, *annotations to Art.4, Directive 79/7*

CIB/4497/2002 is now reported as *R(IB) 5/04.* 4.076
In *Hockenjos v Secretary of State for Social Security (No.2)*, judgment of
December 21, 2004 [2004] EWCA Civ 1749, the Court of Appeal has
allowed the claimant's appeal against the decision of the Commissioner
in *CJSA/4890/2003* and dismissed the Department's cross appeal. It will
be recalled that *Hockenjos v Secretary of State for Social Security (No.1)*,
judgment of May 2, 2001 (and referred to in the annotations to Art.3)
was the decision of the Court of Appeal determining that jobseeker's
allowance was a benefit falling within the material scope of the Directive.
This decision of the Court of Appeal deals with the substance of the
claimant's claim to entitlement to additional amounts in respect of his
children (the child premium) and to the family premium. Though he
had shared care of the children, child benefit was paid to the children's
mother which precluded payment of the additions to the claimant.
All three judges in the Court of Appeal reach the same conclusion by
somewhat different lines of reasoning on the detail of the case. The

Department conceded that the conditions of entitlement for child additions to a jobseeker's allowance, which linked these to entitlement to child benefit, were indirectly discriminatory, but argued that the discrimination could be objectively justified. The claimant was a man with shared care of his children following his separation from his wife. The Department argued that the link with entitlement to child benefit ensured consistency of decision-making. Scott Baker, L.J. delivering the first judgement said:

> "45. According, in my judgment the position is this. The law is set out in the European Court's judgment in *Seymour-Smith*. The Secretary of State must first show that the discriminatory rule reflects a legitimate aim of social policy. Next he must show that the aim is unrelated to any discrimination based on sex and finally that he could reasonably consider that the means chosen are suitable for attaining that aim. Built into this final question is the balance between holding fast to the Community's fundamental principles on the one hand and the Member State's freedom to achieve its own social policy on the other."

Scott Baker, L.J. concludes that reg.77(1), (2), (3) and (5) are discriminatory contrary to Art.4 of the Directive and have not been justified by the Secretary of State. The question of the remedy to be applied once this conclusion was reached clearly troubled the Court of Appeal, and there was an ultimately fruitless excursion into the possible impact of the Apportionment Act 1870. The conclusion reached is that the proper remedy is for the whole allowance to be paid to the claimant in respect of each child, since both children met the test of being members of the claimant's household for whom he was responsible. This is because there is no provision in the jobseeker's allowance scheme permitting the splitting of the additions for children.

pp.1103–1105, *annotations to Art.7*

4.077   Note the directions given by the Commissioner in granting a further stay in *CI/1881/2003* because Mrs Hepple has proceedings pending before the Court of Human Rights, the outcome of which, *inter alia,* "might well be to remove my inhibitions about inviting the European Court of Justice to reconsider its own decision in *Hepple*" (para.5 of Directions of June 3, 2004). The Grand Chamber of the European Court of Human Rights is to hear the *Hepple* case on March 9, 2005.

pp.1103–1105, *annotations to Art.7, Council Directive 79/7/EEC: exception in Art.7(1)(a)*

4.078   In Case C-303/02 *Haackert v Pensionsversicherungsanstalt der Angestellten,* Judgment of March 4, 2004, the Court of Justice ruled that the exception in Art.7(1)(a) applied to early old-age pension schemes with different entitlement ages for men and women because of the close link with the age at which old-age pensions, which were not awarded early, would arise. In the circumstances of the case before the Court, the early old-age pension operated as a substitute for the old-age pension.

pp.1111–1113, *Human Rights Act 1998, s.1*

With effect from June 22, 2004, s.1(1)(c) is amended by the Human 4.079
Rights Act 1998 (Amendment) Order 2004 (SI 2004/1574) to read as
follows: "(c) Article 1 of the Thirteenth Protocol,".

GENERAL NOTE

The reference to Arts 1 and 2 of the Sixth Protocol have been replaced by the 4.080
reference to the Thirteenth Protocol now that this Protocol has been ratified and
entered into force on February 1, 2004. The Protocol abolished the death
penalty in all circumstances, whereas the Sixth Protocol preserved the possibility
of its use in time of war.

pp.1116–1118, *annotations to Human Rights Act 1998, s.3*

In *Ghaidan v Godin-Mendoza* [2004] UKHL 30, the House of Lords 4.081
ruled that the policy reasons for giving a statutory tenancy to the survivor
of a cohabiting heterosexual couple applied equally to the survivor of a
cohabiting homosexual couple. In so holding, they interpreted paras 2
and 3 of Sch.1 to the Rent Act 1977 to secure compatibility with
Convention rights. This avoided less favourable treatment of homosexual couples in the enjoyment of their Convention rights under Art.8
ECHR which could not be objectively justified.

The case is important for its re-affirmation of the approach which
should be adopted in reading and giving effect to primary and sub-
ordinate legislation in a way which is compatible with Convention rights.
Significantly, the judges in the House of Lords did not attempt to write
words into or delete words from the statutory provisions in issue, prefer-
ring simply to indicate what the substantive effect of those provisions
should be (see opinion of Lord Nicholls at para.35). The task of interpretation under s.3 required courts, if necessary, to depart from the
unambiguous meaning of a legislative provision in order to ensure
respect for Convention rights. Lord Steyn said that declarations of
incompatibility under s.4 were remedies of last resort, and that s.3
represents the principal remedial measure. Lord Steyn also indicated
that there had been a tendency to concentrate too much on linguistic
features of particular legislative provisions; what was required was a
broad purposive approach concentrating on the Convention right in
issue. Lord Rodger said:

"123. Attaching decisive importance to the precise adjustments
required to the language of any particular provision would reduce the
exercise envisaged by section 3(1) to a game where the outcome would
depend in part on the particular turn of phrase chosen by the draftsman and in part on the skill of the court in devising brief formulae to
make the provision compatible with Convention rights. The statute
book is the work of many different hands in different parliaments over
hundreds of years and, even today, two different draftsmen might
choose different language to express the same proposition. In enacting
section 3(1), it cannot have been the intention of Parliament to place
those asserting their rights at the mercy of the linguistic choices of the

161

individual who happened to draft the provision in question. What matters is not so much the particular phraseology chosen by the draftsman as the substance of the measure which Parliament has enacted in those words. Equally, it cannot have been the intention of Parliament to place a premium on the skill of those called on to think up a neat way round the draftsman's language. Parliament was not out to devise an entertaining parlour game for lawyers, but, so far as possible, to make legislation operate compatibly with Convention rights. This means concentrating on matters of substance, rather than on matters of mere language.

124. Sometimes it may be possible to isolate a particular phrase which causes the difficulty and to read in words that modify it so as to remove the incompatibility. Or else the court may read in words that qualify the provision as a whole. At other times the appropriate solution may be to read down the provision so that it falls to be given effect in a way that is compatible with the Convention rights in question. In other cases the easiest solution may be to put the offending part of the provision into different words which convey the meaning that will be compatible with those rights. The preferred technique will depend on the particular provision and also, in reality, on the person doing the interpreting. This does not matter since they are simply different means of achieving the same substantive result. However, precisely because section 3(1) is to be operated by many others besides the courts, and because it is concerned with interpreting and not with amending the offending provision, it respectfully seems to me that it would be going too far to insist that those using the section to interpret legislation should match the standards to be expected of a parliamentary draftsman amending the provision: *cf. R. v Lambert* [2002] 2 A.C. 545, 585, para.80 *per* Lord Hope of Craighead. It is enough that the interpretation placed on the provision should be clear, however it may be expressed and whatever the precise means adopted to achieve it."

4.082   The proper approach to the application of s.3 would appear in the light of all the authorities to involve a number of steps. First, it is necessary to identify the legislative provision which it is argued breaches Convention rights: see *R. v A (No.2)* [2002] A.C. 45. Then consideration should be given to whether that provision involves a breach of Convention rights: see *Poplar Housing and Regeneration Community Association Ltd v Donoghue* [2002] Q.B. 48. If there is, then a s.3 interpretation is needed and the focus here should be on compatibility with the Convention right. This can be achieved by reading in Convention rights, that is, by implying words in the legislative provision to secure compatibility with Convention rights; or by reading down, that is, by applying a narrower interpretation in order to secure compatibility. But it is not necessary to specify the precise re-wording of the provision: see *Ghaidan v Godin-Mendoza* above.

The limits of interpretation are reached where the required construction conflicts with the express words of a legislative provision: see *R. (Anderson) v Secretary of State for the Home Department* [2003] 1 A.C.

837. The same conclusion will be reached if there is a conflict with the legislative provision by necessary implication. Finally, the limits of construction are reached when the construction placed on the provision alters the statutory scheme in a fundamental way.

In *R(G) 2/04*, the reported decision in *CG/1467/2001*, the Commissioner, following the decision of the Court of Appeal in *R. (Hooper and others) v Secretary of State for Work and Pensions* [2003] 1 W.L.R. 2623 in this respect—which it is understood is not in issue in the pending appeal to the House of Lords—that the words of the statute admitted of only one interpretation. The effect of this was to preclude a man from claiming widow's benefit in respect of a spouse who died before April 9, 2001. See annotations to Art.14 of the European Convention on Human Rights for more detail on this line of cases.

pp.1118–1120, *annotations to Human Rights Act 1998, s.4*

In its admissibility decision of June 18, 2002 in *Hobbs v United Kingdom* (App.63684/00), the Court of Human Rights ruled that a declaration of incompatibility is not an effective remedy within the meaning of Art.35 of the Convention for the purpose of the rule requiring an applicant to exhaust domestic remedies. The Court rejected the Government's invitation to reconsider this position in its admissibility decision of March 16, 2004 in *Walker v United Kingdom* (App.37212/02). The Court was strongly influenced by the fact that a declaration of incompatibility was not binding on the parties.   **4.083**

CIS/4511/2002 is now reported as *R(IS) 12/04*.

pp.1121–1122, *annotations to s.6, Human Rights Act 1998*

On the concept of "public authority" for the purposes of this Act, see also *Parochial Church Council of the Parish of Aston Cantlow and Wilmcote with Billesley, Warwickshire v Wallbank and others* [2003] UKHL 37; [2003] 3 W.L.R. 283; and *Hampshire County Council v Beer t/a Hammer Trout Farm* [2003] EWCA Civ 1056; [2004] 1 W.L.R. 233.   **4.084**

In the *Aston Cantlow* case, Lord Nicholls said:

"12. What, then, is the touchstone to be used in deciding whether a function is public for this purpose? Clearly there is no single test of universal application. There cannot be, given the diverse nature of governmental functions and the variety of means by which these functions are discharged today. Factors to be taken into account include the extent to which in carrying out the relevant function the body is publicly funded, or is exercising statutory powers, or is taking the place of central government or local authorities, or is providing a public service."

For a detailed consideration of the concept of "public authority" and the way in which the courts are approaching the determination of this issue, see generally *The Meaning of Public Authority under the Human Rights Act*, Seventh Report of the Joint Committee on Human Rights of Session 2003–04 HL Paper 39, HC 382, which can be found at *http://www.*

publications.parliament.uk/pa/jt200304/jtselect/jtrights/39/39.pdf. The Joint Committee expresses some concern about the way the courts are interpreting the concept, but commends the approach adopted by the House of Lords in the *Aston Cantlow* case.

pp.1122–1126, *annotations to Human Rights Act 1998 s.7*

4.085   *CIS/4511/2002* is now reported as *R(IS) 12/04.*

pp.1135–1137, *Human Rights Act 1998, s.21*

4.086   With effect from June 22, 2004, art.2(2) of the Human Rights Act 1998 (Amendment) Order 2004 (SI 2004/1574) omits the definition of the Sixth Protocol in s.21(1) and inserts the following definition after the definition of the Eleventh Protocol: " 'the Thirteenth Protocol' means the protocol to the Convention (concerning the abolition of the death penalty in all circumstances agreed at Vilnius on 3rd May 2002;".

p.1139, *annotations to Art.3, ECHR*

4.087   In *Secretary of State for the Home Department v Limbuela, Tesema and Adam* [2004] EWCA Civ 540, the Court of Appeal ruled that the refusal to provide State support for three asylum seekers who had not applied for asylum within three days of their arrival in the UK under s.55 of the Nationality, Immigration and Asylum Act 2002 engaged their Convention rights under Art.3. Carnwath L.J. said that the case raised the question of the level of abject destitution to which such individuals must sink before their suffering reaches the minimum threshold for Art.3 to bite. Shelter was regarded as a basic amenity and the threat of not having access to shelter in the future could come within the ambit of inhuman and degrading treatment under Art.3. Laws L.J. dissented. Carnwath L.J. said:

> "118. . . . I acknowledge with gratitude the illumination provided by Laws LJ's powerful discussion of the scope of Article 3, and its application in the present context. As he says, the legal reality is a spectrum. At one end is state-authorised violence. At the other are to be found executive decisions in exercise of lawful policy objectives, which have consequences for individuals so severe that 'the Court is bound to limit the State's right to implement the policy on Article 3 grounds'. I agree also with much of his analysis of the consequences of that distinction, and of the correct approach to the task of drawing the line in an individual case.
>
> 119. Laws L.J. accepts that Article 3 may be engaged by a particular 'vulnerability' in the individual, or external circumstances which make it impossible for him to find food and other basic amenities. Where, with respect, I part company from him is in his view that, on the evidence available to us, the judges were not entitled to find that such circumstances existed in the present cases. I would add that I find it difficult not to regard shelter of some form from the elements at night

(even if it is limited as it was in *T*'s case) as a 'basic amenity', at least in winter and bad weather . . . ".

The Secretary of State is appealing to the House of Lords.

The judgment is important because it sets out circumstances within the context of State support for individuals which fall within the ambit of inhuman and degrading treatment in Art.3.

pp.1140–1160, *annotations to Art.6 ECHR*

It is understood that legal aid has been granted in the *Gillies* case, which is now likely to heard by the House of Lords in the second half of 2005. 4.088

While the decision of the House of Lords is awaited in *Gillies*, we have a further authority from the Court of Session on bias and medical members to consider: *Secretary of State for Work and Pensions v Cunningham*, Court of Session, August 6, 2004, reported as *R(DLA) 7/04*. The Deputy Commissioner had ruled that a situation might well have arisen of a reasonable apprehension of bias in circumstances where an examining medical practitioner had sat as the medical member of a tribunal with the chairman at 22 tribunal sessions, with the disability member at 14 tribunal sessions, and with both the chairman and the disability member at three tribunal sessions. The Court of Session agreed. The facts before the Deputy Commissioner were said by the Court of Session to be "readily distinguishable" from those which arose in *Gillies*.

Counsel for the Secretary of State, were the Court to go against him (as it did), asked for clarification as to how far the decision depended on the frequency with which the doctor had sat with the other members of the tribunal. The Court of Session declined to go further than the obvious point that it might have made a difference if the doctor had sat only once with the other members some considerable time before the case in issue.

In its admissibility decision of April 8, 2003 (see para.4.62 of Vol.III) in *Wingrave v United Kingdom* (App.40029/02), the Court of Human Rights had declared inadmissible part of the claim (relating: (1) to a breach of contract claim; (2) to the requirement to make a new claim at age 65 for disability living allowance; and (3) concerning the quality of her representation) but adjourned the issue concerning the length of the proceedings. The appeal had been twice remitted for rehearing by the Commissioners and had taken nearly five years to conclude. The decision on the admissibility of that complaint was adjourned by the Court of Human Rights in its decision of April 8, 2003. By a decision of May 18, 2004, the Court of Human Rights has declared this aspect of the complaint admissible. 4.089

Part of the decision of the Tribunal of Commissioners in *CIB/3645/2002* concerned an argument that the absence of a right of appeal in the social security legislation contravened the claimant's rights under Art.6 of the Convention. As noted at para.2.508 of Vol.III, the Tribunal of Commissioners decided the decision that the claimant was not permanently incapacitated for work at the time of leaving Great Britain for Jamaica concerned the payability of benefit while the claimant was in

Jamaica rather than his entitlement to the benefit. The decision was accordingly not within the scope of s.12(3) of the Social Security Act 1998. Furthermore Art.6 was not relevant because Art.6 had "no part to play in the ambit of substantive rights, as opposed to procedural rights" (para.43), since Art.13(2) of the Social Security (Jamaica) Order 1997 (SI 1997/871) provided a subjective test under which the Secretary of State determined whether benefit was to continue to be payable abroad if he considered the claimant likely to be permanently incapacitated for work when leaving Great Britain.

The Tribunal of Commissioners indicates that it has not come to this decision lightly and adds a rider in para.54 of its decision:

"Finally, we should make clear that our decision is limited to the issues before us. On the basis of the decision of Mr Commissioner Howell QC in *CIB/3654/2002* [this appears to be an erroneous reference, which should be to *CIS/540/2002*, now reported as *R(IS) 6/04*], it may be arguable that that the Human Rights Act and Article 6 of the European Convention may require rights of appeal to be granted against decisions under reciprocal agreement provisions in respect of which rights of appeal had existed previously. There may also be other cases in which it may be arguable that Paragraph 22 of Schedule 2 of the Decisions and Appeals Regulations does not restrict certain rights of appeal without deciding whether the provision is *ultra vires* (as found in *CIB/3586/2000* (starred decision 15/00)). We express no view on the correctness of those decisions."

The claimant is appealing to the Court of Appeal under the name *Campbell v Secretary of State for Work and Pensions*.

CIS/4/2003 is now reported as *R(IS) 15/04*.

pp.1160–1162, *annotations to Art.8 ECHR*

4.090   Some helpful guidance on the application of Art.8 to covert filming is provided by the decision of the Employment Appeal Tribunal in *XXX v YYY and ZZZ*, April 9, 2003, *EAT/0729* and *EAT/0413/2002*. The issue before the employment tribunal related to claims of sex discrimination and victimisation by a nanny, who had been involved in a consensual sexual relationship with the father of the child for whom she was employed to care, which had broken down. The nanny made a covert video recording of events one morning involving herself and the father in the presence of the child; the recording depicts sexual advances made by the father to the nanny. The issue concerned the admissibility of this recording in the proceedings. The EAT was particularly concerned with the rights of the child under Art.8 of the Convention, but also recognised that Art.6 ECHR also came into play in that the applicant (the nanny) was arguing that the admission of the video recording was essential for her to be guaranteed a fair trial under that article. The guidance given by the EAT incorporates the guidance which had been contained in the judgment of the Court of Appeal in *Jones v University of Warwick* [2003] 1 W.L.R. 954, as follows:

"26. Mr Weir [Counsel for the Claimant] argues that unless it was *necessary* for the insurers to take the actions they did, the evidence must inevitably, at least in a case such as this, be held inadmissible. He submits that otherwise the court would be contravening the duty that it is under, pursuant to section 6 of the Human Rights Act not to contravene Article 8. While the court should not ignore the contravention of Article 8, to adopt Mr Weir's approach would fail to recognise that the contravention would still remain that of the insurer's enquiry agent and not that of the court. The court's obligation under section 6 of the Human Rights Act is to 'not itself act in a way which is incompatible with a convention right' (see *Venables v News Group Newspapers Ltd* [2001] 2 W.L.R. 1038 at p.1048/9 paras 24–27).

27. As the Strasbourg jurisprudence makes clear, the Convention does not decide what is to be the consequence of evidence being obtained in breach of Article 8 (see *Schenk v Switzerland* [1988] 13 E.H.R.R. 242 and *PG and JH v United Kingdom* application no. 44787/98 (25/9/2001 paragraph 76). This is a matter, at least initially, for the domestic courts. Once the court has decided the order, which it should make in order to deal with the case justly, in accordance with the overriding objectives set out in Part 1.1 of the CPR in the exercise of its discretion under Part 32.1, then it is required or it is necessary for the court to make that order. Accordingly if the court could be said to have breached Article 8.1 by making the order which it has decided the law requires, it would be acting within Article 8.2 in doing so.

28. That leaves the issue as to how the court should exercise its discretion in the difficult situation confronting the district judge and Judge Harris. The court must try to give effect to what are here the two conflicting public interests. The weight to be attached to each will vary according to the circumstances. The significance of the evidence will differ as will the gravity of the breach of Article 8, according to the facts of the particular case. The decision will depend on all the circumstances. Here, the court cannot ignore the reality of the situation. This is not a case where the conduct of the defendant's insurers is so outrageous that the defence should be struck out. The case, therefore, has to be tried. It would be artificial and undesirable for the actual evidence, which is relevant and admissible, not to be placed before the judge who has the task of trying the case. We accept Mr Owen's [Counsel for the defendants] submission that to exclude the use of the evidence would create a wholly undesirable situation. Fresh medical experts would have to be instructed on both sides. Evidence which is relevant would have to be concealed from them, perhaps resulting in a misdiagnosis; and it would not be possible to cross-examine the claimant appropriately. For these reasons we do not consider it would be right to interfere with the Judge's decision not to exclude the evidence."

In *R. (Smith) v Secretary of State for Defence and Secretary of State for Work and Pensions* [2004] EWHC 1797 (Admin), Wilson J. held that respect for private life under Art.8 encompasses respect for a person's need for financial support "when under as well as over the age of 60". The case concerned an argument by an ex-wife that she was entitled to payment of that part of a pension which was subject to a pension sharing order below the age of 60 since the pension was so payable to her former husband. The judge held that the provisions governing the payment to the ex-wife of the pension at the age of 60 did not breach her rights under Art.8:

> "One cannot say that the impugned provision challenges the principle that the claimant needs financial support before as well as after the age of 60. In making the provision the state has decreed only that provision carved out of pension rights should not result in payment earlier than what is presently regarded, in the context of state provision, as normal pensionable age. In other words pension credits are conferred so as to address later, rather than earlier, need; and, because of the delay in payment suffered by some pension credit members, the real amount of their pension is correspondingly increased. The impugned provision does not derogate from the duty of the divorce court under [the matrimonial legislation] to have regard to a spouse's likely needs prior to the age of 60 in deciding what, of any, order to make for her or his benefit by way of financial provision or property adjustment in addition to the pension sharing order" (para.21(b)).

pp.1163–1173, *annotations to Art.14 ECHR*

4.091   In *Ghaidan v Godin-Mendoza* [2004] UKHL 30, the House of Lords ruled that the policy reasons for giving a statutory tenancy to the survivor of a cohabiting heterosexual couple applied equally to the survivor of a cohabiting homosexual couple. In so holding, they interpreted paras 2 and 3 of Sch.1 to the Rent Act 1977 to secure compatibility with Convention rights. This avoided less favourable treatment of homosexual couples in the enjoyment of their Convention rights under Art.8 ECHR which could not be objectively justified. There may well be implications flowing from this decision into other areas where homosexual couples are treated differently from heterosexual couples.

See also *Secretary of State for Work and Pensions v M; Langley v Bradford Metropolitan District Council and Secretary of State for Work and Pensions* [2004] EWCA Civ 1343; one case concerned the calculation of child support liability and the other a housing benefit case. In the *M* case, M was currently living in a same-sex relationship and the material regulations were treated as applying to her as they apply to members of heterosexual partnerships and marriages. In the *Langley* case, the claimant complained that she was not entitled to housing benefit because she was paying rent to a former cohabiting partner of the opposite sex, whereas she would not have been entitled had she been paying to a former cohabiting partner of the same sex. Her appeal had been dismissed by the Commissioner because there was no material similarity or analogy between her case and that of the comparator she put forward. The Court of Appeal disagrees with his reasoning, though the Court concludes for different reasons that there has been no breach of her Convention rights. The approach of the members of the Court differed in their approach.

Kennedy, L.J., who adopted the submission made to him by the Secretary of State, concluded that housing benefit falls outside the ambit of Art.8 (and so no argument under Art.14 could arise) because there is no obligation under Art.8 to provide the benefit and its provision is not the State's method of demonstrating respect for the home.

Neuberger, L.J. was, however, prepared to accept that it is was argu- **4.092** able that the housing benefit scheme did fall within the ambit of Art.8, without deciding the point; though he did stress that the decision in *Douglas v North Tyneside MBC* [2003] EWCA Civ 1847 could be a substantial barrier to proving even this. However, Ms Langley was not entitled to succeed under Art.14 because, following the reasoning of the Court of Appeal at paras [160]–[163] of *R. (Hooper) v Secretary of State for Work and Pensions* [2003] 1 W.L.R. 2623, because compensating her would achieve no legitimate aim. Her complaint in truth was that reg.7(1)(c)(i) did not apply to same-sex partnerships, not that it does apply to opposite-sex partnerships. But once that point had been reached it would only compound the anomaly that same-sex partnerships fall outside the regulation by saying that opposite-sex partnerships should not fall within it, thus rendering the regulation of no effect whatsoever.

Sedley, L.J. was much clearer in his view that the housing benefit scheme as a whole did come within the ambit of Art.8. He distinguished Laws, L.J.'s comment in *Reynolds* [2003] 3 All E.R. 577 that the income support scheme *per se* does not engage Art.8, by stressing that the housing benefit scheme is a discrete scheme with a particular purpose that does lie within the ambit of Art.8.

However, for him the more precise question which needed to be asked here was whether reg.7(1)(c)(i) came within the ambit of Art.8. It was this particular regulation which Ms Langley was complaining of and it was only this regulation that she was arguing she was a "victim" of under s.7(1) of the Human Rights Act 1998. She was not a victim of the housing benefit scheme as a whole.

Viewed from this perspective the question for Sedley, L.J. was whether the specific anti-abuse provision came within the ambit of Art.8 (respect for the home and family), which it did not. In order to rank as a victim Ms Langley would need to show that, if the regulation included same-sex partners, she would in some appreciable way be better off. That she plainly could not do. The only way she would be better off would be if there were no reg.7(1)(c)(i) at all. But in that circumstance what Ms Langley would be the victim of would not be the discriminatory element of the regulation but the regulation itself; of which no Convention complaint could be made.

In *Malcolm v Mackenzie and Allied Dunbar plc* [2004] EWHC CH 339, **4.093** the High Court considered an argument made by the applicant that he had been the victim of discrimination contrary to Art.14 when read with Art.1 of Protocol 1. The applicant asserted unfair differential treatment of the assets of persons declared bankrupt in that the benefit of a retirement annuity contract of self-employed person vests in the trustee in bankruptcy, whereas an employed person holding benefits under an occupational pension scheme does not lose the benefit of the scheme on

bankruptcy. Much of the discussion in the case concerns the retrospective application of the Human Rights Act 1998, but Lloyd J. does go
on to express his views on the merits of the complaint. He accepts that
the benefits of a retirement annuity contract are possessions for the
purposes of Art.1 of Protocol 1 and so Art.14 is engaged if discrimination prohibited by the article can be shown. However, he disagrees with
the applicant on the choice of comparator, pointing out that the differential treatment does not arise as between employed and self-employed
persons, but between self-employed persons and employed persons who
are members of an occupational pension scheme which includes a forfeiture clause. The judge then opines: "It seems to me that this requires
the introduction of too many different factors for the comparison to be
appropriate or relevant under article 14" (para.61 of judgment). The
judge also concludes that the differential treatment could be objectively
justified.

While expressing the view that he found the judgment of Lloyd J. on
the Convention rights argument "impressive and fairly hard to assail",
Neuberger L.J. has granted leave to appeal to the Court of Appeal on the
grounds that it is conceivable that the Court of Appeal might take a
different view and the point is of some general interest: see [2004]
EWCA Civ 584.

In *Douglas v North Tyneside Metropolitan Borough Council and Secretary
of State for Education and Skills* [2003] EWCA Civ 1847, the claimant
was above the upper age limit for eligibility for a student loan. He argued
that there was unjustifiable discrimination on grounds of age in breach of
Art.14 when read in conjunction with Art.2 of Protocol 1 on the right to
education. The Court of Appeal ruled that tertiary education fell within
the ambit of Art.2 of Protocol 1, and went on to consider the Art.14
complaint. The Court held that student loans were one step removed
from the provision of education, and were not so closely related to the
provision of education as to prevent the claimant from participating. So,
although the provision of tertiary education was within the ambit of
Art.2 of Protocol 1, the provision of student loans to support it was not.
Had the Court concluded that it was, they would have held that the
difference in treatment on grounds of age was justified. In delivering the
judgment of the Court, Scott Baker L.J. said:

> "[62] It is not for the courts to interfere with the Secretary of State's
> funding arrangements provided they are lawfully made and applied.
> Funding arrangements for further education fall within the general
> area where social and economic judgements are required that involve
> the allocation of finite resources and the balancing of competing
> claims. The courts in my judgment have to be careful when consider-
> ing an issue of justification such as would arise in the present case were
> Art.2 to be engaged not to trespass into the discretionary area of
> resource allocation. That is an area that is not justiciable.
>
> [63] I find the following points compelling in favour of the Secretary
> of State's argument that the funding arrangement is justified:
> — Higher education is a scarce resource; it is not available to
>   everybody, as is primary and secondary education.

— The government is entitled to decide the priorities in the allocation of scarce resources.

— The arrangements are entitled to treat older students differently on the ground that the scheme is a loan scheme and the money is expected to be repaid. It is a reasonable assumption that older students have less chance of being in a position to repay than younger students. (The obligation to repay the loan ceases at 65.)

— The age cut-off is part of a larger picture on which a judgement is made.

— There are other measures that may be available to assist a student who is ineligible by way of age for a loan. These are fee waiver and a hardship grant.

[64] For these broad reasons, therefore, I am satisfied that the Secretary of State discharges the burden of justification".

R. (Smith) v Secretary of State for Defence and Secretary of State for Work   **4.094**
and Pensions [2004] EWHC 1797 (Admin), concerned complaint by an ex-wife that there was a breach of Art.14 read in conjunction with Art.1 of Protocol 1 (or Art.8) where a pension payable to the pension holder was payable below the age of 60 but where the pension payable to the ex-wife following a pension sharing order did not take effect until she reached the age of 60. Wilson J. accepted that this was discrimination within Art.14 on grounds of both age and gender, he found that it was justified since the policy objective was to encourage ex-wives under the age of 60 to work until that age—a legitimate aim of the state—and that, if for some reason she could not do so, "she could reasonably expect the divorce court to oblige the ex-husband to provide her with support in respect of that period" (para.32).

The Court of Human Rights has declared admissible a complaint by a man that it is a breach of Art.14 read with Art.1 of Protocol 1 to require a man to pay national insurance contributions beyond the age of 60 when the liability of a woman ceases: *Walker v United Kingdom* (App.37212/02), Decision of March 16, 2004.

The Court of Human Rights has also declared admissible a complaint by a woman that it is a breach of Art.14 read with Art.1 of Protocol 1 in that her entitlement to incapacity benefit ceases at the age of 60 whereas a man in the same situation would continue to receive incapacity benefit until the age of 65. The applicant receives less by way of State retirement pension, to which she became entitled at the age of 60, than she previously received by way of incapacity benefit: *Barrow v United Kingdom* (App.42735/02), Decision of April 27, 2004.

In *CIS/1870/2003* the Commissioner ruled that the payment of social fund funeral payments did not come within the scope of either Art.8, or 9 or Art.1 of Protocol 1. Consequently Art.14 could not be used to attack the restriction on the payment of social fund funeral payments for funerals in Great Britain (or in certain circumstances other EEA countries). However, the decision adopts the European Community law approach to discrimination, and concludes that Art.14 covers indirect discrimination. He says:

"The provision depriving claimants who wish to bury their relatives abroad of all benefit is intrinsically more liable to affect migrants and their families in the group I have sought to identify than those whose families have been here longer, and the result is that the former group are placed at a disadvantage by being deprived of any State assistance at all for funeral arrangements which all sides accept are proper, legitimate and normal for them to seek to make. I follow the ECJ in holding it sufficient that the condition is inherently liable to have such an effect and has actually had exactly that effect in each of these cases and other similar ones involving migrant families" (para.22).

4.095   The Commissioner provides an extensive analysis of what constitutes falling within the ambit of one of the Convention rights such that Art.14 becomes applicable. His conclusion is as follows:

"In my judgment what must be looked for is some direct link to the *freedoms or rights* specified in the substantive primary Article. That is not shown merely by a contextual link between the payment of a cash benefit and some person, family or religious significance associated with the event or purpose on or for which it is paid, or the fact that anyone to whom it is paid will thereby have more possessions" (para.32).

The Commissioner's decision contrasts with that in *CIS/4769/2001* where the appeal proceeded on the basis that Arts 8 and 9 of the Convention were engaged. But that was a concession made by the Secretary of State in that appeal; in this appeal the Secretary of State did not make that concession and invited the Commissioner to depart from the views which had been expressed in *CIS/3280/2001* that Art.8 was engaged because of the importance of funerals in family life. The Commissioner does depart from the views in that case for reasons set out in detail at paras 34–37 of the decision.

The Commissioner in *CSJSA/0125/2004* takes a similar approach:

"The language of the articles is crucial. There are two essentials that have to be satisfied for the facts as established to fall within the ambit. First the matter relied upon must have a direct relationship to the substantive Convention right, in this case article 8. Second the discrimination must be of the type provided for in article 14 and not be discrimination of a sort not covered. On both these issues the claimant fails in this case . . . Just because the Convention gives a right to respect for one's home does not mean that something which is indirectly related to the home, such as payments of interest of a heritably secured debt obtained for the purposes of purchasing the home, falls within the ambit of the Convention right provided by article 8. In my view the provision of housing costs in respect of the payment of interest is too remote from the right secured by the Convention for it to fall within the ambit. Such provision falls outwith what article 8 seeks to secure. Further and in any event for article 8 to be engaged, where there is no positive obligation to provide state assistance, the discrimination asserted would have to be of the type set out in article 14" (para.14).

For a contrasting approach to the ambit of Art.8 see *CH/4574/2003,*   **4.096**
which is under appeal to the Court of Appeal as *W v Peterborough City
Council and the Secretary of State for Work and Pensions.*

Note that in *R(G) 2/04,* the reported decision in *CG/1467/2001,* the
Commissioner rules on a point of interpretation on which he regarded
himself as bound by the decision of the Court of Appeal in the *Hooper*
litigation (which it is understood are not in issue in the pending appeal
to the House of Lords in that litigation) that "no man who claims
widow's benefit in respect of a spouse who died before 9 April 2001 is
entitled under British social security legislation to any payment of widow's benefit" (para.2).

CG/3322/2002 is reported as *R(G) 2/04.*

CIS/4511/2002 is now reported as *R(IS) 12/04.*

pp.1173–1176, *annotations to Art.1 of Protocol 1 ECHR*

In *CP/0281/2002* the Commissioner ruled that there was no breach of   **4.097**
Art.1 of Protocol 1 as a consequence of the requirement under the
Pension Schemes Act 1993 that any additional pension is reduced by the
amount of any guaranteed minimum pension payable to a person.

In *R. (Smith) v Secretary of State for Defence and Secretary of State for
Work and Pensions* [2004] EWHC 1797 (Admin), Wilson J. held that a
non-contributory pension under the Armed Forces Pension Scheme was
a possession within the ambit of Art.1 of Protocol 1. This extended to
the spouse of the pension holder following the making of a pension-
sharing order. However, Art.1 of Protocol 1 does not guarantee a right to
a pension of a particular amount, nor payment from a particular time.
The remainder of the case principally concerned this article when read
in conjunction with Art.14, and is discussed in the annotations to Art.14.
Although the application was declared admissible on other grounds, it
seems implicit in the decision of the Court of Human Rights in *Meyne-
Moskalczuk and others v The Netherlands* (App.53002/99), Decision of
December 9, 2003, that entitlement to a pension arising following the
making of a pension sharing order in matrimonial proceedings will give
rise to a property right within Art.1 of Protocol 1.

In *Van Den Bouwhuijsen and Schuring v The Netherlands* (App.44658/
98), Decision of December 16, 2003, the Court found the application
inadmissible, but affirmed that:

> "entitlement to benefit pursuant to a national insurance scheme may
> constitute a pecuniary right for the purposes of Article 1 of Protocol 1
> without it being necessary to rely solely on the link between entitle-
> ment to benefit and the obligation to pay 'taxes or other contri-
> butions'. However, in order to establish such a pecuniary right,
> the person concerned must satisfy the various conditions set by
> law . . .".

In *Azinas v Cyprus* (App.56679/00) the Court of Human Rights in its   **4.098**
judgment of June 20, 2002 concluded that rights under a non-contributory civil service pension could be "assimilated to a property right"
(para.32). The Court found a violation in circumstances where the

pension benefits were forfeited on dismissal. The Court's decision was referred to the Grand Chamber by the Cyprus Government. It had been hoped that the judgment of the Grand Chamber would have illuminated the scope of Art.1 of Protocol 1 in the context of social security and pensions entitlements, but the outcome in its judgment of April 28, 2004 was that the application was declared inadmissible since the applicant had not exhausted his domestic remedies. The majority does not address the question of the application of Art.1 of Protocol 1. The uncertainty remains. In a Concurring Opinion, Judge Wildhaber, joined by Judges Rozakis and Mularoni, concluded that there was no property right in the pension within Art.1 of Protocol 1 (and even if there was its forfeiture was justified). A Concurring Opinion of Judge Hadjihambis concludes that there was a property right in the pension, but expresses no view over whether the applicant's Convention rights were violated. A Joint Dissenting Opinion of Judges Costa and Garlicki indicates that they would "probably have found" that there was no violation of Art.1 of Protocol 1. Finally a Dissenting Opinion of Judge Ress indicates his agreement with the Judgment of the Chamber of June 20, 2002. The resulting position is that the precise scope of Art.1 of Protocol 1 remains much less clear than before the deliberations of the Grand Chamber.

The issue may be re-visited in the judgment of the Grand Chamber in the cases of *Hepple v United Kingdom*, and *Kimber v United Kingdom*, Apps 65731/01 and 65900/01. These cases are being heard on March 9, 2005.

Kjartan Ásmundsson v Iceland (App.60669/00), Court of Human Rights, October 12, 2004, concerned disability pensions paid to fishermen in Iceland. The applicant had suffered a serious accident while on board a trawler and had received a full disability pension from the Seamen's Pension Fund, a State operated contributory pension scheme for fishermen. The applicant subsequently obtained office work; the pension scheme rules allowed this (without any reduction in the amount of the disability pension) as long as the income from the employment did not exceed the amount of the pension. The rules of the Pension Fund were changed so that the disability test related not just to ability to undertake the same work as before but to undertake work in general. There was a minimum threshold for payment of the disability pension of 35 per cent disablement. The applicant was assessed with 25 per cent disablement. As a consequence payment of his disability pension ceased altogether. The government claimed that the changes to the scheme were needed in order to secure its financial position. The applicant complained that this was a breach of his Convention rights under Art.1 of Protocol 1, or alternatively of that article read together with Art.14. The Court decided the case under Art.1 of Protocol 1.

The Court recapitulated its case law confirming that contributions to a pension fund may create a property right, that payments to social insurance systems are pecuniary rights within Art.1 of Protocol 1, but that the article gives no right to a pension of a particular amount. The question which the Court needed to address was whether the applicant's right to derive benefit from his pension fund had been infringed in a manner resulting in the impairment of the essence of his pension rights. The Court approached this question by looking at whether the scheme as it applied to the applicant reflected a fair balance "between the demands of the general interest of the community and the requirements of the protection of the individual's fundamental rights" (para.40). The Court is sceptical about the financial burden of the scheme since most of the disability pensioners continued to receive benefits at the same level as prior to the changes in the law, and a very small minority lost all their pension entitlement. The Court seems to have been influenced by the differential treatment of different groups of pensioners and comments:

> "the . . . differential treatment in itself suggests that the impugned measure was unjustified for the purposes of Article 14, which consideration must carry great weight in the assessment of the proportionality issue under Article 1 of Protocol 1" (para.43).

The Court concluded that the applicant was made to bear an excessive   **4.099** and disproportionate burden which could not be justified by the legitimate interests of the State. The Court indicates that a proportionate response would have been to reduce the applicant's pension rather than remove it altogether.

pp.1176–1177, *annotations to Art.2 of Protocol 1 ECHR*

In *Douglas v North Tyneside Metropolitan Borough Council and Secretary*   **4.100** *of State for Education and Skills* [2003] EWCA Civ 1847, the Court of Appeal ruled that tertiary education falls within the ambit of Art.2 of Protocol 1. The Court of Appeal held that, although there was no European or domestic authority establishing clearly that tertiary education falls within the ambit of Art.2 of Protocol 1, the Convention was a living instrument and the number of adults in higher education had grown. There was no principle that the article applied only to earlier stages of education, and so tertiary education falls within the ambit of the article. The case turned on the application of Art.14 when read in conjunction with Art.2 of Protocol 1, and is discussed in the update to the annotations on Art.14 above.

p.1177, *Pt III of Sch.1 to the Human Rights Act 1998*

With effect from June 22, 2004, art.2(3) of the Human Rights Act   **4.101** 1998 (Amendment) Order 2004 (SI 2004/1574) substitute the following for Pt 3 of Sch.1 to the Act:

"PART 3

ARTICLE 1 OF THE THIRTEENTH PROTOCOL

ABOLITION OF THE DEATH PENALTY

The death penalty shall be abolished. No one shall be condemned to such penalty or executed."

175

PART V

UPDATING MATERIAL
VOLUME IV

TAX CREDITS AND EMPLOYER-PAID
SOCIAL SECURITY BENEFITS

p.12, *Taxes Management Act 1970, s.12*

With effect from April 6, 2004, the Finance Act 2004, s.30 and Sch.5,   5.001
para.1 replace subs.(4) and add subss.(5) and (6) as follows:

"(4) An enquiry extends to—

   (a) anything contained in the return, or required to be contained in
     the return, including any claim or election included in the
     return,

   (b) . . .

(5) If the notice of enquiry is given as a result of an amendment of the
return under section 9ZA of this Act—

   (a) at a time when it is no longer possible to give notice of enquiry
     under subsection (2)(a) . . . above or

   (b) after an enquiry into the return has been completed,

the enquiry into the return is limited to matters to which the amendment relates or which are affected by the amendment.

(6) In this section "the filing date" means the day mentioned in
section (1A) or, as the case may be, section 8A(1A) of this Act."

p.20, *Taxes Management Act 1970, s.35*

With effect from April 6, 2004, the Finance Act 2004, s.92 reintro-   5.002
duces in modified form the following section:

**"Time limit: income received after year for which they are
assessable**

35.—(1) Where income to which this section applies is received in
a year of assessment subsequent to that for which it is assessable, an
assessment to income tax as respects that income may be made at any
time within six years after the year of assessment in which it is
received.

(2) This section applies to—

   (a) employment income,
   (b) pension income, and
   (c) social security income."

p.33, *Income and Corporation Taxes Act 1988, s.15*

The phrase "ground annuals and feu duties" is repealed from   5.003
s.15(1)1(4)(b) by the Scottish measure SSI 2003/435 with effect from
November 28, 2004.

p.34, *Income and Corporation Taxes Act 1988, s.18*

The Finance Act 2004, s.105(4) adds subs.(6) as follows, with effect   5.004
from January 1, 2004:

"(6) This section is subject to Chapter 6 of Part 3 of the Finance Act 2004 (exemption from income tax for certain interest and royalty payments)."

p.46, *Income and Corporation Taxes Act 1988, s.74*

5.005 Section 74(1)(n) repealed by the Finance Act 2004, s.326 with effect from 1 April 2004.

p.48, *Income and Corporation Taxes Act 1988, s.282A*

5.006 With effect from April 6, 2004, the Finance Act 2004, s.91(2) adds subs.(4A):

"(4A) Subsection (1) above shall not apply to income consisting of a distribution arising from property consisting of—

(a) close company shares to which either the husband or the wife is beneficially entitled to the exclusion of the other, or
(b) close company shares to which they are beneficially entitled in equal or unequal shares."

p.52, *Income and Corporation Taxes Act 1988, s.336*

5.007 The correction of errors provisionally included in the text are confirmed by the Finance Act 2004, Sch.17, para.10(2).

p.62, *Income and Corporation Taxes Act 1988, s.677*

5.008 With effect from April 6, 2004, s.677 is amended as follows by the Finance Act 2004, s.29 and Sch.4, para.1:

"(1) Section 677 of the Taxes Act 1988 (sums paid to settlor otherwise than as income) is amended as follows.

(2) In subsection (2) (the amount of income available up to the end of a year) in paragraph (h) (deduction of amount equal to tax at the rate applicable to trusts on the undistributed income less the income etc referred to in certain paragraphs) for "paragraphs (c), (d), (e), (f) and (g) above" substitute "each of paragraphs (c) to (g) above".

(3) In subsection (7) (tax to be charged under Case VI of Schedule D, but with a set-off for the amount described in paragraph (a) or (b), whichever is the less) for the words from "charged," in paragraph (b) to the end of the subsection substitute

"charged; or
(c) the amount of tax paid by the trustees on the grossed-up amount of so much of the amount of income available up to the end of the year, in relation to the capital sum, as is taken into account under subsection (1) above in relation to that sum in that year (see subsections (7A) to (7C) below), whichever is the least.".

(4) After subsection (7) insert—
"(7A) For the purposes of subsection (7)(c) above—

   (a) any reduction falling to be made under subsection (2)(h) above shall be treated as made against income arising under the settlement in an earlier year of assessment before income arising under the settlement in a later year of assessment; and

   (b) income arising under the settlement in an earlier year of assessment shall be regarded as being taken into account under subsection (1) above before income arising under the settlement in a later year of assessment.

(7B) For the purposes of subsection (7)(c) above—

   (a) the grossed-up amount of any sum is such amount as, after the deduction of tax at the appropriate rate for each part of that sum, would be equal to that sum; and

   (b) the amount of tax paid by the trustees on that grossed-up amount is the amount of tax falling to be deducted under paragraph (a) above.

(7C) For the purposes of subsection (7B) above—

   (a) the appropriate rate for any part of a sum is 0% if—

      (i) the income that falls to be regarded in accordance with subsection (7A) above as representing that part of the sum is income from a source outside the United Kingdom, and

      (ii) the trustees were not resident in the United Kingdom for the relevant year of assessment;

   (b) the appropriate rate for any part of a sum in relation to which paragraph (a) above does not apply is—

      (i) 34%, if the relevant year of assessment is the year 2003–04 or any earlier year of assessment,

      (ii) 40%, if the relevant year of assessment is the year 2004–05 or any subsequent year of assessment.

For the purposes of this subsection the relevant year of assessment in relation to any part of a sum is the year of assessment in which the income to be regarded in accordance with subsection (7A) above as representing that part of the sum arose under the settlement."

p.70, *Income and Corporation Taxes Act 1988, s.832*

The definition of "generally accepted accounting standards" is 5.009
amended by the Finance Act 2004, s.50 to refer to that section and definitions of "international" accounting standards" and "UK generally accepted accounting practice" are added by that section (set out below).

A definition of Scottish "estate in land" is inserted with effect from November 28, 2004 by the Abolition of Feudal Tenure, etc. (Scotland) Act 2000, s.76(1).

p.186, *annotation to Tax Credits Act 2002, s.14(2): initial decisions*

CIS/995/2004 confirms that subs.(2) confers a *power* on the Inland 5.010
Revenue to make enquiries by giving appropriate notice that can only be

invoked *before* the Revenue makes a decision on the claim (para.15). See also paras 16–19 of Mr Commissioner Mesher's decision for criticism of the TC602 standard letter. See further the update to p.489 of main Vol.IV below.

p.206, *Tax Credits Act 2002, s.29*

5.011   In line with this code of practice, the Inland Revenue have made what are termed "hardship payments" to claimants in excess of current entitlement to credits where changes in the level of payment of tax credits are considered to have caused hardship. There has been some doubt expressed about whether such payments are payments of tax credits or are *ex gratia* payments outside the official system. It is understood that the official view is that the payments are payments of tax credits and therefore subject to recovery in the case of overpayments under s.28. The payments are based on decisions to collect smaller amounts of previous overpayments by way of reduction in the level of credits against the current award, made as a payment rather than a reduced reduction for reasons of administrative efficiency.

p.216, *Tax Credits Act 2002, s.38*

5.012   In a "Tax Credits Agenda for Improvement" published jointly by CPAG, the Low Income Tax Reform Group, Citizens Advice, One Parent Families, the Chartered Institute of Taxation and the Institute of Chartered Accountants in England and Wales in September 2004, the bodies jointly asked the Inland Revenue, among other representations, for "adherence to proper procedures when the IR decide to settle an appeal, rather than 'cancelling' the appeal and issuing revised decisions outside the appeal process".

p.293, *Income Tax (Earnings and Pensions) Act 200, Pt 9*

5.013   The Finance Act 2004 contains major amendments to both Pt 9 and to the taxation of pensions and pension funds generally. However, these do not come into effect until April 2006.

p.296, *Income Tax (Earnings and Pensions) Act 2003, s.577*

5.014   The erroneous reference in subs.(2)(b) to s.48 is corrected to s.48A by the Finance Act 2004, Sch.17, para.9(4), and subs.(3) is omitted.

p.312, *Income Tax (Earnings and Pensions) Act 2003, s.677*

5.015   The erroneous entry in Table B relating to compensation payments where child support is reduced because of a change in legislation is omitted by the Finance Act 2004, Sch.17, para.9(5).

pp.378–379, *Working Tax Credit (Entitlement and Maximum Rate)*
Regulations 2002: amendment of reg.14(2)(a)–(c) (meaning of "child
care")

With effect from June 1, 2004, reg.2(2) of the Tax Credits (Miscella-   5.016
neous Amendments No.2) Regulations 2004 (SI 2004/1241) amended
reg.14(2)(a)–(c) to read:

"(2) "Child care" means care provided for a child—

  (a) in England and Wales—
    (i) by persons registered under Part 10A of the Children Act
      1989;
    (ii) in schools or establishments which are exempted from
      registration under Part 10A of the Children Act 1989 by
      virtue of paragraph 1 or 2 of Schedule 9A to that Act;
    (iii) in respect of any period [on or before] the last day he is
      treated as a child for the purposes of this regulation , where
      the care is provided out of school hours, by a school on
      school premises or by a local authority; [. . .]
    (iv) by a child care provider approved by an accredited organi-
      sation within the meaning given by regulation 4 of the Tax
      Credit (New Category of Child Care Provider) Regula-
      tions 1999; [or]
    [(v) by a foster parent under the Fostering Services Regulations
      2002 or the Fostering Services (Wales) Regulations 2003
      in relation to a child other than one whom he is foster-
      ing;]
  (b) in Scotland—
    (i) by a person in circumstances where the care service pro-
      vided by him consists of child minding or of day care of
      children within the meaning of section 2 of the Regulation
      of Care (Scotland) Act 2001 and is registered under Part 1
      of that Act; [. . .]
    (ii) by a local authority in circumstances where the care service
      provided by the local authority consists of child minding or
      of day care of children within the meaning of section 2 of
      the Regulation of Care (Scotland) Act 2001 and is regis-
      tered under Part 2 of that Act; [or]
    [(iii) by a foster carer under the Fostering of Children (Scot-
      land) Regulations 1996 in relation to a child other than one
      whom he is fostering;]
  (c) in Northern Ireland—
    (i) by persons registered under Part XI of the Children
      (Northern Ireland) Order 1995; [. . .]
    (ii) by institutions and establishments exempt from registra-
      tion under that Part by virtue of Article 121 of that Order;
      or
    [(iii) in respect of any period ending on or before the day on
      which he ceases to be a child for the purposes of this
      regulation, where the care is provided out of school hours

by a school on school premises or by an Education and Library Board or a Health and Social Services Trust; or

(iv) by a foster parent under the Foster Placement (Children) Regulations (Northern Ireland) 1996 in relation to a child other than one whom he is fostering; or]".

p.379, *Working Tax Credit (Entitlement and Maximum Rate) Regulations 2002: insertion of reg.14(2)(f) (meaning of "child care")*

5.017   With effect from November 3, 2004, reg.3 of the Tax Credits (Miscellaneous Amendments No.3) Regulations 2004 (SI 2004/2663) inserted after reg.14(2)(e) the following new provision:

"(f) in Wales by a domiciliary care worker under the Domiciliary Care Agencies (Wales) Regulations 2004".

p.410, *Tax Credits (Definition and Calculation of Income) Regulations 2002: amendment of Table 1 in reg.4(4) (payments and benefits disregarded in the calculation of employment income)*

5.018   With effect from November 3, 2004, reg.2 of the Tax Credits (Miscellaneous Amendments No.3) Regulations 2004 (SI 2004/2663) inserted after item 18 the following further disregard:

"**19.** Provision of computer equipment in respect of which no liability to income tax arises by virtue of section 320 of ITEPA."

p.488, *Annotation to Tax Credits (Claims and Notifications) Regulations 2002, reg.3: use of electronic communications*

5.019   See further the decision of Mr Commissioner Mesher in *CIS/995/2004*, discussed in the annotations to main Vol.IV, p.186 above and p.489 below.

p.489, *annotation to Tax Credits (Claims and Notifications) Regulations 2002, reg.5: manner in which claims to be made*

5.020   Mr Commissioner Mesher's decision in *CIS/995/2004* deals with the complex interaction between tax credits and income support and what constitutes a claim for the former. Early in 2003 the claimant in *CIS/995/2004* claimed income support. On January 10, 2003, he also completed an online application form for child tax credit (CTC) and transmitted it to the Inland Revenue. In March 2003 the claimant received a TC602 letter from the Inland Revenue notifying him of his family's CTC entitlement for the 2003/04 tax year and asking him to sign and return the accompanying declaration. Having made further enquiries, the claimant discovered that he would be better off retaining entitlement to income support. He accordingly did not sign and return the TC602 declaration. However, the Revenue started making CTC payments in April 2003 and notified the DWP of this fact. This led the Secretary of State to decide that the claimant was no longer entitled to income support as his income exceeded his applicable amount.

The claimant appealed to a tribunal which disallowed his appeal, holding that reg.7 of the Social Security (Working Tax Credit and Child Tax Credit) Consequential Amendments Regulations 2003 (SI 2003/455) required the DWP to treat the claimant's income as including an amount equivalent to his CTC entitlement. Although finding error in the tribunal's reasoning in other respects, the Commissioner held that the tribunal had come to the only conclusion open to it as a matter of law and on the evidence before it. In particular, the Commissioner rejected the claimant's argument that he had only made a preliminary application for CTC which could not be completed until he had signed and returned the TC602 declaration. On the contrary, the online completion and transmission of the application form, notwithstanding the absence of any written confirmation at the time or later, amounted to a claim. Mr Commissioner Mesher thus held that the claimant had made a valid claim on January 10, 2003, whether in an approved electronic format (and so under regs 3 and 5(2)(a)—a point which did not have to be resolved) or alternatively under the wide power in reg.5(2)(b). A valid award of CTC had then followed. The Commissioner expressly left open the question whether an appeal tribunal or Commissioner has jurisdiction to go behind the Board's determination that a claim had been made.

The informality with which the Inland Revenue will accept renewals claims was emphasised in a public letter to the Institute of Chartered Accountants in England and Wales published on October 1, 2004. Speaking of renewal claims, the Deputy Chairman of the Inland Revenue said:

> "Claimants simply have to confirm or correct the information we hold about their circumstances and report their income for the year just finished. For those not in a position to provide actual income figures at the time they reply, an estimate will be accepted. The information necessary to renew can be accepted by telephone or through our e-portal or by filling in a short paper form."

He added: "I should also make clear, in answer to a concern you raise, **5.021** that renewals information is logged on receipt, even if it has not yet been processed, to make sure the payments continue".

p.501, *Tax Credits (Claims and Notifications) Regulations 2002:*
amendment of reg.21(2)(a) (Requirement to notify changes of circumstances)

With effect from May 1, 2004, reg.3 of the Tax Credits (Miscellaneous **5.022** Amendments No.2) Regulations 2004 (SI 2004/1241) amended reg.21 to read:

> "(a) entitlement to the tax credit ceases by virtue of section 3(4) [or 3(7)] of the Act; or".

185

p.510, *Tax Credits (Claims and Notifications) Regulations 2002: insertion of reg.29A (Form in which evidence of birth or adoption to be provided)*

5.023   With effect from May 1, 2004, reg.4 of the Tax Credits (Miscellaneous Amendments No.2) Regulations 2004 (SI 2004/1241) inserted after before reg.30 a new reg.29A reading as follows:

"Form in which evidence of birth or adoption to be provided

29A. If the Board require the person, or either or both of the persons, by whom a claim is made to provide a certificate of a child's birth or adoption, the certificate so produced must be either an original certificate or a copy authenticated in such manner as would render it admissible in proceedings in any court in the jurisdiction in which the copy was made."

p.535, *Tax Credits (Payments by the Board) Regulations 2002: amendment of reg.3(3) (Child tax credit and child care element—member of a couple prescribed for the purposes of s.24(2) of the Act)*

5.024   With effect from May 1, 2004, reg.5(a) of the Tax Credits (Miscellaneous Amendments No.2) Regulations 2004 (SI 2004/1241) amended reg.3(3) to read:

"(3) The member of a married couple or an unmarried couple [prescribed by this paragraph is—

    (a) where the married or unmarried couple are for the time being resident at the same address—
        (i) the member who is identified by both members of the married couple or unmarried couple as the main carer;
        (ii) in default of a member being so identified, the member who appears to the Board to be the main carer; and
    (b) where—
        (i) the members of the married or unmarried couple are for the time being resident at different addresses, or
        (ii) one member of the married couple or unmarried couple is temporarily absent from the address at which they live together,
the member who appears to the Board to be the main carer.

Here "main carer" means the member of the married couple or unmarried couple who is the main carer for the children and qualifying young persons for whom either or both of the members is or are responsible.]"

p.535, *Tax Credits (Payments by the Board) Regulations 2002: amendment of reg.3(6) (Child tax credit and child care element—member of a couple prescribed for the purposes of s.24(2) of the Act)*

5.025   With effect from May 1, 2004, reg.5(b) of the Tax Credits (Miscellaneous Amendments No.2) Regulations 2004 (SI 2004/1241) amended reg.3(6) to read:

"(6) Where payments are being made to the member of a married couple or an unmarried couple prescribed by virtue of paragraph (3) and the members of the married couple or unmarried couple jointly give notice to the Board that, as a result of a change of circumstances, the payments should be made to the other member as the main carer, the other member shall [, except where the notice appears to the Board to be unreasonable,] be treated as prescribed by virtue of paragraph (3)."

p.567, *Tax Credits (Residence) Regulations 2003: amendment of reg.3 (Circumstances in which a person is treated as not being in the United Kingdom)*

With effect from May 1, 2004, reg.3 of the Tax Credits (Residence) (Amendment) Regulations 2004 (SI 2004/1243) inserted after reg.3(4) a new reg.3(5) reading as follows:　　　　　　　　　　5.026

"(5) A person shall be treated as not being in the United Kingdom for the purposes of Part 1 of the Act where he—

    (a) makes a claim for child tax credit (other than being treated as making a claim under regulation 11 or 12 of the Tax Credits (Claims and Notifications) Regulations 2002 or otherwise), on or after 1st May 2004; and

    (b) does not have a right to reside in the United Kingdom."

This provision ceases to have effect on May 1, 2006, unless revoked with effect from an earlier date (Tax Credits (Residence) (Amendment) Regulations 2004 (SI 2004/1243), reg.1(2)).

pp.679–680, *Statutory Paternity Pay and Statutory Adoption Pay (Weekly Rates) Regulations 2002: amendment of reg.2 (weekly rate of payment of statutory paternity pay)*

With effect from April 4, 2004, reg.2 of the Statutory Paternity Pay and Statutory Adoption Pay (Weekly Rates) (Amendment) Regulations 2004 (SI 2004/925) substituted a new reg.2 as follows:　　　　　　5.027

"Weekly rate of payment of statutory paternity pay

2. The weekly rate of payment of statutory paternity pay shall be the smaller of the following two amounts—

    (a) £102.80;

    (b) 90 per cent. of the normal weekly earnings of the person claiming statutory paternity pay, determined in accordance with regulations 39 and 40 of the Statutory Paternity Pay and Statutory Adoption Pay (General) Regulations 2002."

p.775, *Inland Revenue Codes of Practice and guidance: note*

Leaflet WTC/AP was reissued in October 2004.　　　　　　5.028

PART VI

FORTHCOMING CHANGES AND UP-RATING OF BENEFITS

FORTHCOMING CHANGES

This section aims to give users of Social Security Legislation 2004 some **6.001** information on significant changes coming into force between November 30, 2004—the date to which this Supplement is up to date—and mid-April 2005, the date to which the 2005 edition will be up to date. The information here reflects our understanding of sources available to us as at November 30, 2004, and users should be aware that there will no doubt be further legislative amendment between then and mid-April 2005. This section of the Supplement will at least enable users to access the relevant legislation on the TSO website (*http://www.hmso.gov.uk/ legis.htm*).

Child Trust Funds Act 2004

(2004 c.6)

191

11. Recouping Inland Revenue contributions.
12. Subscription limits.

Tax

13. Relief from income tax and capital gains tax.
14. Insurance companies and friendly societies.

Information etc.

15. Information from account providers etc.
16. Information about children in care of authority.
17. Use of information.
18. Disclosure of information.

Payments after death

19. Payments after death of child.

Penalties

20. Penalties.
21. Decisions, appeals, mitigation and recovery.

Appeals

22. Rights of appeal.
23. Exercise of rights of appeal.
24. Temporary modifications.

Supplementary

25. Northern Ireland.
26. Money.
27. Commencement.
28. Regulations and orders.
29. Interpretation.
30. Extent.
31. Short title.

An Act to make provision about child trust funds and for connected purposes.

INTRODUCTION AND GENERAL NOTE

6.003   The basic scheme of the Child Trust Fund Act 2004 is that all children in the UK born after August 31, 2002 will have a "child trust fund account", which will in effect be a universal savings policy. Building societies and other financial institutions will have to seek Inland Revenue approval to be an "account provider" under this Act. It is a condition of approval that account providers offer equity-based stakeholder accounts (although cash accounts may also be offered). The Treasury will provide an initial endowment of £250 for each child at the point when the account is opened, or £500 in the case of children in low-income families or those who are being looked after by a local authority. The Government's intention is to make a further endowment (of an amount as yet unspecified) when every child reaches the age of seven. Parents, relatives and family friends will be able to make further contributions to the child trust fund account at any time. The minimum such investment is £10 (unless the account provider permits smaller deposits) and the maximum annual aggregate contribution by family and friends is £1,200. Subject to some very narrow exceptions, no withdrawals will be permitted until the child is 18, so that the child reaches adulthood with a "nest-egg" which can then be re-invested, spent on education or setting up in business, etc. The cost of the scheme is estimated to be in the order of £4 billion over 18 years.

The Government has set out four objectives for child trust fund accounts. These are "to help people understand the benefits of saving and investing; to encourage parents and children to develop the savings habit; to ensure that all children have a financial asset at the start of their adult life; and to build on financial education and help people make better financial choices throughout their lives" (Lord McIntosh of Haringey, Parliamentary Under-Secretary of State, *Hansard* HL Debates Vol.658, col.351, February 26, 2004). The Child Trust Fund Act may thus be seen as an example of the Government's commitment to the principles of "asset-based welfare" and "progressive universalism". It will, of course, take some time to assess whether the scheme fulfils its goals.

The idea of child trust funds emerged through the work of the Institute of Public Policy Research (IPPR) in 2000 and was canvassed by the Treasury in its consultation paper *Savings and Assets for All*, The Modernisation of Britain's Tax and benefit System, Number 8 (April 2001). The proposal also appeared in the Labour Party's 2001 general election manifesto. The Government set out its proposals more fully in the Treasury papers *Delivering Saving and Assets* (November 2001) and especially in *Detailed proposals for the Child Trust Fund* (October 2003). The House of Commons Treasury Committee has issued a report supporting the initiative, although making some further recommendations: *Child Trusts Funds* (Second Report of Session 2003–04, HC 86), and see further *Government Response to the Committee's Second Report on Child Trust Funds* (HC 86) (First Special Report of Session 2003–04, HC 387). In the 2003 Budget the Chancellor of the Exchequer announced the Government's intention that the scheme should commence operations in April 2005 (but confirming that it would also apply to all children born after August 31, 2002).

Section 1 of the Act explains what is meant by a child trust fund, whilst s.2 **6.004** defines the crucial qualifying category of "eligible children". The nature and management of child trust fund accounts is governed by s.3. Funds in such accounts are inalienable (s.4). The expectation is that accounts will be opened by a "responsible person", typically a parent, or by the child (in the case of a child aged 16 or over, who, for example, has just arrived in the country); see s.5, which makes the award of child benefit the trigger for entitlement to a child trust fund account. The fallback position is that the Inland Revenue will open an account (s.6) for any child lacking a child trust fund. Accounts may be transferred to another financial institution (s.7). The initial and supplementary Treasury contributions to be made at the opening of the account are governed by ss.8 and 9. All children receive the initial contribution under s.8 (children being looked after by local authorities receive a higher rate) and children in low-income families qualify for the supplementary contribution under s.9. Section 10 makes provision for further Treasury contributions to be made at some late date (or dates). Where Treasury contributions have been credited in error, they can be recovered by virtue of s.11. Section 12 deals with contributions by parents and others to child trust fund accounts. The tax position is covered by ss.13 and 14 while ss.15–18 make provision for the disclosure and exchange of information relating to accounts. Section 19 makes special provision for the situation where a payment is due after a child beneficiary has died. Sections 20 and 21 concern penalties and ss.22–24 set out appeal rights. The remaining sections of the Act are supplementary in nature (ss.25–31). The first regulations under the Act are the Child Trust Funds Regulations 2004 (SI 2004/1450).

Commencement and extent

6.005   The supplementary provisions in this Act (ss.25–31) came into force on Royal Assent (May 13, 2004): see s.27. Various procedural provisions came into force on January 1, 2005: Child Trust Funds Act 2004 (Commencement No.1) order 2004 (SI 2004/2422, C.103). The remainder of the Act will be brought into force by Order. The Child Trust Funds Regulations 2004 (SI 2004/1450) came into force for various purposes on January 1, 2005 and for remaining purposes on "the appointed day" (reg.1). As it is anticipated that this will be April 6, 2005, they will appear in the next main Vol.IV. The Act extends to the whole of the UK (see further ss.25 and 30).

Introductory

Child trust funds

6.006   **1.**—(1) This Act makes provision about child trust funds and related matters.

(2) In this Act "child trust fund" means an account which—

(a) is held by a child who is or has been an eligible child (see section 2),

(b) satisfies the requirements imposed by and by virtue of this Act (see section 3), and

(c) has been opened in accordance with this Act (see sections 5 and 6).

(3) The matters dealt with by and under this Act are to be under the care and management of the Inland Revenue.

DEFINITIONS

6.007   "child": s.29.
"child trust fund": subs.(2) and s.29.
"eligible child": ss.2 and 29.
"Inland Revenue": s.29.

GENERAL NOTE

6.008   This is a genuinely introductory section.

Subs. (1)

6.009   This provision is no more illuminating than the long title to the Act.

Subs. (2)

6.010   This is more helpful than subs.(1) in that it stipulates the three defining characteristics of a child trust fund—that it be held by an "eligible child" (see s.2), that it meet the statutory requirements (see s.3) and that it has been opened in the appropriate manner (either by a "responsible person" (typically a parent) under s.5 or by the Revenue under s.6).

Subs. (3)

This reflects a standard principle of revenue law (see, *e.g.* Taxes Management **6.011** Act 1970, s.1(1)), namely that such matters are "under the care and management of the Inland Revenue". The only difference is one of nomenclature in the reference to "the Inland Revenue", rather than the more usual statutory formula of "the Board". This principle enables the Revenue to apply the law with a degree of administrative flexibility in appropriate cases. For example, in the context of taxation, this is the basis upon which the Revenue has traditionally promulgated extra-statutory concessions and reached settlements in disputes with taxpayers.

Eligible children

2.—(1) For the purposes of this Act a child is an "eligible child" if the **6.012** child was born after 31st August 2002 and either—
  (a) a person is entitled to child benefit in respect of the child, or
  (b) entitlement to child benefit in respect of the child is excluded by the provisions specified in subsection (2)(a) or (b) (children in care of authority),
but subject as follows.
  (2) The provisions referred to in subsection (1)(b) are—
  (a) paragraph 1(c) of Schedule 9 to the Social Security Contributions and Benefits Act 1992 (c. 4) and regulations made under it, and
  (b) paragraph 1(1)(f) of Schedule 9 to the Social Security Contributions and Benefits (Northern Ireland) Act 1992 (c. 7) and regulations made under it.
  (3) Where entitlement to child benefit in respect of a child is excluded because of a directly applicable Community provision or an international agreement, subsection (1) applies as if that exclusion did not apply.
  (4) Where a person is entitled to child benefit in respect of a child only because of a directly applicable Community provision or an international agreement, subsection (1) applies as if the person were not so entitled.
  (5) A child who—
  (a) does not have the right of abode in the United Kingdom within the meaning given by section 2 of the Immigration Act 1971 (c. 77),
  (b) is not a qualified person, or a family member of a qualified person, within the meaning of the Immigration (European Economic Area) Regulations 2000 (S.I. 2000/2326), and
  (c) is not settled in the United Kingdom within the meaning given by section 33(2A) of the Immigration Act 1971,
is not an eligible child.
  (6) A person is not to be regarded for the purposes of subsection (1)(a) as entitled to child benefit in respect of a child (otherwise than by virtue of subsection (3)) unless it has been decided in accordance with—
  (a) Chapter 2 of Part 1 of the Social Security Act 1998 (c. 14), or

(b) Chapter 2 of Part 2 of the Social Security (Northern Ireland) Order 1998 (S.I. 1998/1506 (N.I. 10)),

that the person is so entitled (and that decision has not been over-turned).

(7) Regulations may amend subsection (1) by substituting for the reference to 31st August 2002 a reference to an earlier date.

DEFINITIONS

6.013   "child": s.29.
"eligible child": subs.(1) and s.29.

GENERAL NOTE

6.014   This section defines the concept of an "eligible child", the first of the three fundamental features of a child trust fund. The basic definition is to be found in subs.(1), as expanded by subs.(2) to deal with the special case of children being looked after by a local authority. Cases that have an international dimension are covered by subss.(3)–(5). Subsection (6) acts as a definition provision for subs.(1). Subsection (7) provides the potential for the scope of the child trust fund scheme to be expanded to include children born before the cut-off date for eligibility for a child trust fund.

Subs. (1)

6.015   This is the core definition of who is an "eligible child". There are two basic rules. First, the child must have been born *after* August 31, 2002. This date was chosen to align entitlement with the school year (at least in England and Wales), so that all pupils in any given school year (after that date) would be equally entitled. There will, however, be cases involving siblings born either side of the eligibility date: for the position of children who were born *before* September 1, 2002, see further the annotation to subs.(7) below. Secondly, *either* someone must be entitled to child benefit for that child (subs.(1)(a); see further subs.(6)) *or* that person's entitlement is excluded because the child is being looked after by a local authority (subss.(1)(b) and (2)). Thus in general terms, and subject to that special case, entitlement to child benefit is employed as a gateway to eligibility for a child trust fund. Subsections (3)–(5) make special provision for cases with an international dimension.

Subs. (2)

6.016   The case of a child being looked after by a local authority is the only situation in which the rule requiring that a person be entitled to child benefit in respect of the child is waived. It must follow that in the other situations set out in SSCBA 1992, Sch.9 in which there is no entitlement to child benefit, there is also no entitlement to a child trust fund. These situations include children in detention (but see s.10(4)) and married children. These exclusions, and particularly the latter, may eventually affect a handful of children who are recent immigrants to the country.

Subs. (3)

6.017   There will be some children who live in the UK but in respect of whom child benefit is not payable because of EU law or an international agreement. This provision ensures that such children remain eligible for a child trust fund, notwithstanding that there is no child benefit entitlement. In practice this will apply most commonly to some children who live in Northern Ireland but whose parent works in the Republic of Ireland. In such circumstances, under the EU rules governing the benefit entitlement of migrant workers in Regulation 1408/71, child benefit is payable by the benefit authorities in the Republic. As a result of subs.(3) such children are eligible for a child trust fund account.

Subs. (4)

This deals with the converse position to that in subs.(3). In some cases there **6.018** is entitlement to child benefit in the UK solely because of provisions in EU law or under an international agreement. This would apply where a citizen and resident of the Republic of Ireland (or any other EU country) works in the UK but his or her child lives in the Republic (or other member state). Again, EU Regulation 1408/71 provides that child benefit is payable by the UK authorities. This subsection provides, in effect, that children in this type of case will not be eligible for a child trust fund, unless and until they come to live in the UK. This will affect fewer than 500 children, according to official estimates. The Government's view is that "there is no case for the UK Government to pay endowments to encourage saving for and by children whose ties are not within the UK" (Ruth Kelly, Financial Secretary to the Treasury, Standing Committee A, col.37, January 6, 2004). This exclusion will not affect the special position of the children of Crown servants, such as army personnel, who are entitled to child benefit when stationed overseas by virtue of a provision in purely domestic law (Child Benefit (General) Regulations 2003 (SI 2003/493), reg.30.

However, it is by no means certain that the exclusion of EU workers (and their children) who reside outside but work in the UK from eligibility for child trust funds will necessarily survive legal scrutiny. There are a number of different avenues that might be used to challenge the validity of this provision under EU law. First, Art.7(2) of EU Regulation 1612/68 requires migrant workers to "enjoy the same social and tax advantages as national workers". Of course, one of the fundamental purposes of the child trust fund scheme is to benefit the child, rather than the worker. Indeed, case law demonstrates that the social or tax advantage must be of some direct or indirect benefit to the worker, and not just to a family member (*Centre Public d'Aide Sociale de Courcelles v Lebon*, Case 316/85 [1987] E.C.R. 3261). But a broad view of the child trust fund scheme might meet this requirement. See also *Reina v Landeskredit Bank Baden-Würt-temberg*, Case 65/81 [1982] E.C.R. 33, in which it was held that an interest-free childbirth loan granted only to German nationals was a social advantage within Art.7(2), and so could not be denied to an Italian couple. Although one of the fundamental objectives of the child trust fund scheme is to benefit *children* by providing them with a valuable asset on attaining their majority, it does not require too much imagination to see that the scheme might be construed as being of indirect benefit to the parent-worker. Yet the other purposes of the 2004 Act are framed in terms of domestic policy imperatives, such as encouraging savings, which have no obvious linkage with the free movement of labour. Moreover, the ECJ jurisprudence on Art.7(2) has typically concerned the migrant worker who goes both to work and *live* in another Member State, and not merely to work there; the problem identified in this note is strictly more to do with "frontier workers" than "migrant workers". On that basis, therefore, it may be that s.2(4) is not inconsistent with Art.7(2) of Regulation 1612/68.

Even if this is the case, it does not necessarily follow that s.2(4) is EU-compliant. A second or parallel type of challenge might be made on the basis that the child trust fund scheme confers a "family benefit" within the scope of Regulation 1408/71, so bringing into play Ch.7 of that Regulation. Given the linkage between entitlement to child benefit and eligibility for a child trust fund payment, this point is at least arguable. Finally, there remains the broader argument that this provision in the 2004 Act is in breach of Art.12 of the Treaty itself, which prohibits "within the scope of the application" of the Treaty "any discrimination on grounds of nationality". Section 2(4) makes no express reference to parents' nationality, but may be viewed as indirectly discriminatory in that its operation in practice is more likely to affect (for example) Irish nationals than British nationals. In recent years the ECJ has demonstrated greater willingness to invoke Art.12 for the benefit of citizens of other Member States (see, *e.g.* *Martinez Sala* [1998] E.C.R. I-2691 and Case C-184/99 *Grzelcyk* [2001] E.C.R. I-6193; and see further R. C. A. White, "Residence, Benefit Entitlement and Community Law" [2005] 12 *Journal of Social Security Law* 10).

Subs. (5)

6.019   A child who lacks a proper immigration status cannot be an "eligible child". This covers children who, under the Immigration Act 1971, have no right of abode or are not settled in the UK. However, subs.(5)(c) may give rise to problems in the context of citizenship of the Union: see further the Advocate-General's Opinion of November 11, 2004 in Case C-209/03 *Bidar*. Children who have no entitlement to reside in the UK under EEA law are likewise excluded from access to the child trust fund scheme.

Subs. (6)

6.020   This provides that a person is not entitled to child benefit until a decision has been taken to that effect (and has not been overturned) in accordance with the SSA Act 1998 (or its Northern Ireland equivalent). Thus the Revenue's decision to award child benefit acts as the trigger for eligibility for a child trust fund account.

Subs. (7)

6.021   For the purposes of this Act a child is only an "eligible child" if born after August 31, 2002 (subs.(1)). This provision allows the Government to use secondary legislation to substitute an earlier date for the purpose of this definition, thus bringing older children into the scope of eligibility for a child trust fund account. Any such regulations will be subject to the affirmative procedure (see s.28(5) and (6)(a)). There are obvious arguments in favour of such an extension in the scheme's remit, not least the fact that under the present arrangements older siblings are potentially disadvantaged, and parents and other relatives may naturally wish to make equal financial provision for children in the same family, irrespective of the accident of their date of birth. This problem will be particularly acute in the case of twins, and doubtless there are some, where one twin was born in the last minutes of August 31, 2002 and the younger twin arrived after the stroke of midnight. The House of Commons Treasury Committee recommended that consideration be given to extending the scope of the children to include older children, but without Government endowments (*Second Report*, Session 2003–04, HC 86, para.34). The Government has not, to date, demonstrated any significant enthusiasm for extending the remit of the scheme even in this limited way, noting the potential burden on providers.

Requirements to be satisfied

6.022   **3.**—(1) A child trust fund may be held only with a person (referred to in this Act as an "account provider") who has been approved by the Inland Revenue in accordance with regulations.

(2) An account is not a child trust fund unless it is an account of one of the descriptions prescribed by regulations.

(3) The provision which may be made by regulations under subsection (1) includes making approval of an account provider dependent on the person undertaking to provide accounts of such of the descriptions for which provision is made by regulations under subsection (2) as is prescribed by the regulations.

(4) The terms of a child trust fund must—

(a) secure that it is held in the name of a child,

(b) secure that the child is beneficially entitled to the investments under it,

(c) secure that all income and gains arising on investments under it constitute investments under it,

(d) prevent withdrawals from it except as permitted by regulations, and

(e) provide that instructions may be given to the account provider with respect to its management only by the person who has the authority to manage it.

(5) Regulations may impose other requirements which must be satisfied in relation to child trust funds.

(6) The person who has the authority to manage a child trust fund held by a child—

(a) if the child is 16 or over, is the child, and

(b) if the child is under 16, is the person who has that authority by virtue of subsection (7) (but subject to subsection (10)).

(7) If there is one person who is a responsible person in relation to the child, that person has that authority; and if there is more than one person who is such a person, which of them has that authority is to be determined in accordance with regulations.

(8) For the purposes of this Act a person is a responsible person in relation to a child under 16 if the person has parental responsibility in relation to the child and is not—

(a) a local authority or, in Northern Ireland, an authority within the meaning of the Children (Northern Ireland) Order 1995 (S.I. 1995/755 (N.I. 2)), or

(b) a person under 16.

(9) "Parental responsibility" means—

(a) parental responsibility within the meaning of the Children Act 1989 (c. 41) or the Children (Northern Ireland) Order 1995, or

(b) parental responsibilities within the meaning of the Children (Scotland) Act 1995 (c. 36).

(10) Regulations may provide that, in circumstances prescribed by the regulations, the person who has the authority to manage a child trust fund held by a child under 16 is to be the Official Solicitor (in England and Wales or Northern Ireland) or the Accountant of Court (in Scotland).

(11) A person who has the authority to manage a child trust fund by virtue of subsection (10) is entitled to give any instructions to the account provider with respect to its management which appear to the person who has that authority to be for the benefit of the child.

(12) Where a contract is entered into by or on behalf of a child who is 16 or over in connection with a child trust fund—

(a) held by the child, or

(b) held by another child in relation to whom the child has parental responsibility,

the contract has effect as if the child had been 18 or over when it was entered into.

DEFINITIONS

6.023   "account provider": subs.(1) and s.29.
"child": s.29.
"child trust fund": s.29.
"Inland Revenue": s.29.
"parental responsibility": subs.(9).
"responsible person": subs.(8).

GENERAL NOTE

6.024   This section sets out various administrative and procedural requirements which must be satisfied in order for a child trust fund account to come into existence. Only authorised financial institutions may offer child trust fund accounts (subs.(1)) and such accounts must meet a number of criteria (subss.(2)–(5)). This section also defines who has the authority to manage the child's account. This will usually be a person with parental responsibility or, in the case of a child aged at least 16, the child him or herself (subss.(6)–(12)).

Subs. (1)

6.025   Financial institutions, known as "account providers" in this Act, must be approved by the Inland Revenue before they can offer child trust fund accounts. The details of the approval process, which are set out in regulations (see Child Trust Funds Regulations 2004, regs 14–17 and 19–20), are modeled on those that apply to Individual Savings Accounts (ISAs). Institutions denied approval have a right of appeal (see s.22(1)).

Subs. (2)

6.026   Approval operates at two levels. First, the account provider itself must be approved by the Revenue under subs.(1). Secondly, by virtue of this subsection, only certain types of accounts may qualify as child trust fund accounts. In order to qualify an account must meet the criteria which are set out in regulations and are based on the arrangements governing ISAs (see Child Trust Funds Regulations 2004, reg.8).

Subs. (3)

6.027   This provision means that the regulations governing the approval of financial institutions may require account providers to provide particular types of account as a condition of such approval. The general rule is that, in order to be authorised as an account provider for the purposes of the child trust fund scheme, institutions must offer stakeholder accounts to the general public (see Child Trust Funds Regulations 2004, reg.14(2)(b)(i)). The characteristics of a stakeholder account are defined in the Schedule to the Regulations. The policy justification for this requirement is that it will enable beneficiaries to gain from the potentially higher returns from equities as a long-term investment. Further, the risk of a fall in the value of equities is reduced by the requirement to spread the investment over a number of companies (*ibid.*, para.2(2)(c)) and to transfer the investment to other assets (*e.g.* cash or gilts) as the maturity date nears.

Subs. (4)

This provision sets out the core requirements which must be met in order for an account to qualify for the purposes of the child trust fund scheme. For further details, see Child Trust Funds Regulations 2004, reg.8. **6.028**

The general rule is that no withdrawals are permitted from a child trust fund account before the child attains 18 (subs.(4)(d)). The Government's argument is that this restriction is essential if such accounts are to achieve their long-term goals. The only exceptions to this principle in the regulations as they currently stand, relate to withdrawals on closure in the event of the child's death and to deductions for management charges due (Child Trust Funds Regulations 2004, reg.18; there is a cap of 1.5 per cent on administration fees: *ibid.*, Sch., para.3(2)). However, following sustained pressure in Parliament, the Government conceded that a further exception should be made in the case of children suffering from a terminal illness. See now Child Trust Funds Regulations 2004, reg.18A. In contrast to the tight restrictions on withdrawals before the age of 18, there are no controls whatsoever on how young adults apply their child trust fund account holdings on reaching that age.

Subs. (5)

For further details, see Child Trust Funds Regulations 2004, reg.8. **6.029**

Subs. (6)

The effect of this provision, taken together with the definitions and qualifications in the following subsections, is that the child trust fund account is managed by the child, if he or she is 16 or over, and otherwise by the person with parental responsibility in respect of that child. This provision was inserted as a government amendment to the original Bill, which had given 16 and 17 year olds in Scotland the right to manage their accounts, but not their peers south of the border (reflecting the special rules in Scots law relating to the age of majority). Following debate, the Government accepted that it was difficult to sustain this distinction in the context of the child trust fund, and so brought forward this provision to ensure that all 16 and 17 year olds in the UK have the right to manage their child trust fund account. Such individuals are deemed to have full contractual authority to manage their accounts by virtue of subs.(12). They will not be able to withdraw funds until they reach the age of 18 (see subs.(4)(d)). **6.030**

Subss. (7)–(9)

In the case of children under the age of 16, the "responsible person" is designated as the individual with the authority to manage the child trust fund account (subs.(7)). The basic rule is that the "responsible person" in respect of a child under 16 is the person with parental responsibility for that child under the Children Act 1989 (or the relevant legislation for other parts of the UK: see subs.(9)). There are two exceptions to this rule (subs.(8)): first, a local authority (which may have parental responsibility by virtue of a care order) cannot be a "responsible person"; secondly, a young parent under the age of 16 cannot assume that role. It follows, for example, that the child trust fund accounts of both a 15-year-old mother and her baby will have to be managed by a third party. **6.031**

It is common, of course, for two individuals to share parental responsibility for a child, as in the case of a married couple (Children Act 1989, s.2(1)). In such cases the voucher will be sent to the holder of the child benefit award (see s.5 and Child Trust Funds Regulations 2004, reg.3(2)). Moreover, there can be only one person with authority to manage the child trust fund account, known as the "registered contact" (*ibid.*, reg.8(1)(d)). Typically this will be a "single responsible person", *i.e.* a person with parental responsibility (see further *ibid.*, reg.13).

Subs. (10)

6.032 This was another government amendment to the original Bill. It is designed to deal with the problem created by the lack of a "responsible person" for some children in local authority care. A local authority cannot be a responsible person (subs.(8)(a)). In the case of most children being looked after by a local authority, this will not matter, as the child's parent will retain parental responsibility and so be a responsible person. However, there will be a minority of cases in which no individual person holds parental responsibility (*e.g.* some orphans in care). The Government has announced that the Official Solicitor (in England, Wales and Northern Ireland) or the Accountant of Court (in Scotland) will undertake the function of managing the accounts of children in care for whom there is no one with parental responsibility. The relevant regulations have not yet been laid.

Inalienability

6.033 **4.**—(1) Any assignment of, or agreement to assign, investments under a child trust fund, and any charge on or agreement to charge any such investments, is void.

(2) On the bankruptcy of a child by whom a child trust fund is held, the entitlement to investments under it does not pass to any trustee or other person acting on behalf of the child's creditors.

(3) "Assignment" includes assignation; and "assign" is to be construed accordingly.

(4) "Charge on or agreement to charge" includes a right in security over or an agreement to create a right in security over.

(5) "Bankruptcy", in relation to a child, includes the sequestration of the child's estate.

DEFINITIONS

6.034 "assign": subs.(3).
"assignment": subs.(3).
"bankruptcy": subs.(5).
"charge on or agreement to charge": subs.(4).
"child trust fund": s.29.

GENERAL NOTE

6.035 The principle of the inalienability of social security benefits is enshrined in SSAA 1992, s.187 (see also Tax Credits Act 2002, s.45). This section provides, in similar fashion, for the inalienability of investments held under a child trust fund. The parallel provision in SSAA 1992, s.187 was applied (in the Scottish context) in *Mulvey v Secretary of State for Social Security* 1997 S.C. (H.L.) 105, where the House of Lords held that the bankrupt's right to income support could not be owed to the permanent trustee (the Scottish equivalent of a trustee in bankruptcy). However, the House of Lords held that deductions could lawfully be made from income support to pay a social fund debt incurred prior to sequestration.

Opening and transfers

Opening by responsible person or child

5.—(1) In the case of each child who is first an eligible child by virtue   6.036
of section 2(1)(a) the Inland Revenue must issue, in a manner prescribed
by regulations, a voucher in such form as is so prescribed.

(2) The voucher must be issued to the person who is entitled to child
benefit in respect of the child (or, in the case of a child who is such an
eligible child because of section 2(3), to a responsible person).

(3) An application may be made—
(a) if the child is 16 or over, by the child, or
(b) otherwise, by a responsible person,
to open for the child with an account provider a child trust fund of any
description provided by the account provider.

(4) The application is to be made—
(a) within such period beginning with the day on which the voucher
    is issued as is prescribed by regulations, and
(b) in accordance with regulations.

(5) When the application has been made the account provider
must—
(a) open, in accordance with regulations, a child trust fund of that
    description for the child, and
(b) inform the Inland Revenue in accordance with regulations.

DEFINITIONS

"account provider": s.29.   6.037
"child": s.29.
"child trust fund": s.29.
"eligible child": s.2(1) and s.29.
"Inland Revenue": s.29.
"responsible person": ss.3(8) and 29.

GENERAL NOTE

This section sets out the framework within which child trust fund accounts are   6.038
to be opened, typically by the "responsible person" (as defined by s.3(8)) and in
exceptional cases by the child (assuming he or she is 16 or over). The default
position is that an account must be opened by the Inland Revenue (see further
s.6).

Subs. (1)

This places a duty on the Inland Revenue to issue a voucher in respect of any   6.039
eligible child (within the normal definition in s.2(1)(a)). The issue of the voucher
will be triggered by the award of child benefit (which, as a result of the Tax
Credits Act 2002, is now administered by the Revenue rather than the Department for Work and Pensions). See further Child Trust Funds Regulations 2004,
reg.3.

Subs. (2)

The voucher must be issued to the individual who is entitled to child benefit.   6.040
The Government has announced that the voucher will be in the amount of the

initial Treasury contribution to be paid to all eligible children (£250). It should be noted that the process of issuing vouchers is envisaged to be an automatic process—there is no requirement in the legislation for the parent or other responsible person to make an independent claim for a child trust fund account voucher. In the special cross-border situation where the child lives in the UK but the parent works in another EU member state (*e.g.* the Republic of Ireland) there will be no child benefit recipient in this jurisdiction (see annotation to s.2(3)). Accordingly in such cases the voucher must be issued to a responsible person for that child.

Subs. (3)

6.041   This enables the "responsible person" to apply to open a child trust fund account with an approved account provider (see further subs.(4)). As originally drafted, the Bill would have required the responsible person physically to present the voucher to the account provider. As a result of a government amendment, the details of this procedure are now left to regulations. The Child Trust Funds Regulations 2004 still envisage a physical transfer of the voucher (reg.5(1), condition 1), but may in the future make provision for an entirely online application process. The "responsible person" is not, as such, under a statutory duty to make such an application. If he or she fails to do so, the default position is that ultimately the Inland Revenue will step in (see further s.6). In exceptional cases a child aged 16 or 17 may make an application to open a child trust fund account in his or her own name. The most likely circumstance in which this will arise is in the future where a child (born after August 31, 2002) moves to the UK at the age of 16 having never previously had an entitlement to a child trust fund account.

Subs. (4)

6.042   The application procedure is set out in regulations (see Child Trust Funds Regulations 2004, regs 5 and 13). The responsible person can select both the account provider and the type of account for the child trust fund. The voucher issued by the Inland Revenue will be valid for one year from the date of issue (*ibid.*, reg.3(2)), so applicants have a year in which to make the application. If they fail to do so, the Revenue's default duty under s.6 arises.

Subs. (5)

6.043   Once a valid application has been made, an account provider is required to open a child trust fund account for the child in question and to inform the Revenue that it has done so. The Child Trust Funds Regulations 2004 require institutions to make both fortnightly and annual returns of such information to the Revenue (regs 30 and 32).

Opening by Inland Revenue

6.044   **6.**—(1) In the case of each child to whom this section applies, the Inland Revenue must apply to open for the child with an account provider selected in accordance with regulations a child trust fund of a description so selected.
(2) The application is to be made in accordance with regulations.
(3) The account provider must—
(a) open, in accordance with regulations, a child trust fund of that description for the child, and
(b) inform the Inland Revenue in accordance with regulations.

(4) This section applies—

(a) to a child in respect of whom a voucher is issued under section 5(1) but in whose case subsection (5) is satisfied, and

(b) to a child who is first an eligible child by virtue of section 2(1)(b).

(5) This subsection is satisfied in the case of a child if—

(a) the period prescribed under section 5(4) expires without a child trust fund having been opened for the child, or

(b) the child is under 16 and it appears to the Inland Revenue that there is no-one who is a responsible person in relation to the child.

(6) No liability is to arise in respect of the selection of an account provider, or a description of child trust fund, in accordance with regulations under this section.

DEFINITIONS

"account provider": s.29. **6.045**
"child": s.29.
"child trust fund": s.29.
"eligible child": s.2(1) and s.29.
"Inland Revenue": s.29.
"responsible person": ss.3(8) and 29.

GENERAL NOTE

Normally a child's parent (or other adult who is the child benefit recipient), as **6.046** a "responsible person", will make an application for a child trust fund account in accordance with s.5. There will inevitably be cases where no such application is made. This section therefore performs a "mop-up" function, placing the onus on the Revenue to ensure that accounts are opened for such children who would otherwise miss out. The Revenue's obligation under subs.(1) to open a child trust fund account arises in two types of case. The first is where either, following an award of child benefit, a voucher has been issued to the "responsible person" but no application has been made to open a child trust fund account for that child within the required period (12 months) or there appears to be no "responsible person" for that child (subss.(4)(a) and (5)). The second is where the child is being looked after by a local authority and so there is no individual entitled to child benefit (subs.(4)(b)).

Subs. (1)

In cases to which this section applies (see subss.(4) and (5) and the General **6.047** Note), the Inland Revenue *must* take the initiative and apply to open a child trust fund account for the child in question. The details of the procedure to be adopted are set out in the Child Trust Funds Regulations 2004, reg.6. Account providers are not required to offer these default Revenue-allocated accounts under this arrangement. However, *if* institutions do agree to offer such accounts, they must then accept any Revenue application to open such an account (see subs.(3) and Child Trust Funds Regulations 2004, reg.6(2)). The Revenue will maintain a list of account providers willing to offer such accounts, and select account holders in rotation to ensure parity of treatment (*ibid.*, reg.6(3)). If account holders offer more than one type of stakeholder account, the account will likewise be chosen in rotation (*ibid.*, reg.6(4)). The legislation expressly exempts the Revenue from any liability in respect of such decisions (subs.(6)). In these cases the Revenue's role is furthermore limited to *opening* the account; it will have no role in *managing* the account in such a case. It will always be open to parents to transfer the account to another provider (s.7).

Subs. (2)

6.048   See further Child Trust Funds Regulations 2004, reg.6.

Subs. (3)

6.049   This is in parallel terms to the obligation imposed on account providers by s.5(5).

Subss. (4) and (5)

6.050   See the General Note to this section.

Subs. (6)

6.051   See the annotation to subs.(1).

Transfers

6.052   7.—Regulations may make provision about the circumstances in which—

   (a) a child trust fund which is an account of one of the descriptions prescribed by regulations may become an account of another of those descriptions, and
   (b) a child trust fund held with one account provider may be transferred to another.

DEFINITIONS

6.053   "account provider": s.29.
         "child trust fund": s.29.

GENERAL NOTE

6.054   This allows regulations to be made which permit the responsible person to change the type of child trust fund account (*e.g.* from a cash to a stakeholder account) and to move from one provider to another. The procedural rules for transfers are similar to those relating to transfers of ISA accounts, but require transfers to be free of charge (save for share dealing costs); see further Child Trust Funds Regulations 2004, reg.21.

Contributions and subscriptions

Initial contribution by Inland Revenue

6.055   8.—(1) The Inland Revenue must pay to an account provider such amount as is prescribed by regulations if the account provider has—

   (a) informed the Inland Revenue under section 5(5) or 6(3) that a child trust fund has been opened, and
   (b) made a claim to the Inland Revenue in accordance with regulations.

(2) On receipt of the payment the account provider must credit the child trust fund with the amount of the payment.

DEFINITIONS

"account provider": s.29. 6.056
"child trust fund": s.29.
"Inland Revenue": s.29.

GENERAL NOTE

This section explains how the initial Treasury contribution of £250 stated on 6.057
the voucher issued to the child benefit recipient is actually converted, albeit indirectly, into cash (the voucher itself cannot be exchanged for money: see Child Trust Funds Regulations 2004, reg.3(1)). Once a child trust fund account has been opened, either in the normal way (s.5) or through the process of Revenue allocation (s.6), the account provider is required to notify the Revenue. Account providers then make a claim to the Revenue (these are to be made on a fortnightly basis—see Child Trust Funds Regulations 2004, reg.30. The Revenue must in turn pay the account holder "such amount as is prescribed by regulations" by way of an initial contribution (subs.(1)), which the account holder must credit to the relevant account (subs.(2)). Children born into the poorest families may also qualify for a "supplementary contribution" under s.9. There is, moreover, the prospect of a further Treasury contribution for all eligible children when they reach the age of seven (see s.10).

The regulations describe the "initial" and "supplementary" contributions as "Government contributions" (Child Trust Funds Regulations 2004, reg.7). The basic rule for children born on or after the appointed day (anticipated to be April 6, 2005) is that the initial contribution will be £250, or £500 for those in local authority care (*ibid.*, reg.7(4)). Slightly higher amounts have been prescribed for those born on or after September 1, 2002 (the first date on which a child could qualify as an eligible child under s.2(1)) but before the appointed day. These higher amounts are designed to reflect the fact that these children have not had the benefit of interest on their investments to date. The rates are £277 for children born after August 31, 2002 but before the end of the 2002/03 tax year, £268 for those born in the 2003/04 tax year, and £256 for those born between April 6, 2004 and the appointed day (*ibid.*, reg.7(2)). For children in care, the equivalent figures are £553, £536 and £512.

Supplementary contribution by Inland Revenue

9.—(1) If this section applies to a child the Inland Revenue must 6.058
inform the account provider with whom a child trust fund is held by the child that this section applies to the child.

(2) If the account provider makes a claim to the Inland Revenue in accordance with regulations, the Inland Revenue must pay to the account provider such amount as is prescribed by regulations.

(3) On receipt of the payment the account provider must credit the child trust fund with the amount of the payment.

(4) This section applies to a child if—

(a) a child trust fund is held by the child,

(b) the child was first an eligible child by virtue of section 2(1)(a), and

(c) the condition in subsection (5) is satisfied in relation to the child.

(5) That condition is that it has been determined in accordance with the provision made by and by virtue of sections 18 to 21 of the Tax Credits Act 2002 (c. 21)—

 (a) that a person was, or persons were, entitled to child tax credit in respect of the child for the child benefit commencement date, and

 (b) that either the relevant income of the person or persons for the tax year in which that date fell does not exceed the income threshold or the person, or either of the persons, was entitled to a relevant social security benefit for that date,

and that determination has not been overturned.

 (6) In subsection (5)(b)—

"the income threshold" has the meaning given by section 7(1)(a) of the Tax Credits Act 2002,

"the relevant income", in relation to a person or persons and a tax year, has the meaning given by section 7(3) of that Act in relation to a claim by the person or persons for a tax credit for the tax year,

"relevant social security benefit" means any social security benefit prescribed for the purposes of section 7(2) of that Act, and

"tax year" means a period beginning with 6th April in one year and ending with 5th April in the next.

 (7) If the child benefit commencement date is earlier than 6th April 2005, this section applies in relation to the child even if the condition in subsection (5) is not satisfied in relation to the child provided that the condition in subsection (8) is so satisfied.

 (8) That condition is that—

 (a) income support, or income-based jobseeker's allowance, was paid for the child benefit commencement date to a person whose applicable amount included an amount in respect of the child, or

 (b) working families' tax credit, or disabled person's tax credit, was paid for that date to a person whose appropriate maximum working families' tax credit, or appropriate maximum disabled person's tax credit, included a credit in respect of the child.

 (9) If the child benefit commencement date is earlier than 6th April 2003, subsection (5) has effect as if—

 (a) the reference in paragraph (a) to the child benefit commencement date were to any date in the tax year beginning with 6th April 2003,

 (b) the reference in paragraph (b) to the tax year in which the child benefit commencement date fell were to the tax year beginning with 6th April 2003, and

 (c) the reference in paragraph (b) to being entitled to a relevant social security benefit for the child benefit commencement date were to being so entitled for any date in that tax year for which the person was, or the persons were, entitled to child tax credit in respect of the child.

 (10) "Child benefit commencement date", in relation to a child, means—

(a) the first day for which child benefit was paid in respect of the child (otherwise than because of a directly applicable Community provision or an international agreement), or

(b) in the case of a child to whom section 2(3) applies or section 2(5) has applied, such day as is prescribed by regulations.

DEFINITIONS

"account provider": s.29.   **6.059**
"child": s.29.
"child benefit commencement date": subs.(10)
"child trust fund": s.29.
"eligible child": ss.2(1) and 29.
"income threshold": subs.(6)
"Inland Revenue": s.29.
"relevant income": subs.(6).
"relevant social security benefit": subs.(6).
"tax year": subs.(6).

GENERAL NOTE

In addition to the initial contribution under s.8, children born into families on   **6.060**
low incomes will be eligible for a "supplementary contribution" to boost their
child trust fund account investment at the outset. This section sets out the rules
governing the award of the supplementary contribution. Subsections (1)–(3)
specify the procedure to be followed. Subsection (4) spells out the criteria for
receipt of the supplementary condition. Children being looked after in local
authority care will *not* qualify for this extra amount (see subs.(4)(b)), but they
will in any event qualify for an equivalent amount under s.8 by virtue of their
status. The means-test is explained in subs.(5), with various terms defined by
subss.(6) and (10). Subsections (7)–(9) deal with various awkward transitional
cases.

Subs. (1)

There is no need for parents on low incomes to claim the supplementary   **6.061**
contribution; indeed, there is no facility for them to do so. Instead, the legislation
requires the Revenue to inform the account provider if a child is eligible for the
supplementary contribution. The Revenue will have this information as it is
responsible for administering child tax credit under the Tax Credits Act 2002,
which acts as the trigger for entitlement to the extra Treasury contribution (see
subss.(4)(c) and (5)).

Subss. (2) and (3)

Having been informed that the child in question is eligible for the supplemen-   **6.062**
tary contribution, the account provider may then make a claim for that extra
amount (subs.(2); see Child Trust Funds Regulations 2004, reg.30(6)(b)). This
section then requires the Revenue to pay the account provider the appropriate
amount by way of a supplementary contribution. In the case of children born
after the appointed day, this is a further £250 (*ibid.*, reg.7(7)), making £500 in
total. The amounts are increased for those born on or after September 1, 2002
but before the appointed day (*ibid.*, reg.7(6)). The account provider must then
credit the extra amount to the child's account (subs.(3)). Subsequent regulations
amending the amount of the supplementary contribution under subs.(2) will be
subject to the affirmative procedure (see s.28(5) and (6)(b)).

Subs. (4)

6.063   This sets out the criteria for the award of the supplementary contribution. The child must have a child trust fund account, have qualified on the basis of an award of child benefit, and meet the child tax credit means-test set out in subs.(5). The second of these requirements has the effect of excluding children who initially qualified for an account because they were in care (see s.2(1)(b)), as they will, in any event, receive the higher initial contribution (see annotation to s.8).

Subs. (5)

6.064   This provision sets out the means-test which determines whether a child is eligible to receive the supplementary as well as the initial Treasury contribution. Two separate conditions must each be satisfied. In the case of both these requirements, the determination of entitlement must have been a final one in accordance with ss.18–21 of the Tax Credits Act 2002 and must not have been overturned.

The first condition is that someone was entitled to child tax credit for the child in question at the date when child benefit was first paid (known as the "child benefit commencement date": see subs.(10)). The second requirement is that *either* their income does not exceed the child tax credit income threshold for the tax year in issue *or* that person is entitled to a "relevant social security benefit". The statutory authority for the child tax credit income threshold is Tax Credits Act 2002, s.7(1)(a) (see subs.(6)). The annual amount of this threshold is prescribed in regulations, and for the 2004/05 tax year is £13,480 (Tax Credits (Income Threshold and Determination of Rates) Regulations 2002 (SI 2002/2008), reg.3(3), as amended by Tax Credits Up-rating Regulations 2004 (SI 2004/941), reg.4. The expression "relevant social security benefit" is defined by reference to Tax Credits Act 2002, s.7(2) (see subs.(6)), and so includes only income support, income-based jobseeker's allowance and pension credit (Tax Credits (Income Threshold and Determination of Rates) Regulations 2002 (SI 2002/2008), reg.4, as amended by Tax Credits (Miscellaneous Amendments No.2) Regulations 2003 (SI 2003/2815), reg.18).

These tests require some modification so that they operate in the desired fashion for eligible children born in the transitional period between August 31, 2002 and April 6, 2005. There are two sets of special transitional rules contained in subss.(7)–(9).

Subss. (7) and (8)

6.065   The first transitional problem relates to the phasing in of child tax credit for families in receipt of income support or income-based jobseeker's allowance. Child tax credit, payable under the Tax Credits Act 2002, came into force on April 6, 2003, at least so far as new claimants and those claiming working tax credit (the successor to working families' tax credit) were concerned. Originally it was anticipated that families already in receipt of income support or income-based jobseeker's allowance would move over to child tax credit a year later on April 6, 2004. In fact, only new claimants of these benefits have received child tax credit from that date, with the process of "migration" for existing benefits cases now starting in October 2004, with a view to such transfers being completed by the end of the 2004/05 tax year. (In the meantime all such families will receive the cash equivalent of child tax credit through their existing benefits.) Some families will therefore not meet the strict terms of subs.(5) because, although they were getting income support or income-based jobseeker's allowance at the material time, they were not yet, as a result of this phasing process, receiving child tax credit. Subsections (7) and (8) deal with this by disapplying the means-test based on entitlement to child tax credit in subs.(5). Instead, they provide alternatively that it is sufficient that a child born before April 6, 2005 was in a household which received one of the means-tested benefits or tax credits listed in subs.(8) in respect of that child.

Subs.(9)

This deals with a separate transitional problem relating to children born   **6.066** between September 1, 2002 and April 5, 2003. The first condition in the means-test (subs.(5)(a)) is that a person was entitled to child tax credit in respect of the child when child benefit was first paid. However, child tax credit did not come into operation until April 6, 2003, and so subs.(5)(a) cannot be satisfied if child benefit was payable *before* that date. There are also knock-on problems in terms of complying with subs.(5)(b) in such cases. This sub-section resolves these problems by deeming the child benefit commencement date (and hence the entitlement to child tax credit) as having been in the 2003/04 tax year.

Further contributions by Inland Revenue

10.—(1) Regulations may make provision for the making by the   **6.067** Inland Revenue in the circumstances mentioned in subsection (2) of payments to account providers of child trust funds held by—

(a) eligible children, or

(b) any description of eligible children,

of amounts prescribed by, or determined in accordance with, regulations.

(2) The circumstances referred to in subsection (1) are—

(a) the children attaining such age as may be prescribed by the regulations, or

(b) such other circumstances as may be so prescribed.

(3) The regulations must include provision—

(a) for making account providers aware that such amounts are payable,

(b) about the claiming of such payments by account providers, and

(c) about the crediting of child trust funds by account providers with the amount of such payments.

(4) For the purposes of this section, a child is to be treated as being an eligible child if entitlement to child benefit in respect of the child is excluded by—

(a) paragraph 1(a) of Schedule 9 to the Social Security Contributions and Benefits Act 1992 (c. 4) (children in custody), or

(b) paragraph 1(1)(a) to (d) of Schedule 9 to the Social Security Contributions and Benefits (Northern Ireland) Act 1992 (c. 7) (corresponding provision for Northern Ireland).

DEFINITIONS

"account provider": s.29.   **6.068**
"child": s.29.
"child trust fund": s.29.
"eligible child": ss.2(1) and 29.
"Inland Revenue": s.29.

GENERAL NOTE

6.069   This is an enabling measure, allowing regulations to be made which may provide for a further Treasury contribution to be credited to the child's account at a later date. Any regulations made under subss.(1) or (2) will be subject to the affirmative procedure (see s.28(5) and (6)(a)).

Subs.(1) and (2)

6.070   The powers enshrined in the section are expressed in broad terms—thus regulations may provide that further contributions are made to all eligible children, or just to a sub-set of them (subs.(1)). The trigger for a further contribution may be when the child attains a particular age, as set out in regulations, or some other factor (subs.(2)). At present these details are not contained in the Child Trust Funds Regulations 2004 but will be announced at a later date. The Government's stated intention is that there will be one further contribution which will be payable to all eligible children at the age of 7 (rather than 3 payments at ages 5, 11 and 16, as suggested in *Savings and Assets for All*). It follows that the first such further payments will not become due until 2009. The rationale for the further contribution is that it will enable additional endowment funds to be targeted on those most in need. It will also help to keep the accounts "live" by reminding both children and their parents of the existence and growth of such funds. Note also that account providers will have to issue annual account statements (Child Trust Funds Regulations 2004, reg.10).

Subs.(3)

6.071   As well as specifying matters such as the amount of the further contribution and the age at which it becomes payable, the regulations which are to be made nearer the time must also address the various procedural matters referred to in this sub-section.

Subs.(4)

6.072   A child will remain an eligible child for these purposes even if there is no child benefit entitlement at the date when the further contribution becomes payable because he or she is detained in custody. Clearly children aged seven are not going to be in custody. However, a future government might decide to make further Treasury contributions to children at the age of 12 or over, when this could become an issue. The Government's view, as a matter of principle, was that it was not justifiable "to disadvantage such children on the grounds that they were in custody on a particular birthday". Such an exclusion from the further contribution might also result in anomalies depending on the length of time the child was in custody and when their birthday fell.

Recouping Inland Revenue contributions

6.073   **11.**—(1) Regulations may make provision requiring that, in circumstances prescribed by the regulations, a person of a description so prescribed is to account to the Inland Revenue for amounts credited to a child trust fund in respect of Inland Revenue contributions (together with any income and gains arising in consequence of the crediting of those amounts).

(2) "Inland Revenue contributions" means payments made by the Inland Revenue which were required to be made under or by virtue of sections 8 to 10 or which the Inland Revenue considered were required to be so made.

"child trust fund": s.29.   **6.074**
"Inland Revenue": s.29
"Inland Revenue contributions": subs.(2).

GENERAL NOTE

In some cases payments will be made under ss.8, 9 or 10 which should not   **6.075**
have been so credited; in social security parlance these would be described as
overpayments. This section allows the Treasury to make regulations governing
the recovery of such payments, *e.g.* where more than one account has been
opened or where the child in question was never an eligible child within s.2. The
intention is that recovery will be possible from the account provider, the child,
the registered contact (typically the parent) and anyone into whose hands the
funds have come.

Subscription limits

12.—(1) No subscription may be made to a child trust fund otherwise   **6.076**
than by way of a monetary payment.
(2) Regulations may prescribe the maximum amount that may be
subscribed to a child trust fund in each year (otherwise than by way of
credits made under or by virtue of this Act or income or gains arising on
investments under the child trust fund).
(3) "Year", in relation to a child trust fund held by a child,
means—
(a) the period beginning with the day on which the child trust fund is
opened and ending immediately before the child's next birthday,
and
(b) each succeeding period of twelve months.

DEFINITIONS

"child trust fund": s.29.   **6.077**
"year": subs.(3).

GENERAL NOTE

Whereas ss.8–11 are all concerned with Treasury contributions to a   **6.078**
child trust fund account, this section deals with contributions to such
accounts by others, for example a child's family and friends. Such non-
governmental contributions may only be in money terms (subs.(1)), and
so shares cannot be transferred to a child trust fund account. There will
also be an annual aggregate limit on such non-governmental contributions, prescribed by regulations made under subs.(2). This cap is to be
£1,200 a year at the outset (Child Trust Fund Regulations 2004,
reg.9(2); there is no facility to carry over any unused allowance to a
following year (*ibid.*, reg.9(3)). A year, in this context, means each year
from the date of the individual child's birthday (subs.(3)), not each
calendar year or each tax year. The minimum contribution on any one
transaction is £10, unless the account provider permits a smaller amount
(Child Trust Fund Regulations 2004, Sch., para.2(4)).
There is no provision in the Act for automatic indexation of the annual
aggregate limit; the Government intends to treat the cap in the same way

as the ISA limit, so any up-rating will be announced in the Budget or simply through regulations.

Tax

Relief from income tax and capital gains tax

6.079   **13.**—(1) Regulations may make provision for and in connection with giving relief from—

    (a) income tax, and

    (b) capital gains tax,

in respect of investments under child trust funds.

    (2) The regulations may, in particular, include—

    (a) provision for securing that losses are disregarded for the purposes of capital gains tax where they accrue on the disposal of investments under child trust funds, and

    (b) provision dealing with anything which, apart from the regulations, would have been regarded for those purposes as an indistinguishable part of the same asset.

    (3) The regulations may specify how tax relief is to be claimed by persons entitled to it or by account providers on their behalf.

    (4) The regulations may include provision requiring that, in circumstances prescribed by the regulations, the person prescribed by the regulations is to account to the Inland Revenue for—

    (a) tax from which relief has been given under the regulations, and

    (b) income or gains arising in consequence of the giving of relief under the regulations,

or for an amount determined in accordance with the regulations in respect of such tax.

    (5) Provision made by virtue of this section may disapply, or modify the effect of, any enactment relating to income tax or capital gains tax.

DEFINITIONS

6.080   "account provider": s.29.

    "child trust fund": s.29.

    "Inland Revenue": s.29.

GENERAL NOTE

6.081   This section is concerned with the tax treatment of investments held in child trust funds. It allows regulations to make provision for relief in respect of income tax and capital gains tax (subs.(1)), and how such tax relief should be claimed (subs.(3)). Such regulations may effectively ring-fence child trust fund investments from any other investments held by the child concerned; this will mean that any capital losses arising on the disposal of child trust fund investments will not be deductible from any capital gains outside the child trust fund (sub-s.(2)(a)). Regulations will also provide for the separate identification of disposals of shares within and outside a child trust fund (subs.(2)(b)). Regulations may provide for the repayment of tax relief that is given in circumstances where it should not have been (subs.(4)). Subsection (5) is a general power that enables regulations to modify income tax and capital gains tax legislation for child trust fund accounts (see generally Child Trust Funds Regulations 2004, Pt 3 and especially regs 24 and 36).

Insurance companies and friendly societies

14.—(1) Subsections (1) and (5) to (9) of section 333B of the Income and Corporation Taxes Act 1988 (c. 1) (involvement of insurance companies and friendly societies with ISAs) have effect in relation to insurance companies and friendly societies as if child trust fund business were section 333 business (within the meaning of section 333B).

6.082

(2) "Child trust fund business", in relation to an insurance company or friendly society, means business of the insurance company or friendly society that is attributable to child trust funds.

DEFINITIONS

"child trust fund": s.29.
"child trust fund business": subs.(2).

6.083

GENERAL NOTE

This section enables the income and gains made on investments held in child trust fund accounts provided in the form of life insurance policies to be free from corporation tax. This will not prevent the profits made by insurance companies and friendly societies on such business from being taxed. See further Child Trust Funds (Insurance Companies) Regulations 2004 (SI 2004/2680).

6.084

Information etc.

Information from account providers etc.

15.—(1) Regulations may require, or authorise officers of the Inland Revenue to require, any relevant person—

6.085

    (a) to make documents available for inspection on behalf of the Inland Revenue, or

    (b) to provide to the Inland Revenue any information,

relating to, or to investments which are or have been held under, a child trust fund.

(2) The following are relevant persons—

    (a) anyone who is or has been the account provider in relation to the child trust fund,

    (b) the person by whom the child trust fund is or was held,

    (c) the person (if any) to whom a voucher was issued under section 5(1) in respect of the child by whom the child trust fund is or was held,

    (d) the person who applied to open the child trust fund (unless it was opened by the Inland Revenue),

    (e) anyone who has given instructions with respect to the management of the child trust fund, and

    (f) anyone entitled to child benefit in respect of the child.

(3) The regulations may include provision requiring documents to be made available or information to be provided—

    (a) in the manner and form, and

    (b) by the time and at the place,

prescribed by or under the regulations.

DEFINITIONS

6.086   "account provider": s.29.

    "child": s.29.

    "child trust fund": s.29.

    "Inland Revenue": s.29.

    "relevant person": subs.(2).

GENERAL NOTE

6.087   This section enables the Treasury to make regulations requiring account providers and other "relevant persons" (as defined by subs.(2)) to supply information or make documents available for inspection (and subject to requirements stipulated under subs.(3)). The Child Trust Funds Regulations 2004 require account holders to supply the Inland Revenue with both fortnightly and annual returns (regs 30 and 32). The fortnightly returns will both act as a claim for payment of the government contributions and enable the Inland Revenue to identify children for whom accounts have not been opened.

Information about children in care of authority

6.088   **16.**—(1) Regulations may require, or authorise officers of the Inland Revenue to require, an authority—

    (a) to make documents available for inspection on behalf of the Inland Revenue, or

    (b) to provide to the Inland Revenue any information,

which the Inland Revenue may require for the discharge of any function relating to child trust funds and which is information to which subsection (2) applies.

(2) This subsection applies to information relating to a child who falls or has fallen within—

    (a) paragraph 1(c) of Schedule 9 to the Social Security Contributions and Benefits Act 1992 (c. 4), or

    (b) paragraph 1(1)(f) of Schedule 9 to the Social Security Contributions and Benefits (Northern Ireland) Act 1992 (c. 7),

by reason of being, or having been, in the care of the authority in circumstances prescribed by regulations under that provision.

(3) The regulations may include provision requiring documents to be made available or information to be provided—

    (a) in the manner and form, and

    (b) by the time and at the place,

prescribed by or under the regulations.

DEFINITIONS

6.089   "child": s.29.

    "child trust fund": s.29.

    "Inland Revenue": s.29.

GENERAL NOTE

The normal rule is that a child is an "eligible child" if child benefit is payable   **6.090**
in respect of him or her (s.2(1)(a)). Receipt of child benefit thus acts as a
passport to entitlement to the child trust fund. The Inland Revenue is also
responsible for administering child benefit and accordingly has access to all the
relevant information in such cases. However, child benefit cannot be claimed for
children in local authority care, for whom special provision has to be made to
make them "eligible children" (ss.2(1)(b) and 2(2)). As these children will not
appear in the records of current child benefit payments, the Inland Revenue will
have to obtain the necessary information direct from local authorities. This
section accordingly enables the Treasury to make regulations requiring local
authorities to provide the information necessary to arrange for a child trust fund
account to be opened or for further contributions to be made. Local authorities
are required to make monthly returns (Child Trust Funds Regulations 2004,
reg.33).

Use of information

17.—(1) Information held for the purposes of any function relating to   **6.091**
child trust funds—

(a) by the Inland Revenue, or

(b) by a person providing services to the Inland Revenue, in connection with the provision of those services,

may be used, or supplied to any person providing services to the Inland
Revenue, for the purposes of, or for any purposes connected with, the
exercise of any such function.

(2) Information held for the purposes of any function relating to child
trust funds—

(a) by the Inland Revenue, or

(b) by a person providing services to the Inland Revenue, in connection with the provision of those services,

may be used, or supplied to any person providing services to the Inland
Revenue, for the purposes of, or for any purposes connected with, the
exercise of any other function of the Inland Revenue.

(3) Information held for the purposes of any function other than those
relating to child trust funds—

(a) by the Inland Revenue, or

(b) by a person providing services to the Inland Revenue, in connection with the provision of those services,

may be used, or supplied to any person providing services to the Inland
Revenue, for the purposes of, or for any purposes connected with, the
exercise of any function of the Inland Revenue relating to child trust
funds.

(4) Information held by the Secretary of State or the Department for
Social Development in Northern Ireland, or any person providing services to the Secretary of State or that Department, may be supplied
to—

(a) the Inland Revenue, or

(b) a person providing services to the Inland Revenue, in connection
with the provision of those services,

for use for the purposes of, or for any purposes connected with, the exercise of any function of the Inland Revenue relating to child trust funds.

DEFINITIONS

6.092   "child trust fund": s.29.
   "Inland Revenue": s.29.

GENERAL NOTE

6.093   This section allows information relating to child trust funds to be shared both within government and between government departments and their contractors (typically their IT providers). Subsection (1) allows information relating to child trust funds to be used for purposes relating to such funds. Subsection (2), on the other hand, enables such information to be used for other (non-child trust fund) purposes by the Inland Revenue (*e.g.* official evaluations of savings policies). Subsection (3) permits information held by the Inland Revenue in connection with other purposes to be used for child trust fund purposes. This allows the Inland Revenue to access information about a person's child tax credit status in order to determine eligibility for the supplementary contribution (see s.9(5)). Finally, subs.(4) allows other government departments to provide information to the Inland Revenue (or its contractors) for reasons connected with child trust funds. In particular, this will enable the Inland Revenue to obtain information from the Department for Work and Pensions about a person's benefit status. This will be relevant to determining entitlement to the supplementary condition in respect of children born on or after September 1, 2002 but before child tax credit became payable to the household in question.

Disclosure of information

6.094   **18.**—*[omitted]*

GENERAL NOTE

6.095   This section amends the Finance Act 1989, s.182 and so brings the child trust fund scheme within the existing statutory provisions which deal with the confidentiality of personal information held by the Inland Revenue, and the exceptions to that principle.

Payments after death

Payments after death of child

6.096   **19.**—(1) Where a relevant child dies, the Inland Revenue may make a payment to the personal representatives of the child if any one or more of the conditions specified in subsection (3) is satisfied.

(2) "Relevant child" means a child who is or has been an eligible child (or would have been had this Act come into force on the date referred to in section 2(1)).

(3) The conditions are—

(a) that either no payment had been made under section 8 by the Inland Revenue or, if one had, the amount of the payment had not been credited to the child trust fund held by the child,

(b) that section 9 applied to the child (or would have had this Act come into force on the date referred to in section 2(1)) but either no payment had been made under that section by the Inland Revenue or, if one had, the amount of the payment had not been credited to the child trust fund held by the child, and

(c) that the Inland Revenue was required by regulations under section 10 to make a payment in respect of the child but either the payment had not been made or, if it had, the amount of the payment had not been credited to the child trust fund held by the child.

(4) The amount of the payment is to be equal to the amount of the payment or payments which had not been made or credited.

DEFINTIONS

"child": s.29.   6.097
"child trust fund": s.29.
"eligible child": s.29.
"Inland Revenue": s.29.
"relevant child": subs.(2).

GENERAL NOTE

This section gives the Inland Revenue the power to make child trust fund   6.098
payments in respect of children born after August 31, 2002 but who have died
before such payments have been credited to an account. Any one (or more) of
three requirements must be satisfied. These are: (1) that no initial contribution
has been paid under s.8 (or it has not been credited to the account); (2) that the
child was entitled to a supplementary contribution under s.9 but this had not
been paid or credited to the account, or (3) that a further contribution was due
under s.10 but again had not been paid or credited (subs.(3)). The amount
payable is a sum equal to the amount of the outstanding payment(s) (subs.(4))
and is payable to the child's personal representatives (subs.(1)). Note that there
is no absolute right to such a payment; the Inland Revenue *may* make such a
payment. The element of discretion has been inserted to allow the Revenue to
refuse to make payments in cases where the child has been unlawfully killed by
the parent. The personal representatives have a right of appeal in the event of a
dispute about payment (s.22(5)).

Penalties

Penalties

20.—(1) A penalty of £300 may be imposed on any person who   6.099
fraudulently—

(a) applies to open a child trust fund,

(b) makes a withdrawal from a child trust fund otherwise than as permitted by regulations under section 3(4)(d), or

(c) secures the opening of a child trust fund by the Inland Revenue.

(2) A penalty not exceeding £3,000 may be imposed on—

    (a) an account provider who fraudulently or negligently makes an incorrect statement or declaration in connection with a claim under section 8 or 9 or regulations under section 10 or 13, and

    (b) any person who fraudulently or negligently provides incorrect information in response to a requirement imposed by or under regulations under section 15.

(3) Penalties may be imposed on—

    (a) an account provider who fails to make a claim under section 8 or 9 or regulations under section 10 by the time required by regulations under the section concerned, and

    (b) any person who fails to make a document available, or provide information, in accordance with regulations under section 15.

(4) The penalties which may be imposed under subsection (3) are—

    (a) a penalty not exceeding £300, and

    (b) if the failure continues after a penalty under paragraph (a) is imposed, a further penalty or penalties not exceeding £60 for each day on which the failure continues after the day on which the penalty under that paragraph was imposed (but excluding any day for which a penalty under this paragraph has already been imposed).

(5) No penalty under subsection (3) may be imposed on a person in respect of a failure after the failure has been remedied.

(6) For the purposes of subsection (3) a person is to be taken not to have failed to make a claim, make available a document or provide information which must be made, made available or provided by a particular time—

    (a) if the person made it, made it available or provided it within such further time (if any) as the Inland Revenue may have allowed,

    (b) if the person had a reasonable excuse for not making it, making it available or providing it by that time, or

    (c) if, after having had such an excuse, the person made it, made it available or provided it without unreasonable delay.

(7) A penalty may be imposed on an account provider in respect of—

    (a) the provision by the account provider, as a child trust fund, of an account which does not meet the condition in subsection (8),

    (b) a failure by the account provider to comply with section 8(2) or 9(3) or with a requirement imposed on the account provider by regulations under section 5(5), 6(3), 7 or 10(3), or

    (c) a breach of section 12(1), or regulations under section 12(2), in relation to a child trust fund held with the account provider.

(8) An account meets the condition referred to in subsection (7)(a) if—

    (a) it is of one of the descriptions prescribed by regulations under section 3(2),

    (b) section 3(4) is complied with in relation to it, and

    (c) the requirements imposed by regulations under section 3(5) are satisfied in relation to it.

(9) The penalty which may be imposed under subsection (7) on the account provider is a penalty not exceeding—

220

(a) £300, or

(b) £1 in respect of each account affected by the matter, or any of the matters, in respect of which the penalty is imposed,

whichever is greater.

DEFINITIONS

"account provider": s.29.   **6.100**
"child trust fund": s.29.
"Inland Revenue": s.29.

GENERAL NOTE

This section makes provision for penalties to be imposed in connection with   **6.101**
child trust fund applications and related matters. Individuals who fraudulently apply to open or secure the opening of an account, or make an account withdrawal, are subject to a penalty of £300 (subs.(1)). Account providers and others who make fraudulent or negligent statements or declarations are liable to a penalty not exceeding £3,000 (subs.(2)). Account providers and others are also liable to a £300 penalty (and £60 per day thereafter for continued non-compliance) for failing to make claims in respect of reimbursements or for failing to provide information or produce documentation (subss.(3) and (4); see further subss.(5) and (6)). Subsections (7)–(9) make further provision for penalties to be imposed on account providers in respect of non-compliance with various statutory requirements.

Any penalties under this section are imposed by the Inland Revenue (s.21(1)), subject to the various procedural requirements in s.21. There is a right of appeal against any decision to impose a penalty, or its amount (s.22(6)).

Decisions, appeals, mitigation and recovery

21.—(1) It is for the Inland Revenue to impose a penalty under section   **6.102**
20.

(2) If the Inland Revenue decide to impose such a penalty the decision must (subject to the permitted maximum) set it at such amount as, in their opinion, is appropriate.

(3) A decision to impose such a penalty may not be made after the end of the period of six years beginning with the date on which the penalty was incurred or began to be incurred.

(4) The Inland Revenue must give notice of such a decision to the person on whom the penalty is imposed.

(5) The notice must state the date on which it is given and give details of the right to appeal against the decision under section 22.

(6) After the notice has been given, the decision must not be altered except on appeal.

(7) But the Inland Revenue may, in their discretion, mitigate any penalty under section 20.

(8) A penalty under section 20 becomes payable at the end of the period of 30 days beginning with the date on which notice of the decision is given.

(9) On an appeal under section 22 against a decision under this section, the General Commissioners or Special Commissioners may—

(a) if it appears that no penalty has been incurred, set the decision aside,

(b) if the amount set appears to be appropriate, confirm the decision,

(c) if the amount set appears to be excessive, reduce it to such other amount (including nil) as they consider appropriate, or

(d) if the amount set appears to be insufficient, increase it to such amount not exceeding the permitted maximum as they consider appropriate.

(10) An appeal from a decision of the Commissioners under subsection (9) lies, at the instance of the person on whom the penalty was imposed, to—

(a) the High Court, or

(b) in Scotland, the Court of Session as the Court of Exchequer in Scotland,

and on such an appeal the court has a similar jurisdiction to that conferred on the Commissioners by that subsection.

(11) A penalty is to be treated for the purposes of Part 6 of the Taxes Management Act 1970 (c. 9) (collection and recovery) as if it were tax charged in an assessment and due and payable.

DEFINTIONS

6.103   "General Commissioners": s.29.
"Inland Revenue": s.29.
"Special Commissioners": s.29.

GENERAL NOTE

6.104   This section deals with procedural matters relating to penalties under s.20 and appeals from such decisions. The Inland Revenue has a broad discretion so far as the amount of any such penalty is concerned (subs.(2); see also the Revenue's power under subs.(7) to mitigate any penalty). There is a six-year limitation period (subs.(3)). Although subs.(9) refers to penalty appeals being determined by the General or Special Commissioners, with a right of appeal to the High Court or the Court of Session (subs.(10)), in practice these appeals will, for the time being at least, be heard by (social security) appeal tribunals and Social Security Commissioners (see s.24, temporarily modifying s.23). The same type of "temporary modification" currently applies to appeals under the Tax Credits Act 2002.

Appeals

Rights of appeal

6.105   **22.**—(1) A person may appeal against—

(a) a decision by the Inland Revenue not to approve the person as an account provider, or

(b) a decision by the Inland Revenue to withdraw the person's approval as an account provider.

(2) A person who is a relevant person in relation to a child may appeal against a decision by the Inland Revenue—

(a) not to issue a voucher under section 5 in relation to the child,

(b) not to open a child trust fund for the child under section 6,

(c) not to make a payment under section 8 or 9 in respect of the child, or

(d) not to make a payment under regulations under section 10 in respect of the child.

(3) "Relevant person", in relation to a child, means—

(a) the person (if any) entitled to child benefit in respect of the child,

(b) anyone who applied to open a child trust fund for the child, and

(c) anyone who has, at any time, given instructions with respect to the management of the child trust fund held by the child.

(4) A person who is required by the Inland Revenue to account for an amount under regulations under section 11 or 13 may appeal against the decision to impose the requirement.

(5) The personal representatives of a child who has died may appeal against a decision by the Inland Revenue not to make a payment to them under section 19.

(6) A person on whom a penalty under section 20 is imposed may appeal against the decision to impose the penalty or its amount.

DEFINTIONS

"account provider": s.29.   6.106
"child": s.29.
"child trust fund": s.29.
"Inland Revenue": s.29.
"relevant person": subs.(3).

GENERAL NOTE

This section sets out the categories of person who can appeal against a   6.107
decision relating to the child trust fund. In so far as there are any appeals, most appeals will presumably be brought by individuals and will concern the entitlement to child trust fund payments in individual cases (subs.(2)). However, companies who are refused permission by the Inland Revenue to act as account providers also have a right of appeal (subs.(1)). Subsections (4)–(6) ensure that various other persons have a right of appeal as appropriate. In particular, subs.(6) provides that any person on whom a penalty is imposed has a right of appeal against both the decision to levy the penalty and also the amount. The tribunal's powers on hearing appeals under this section are set out in s.21(9). In the short to medium term, child trust fund appeals will be heard by appeal tribunals and, on further appeal, by the Social Security Commissioners (s.24, temporarily modifying s.23: see General Note to s.21).

Exercise of rights of appeal

23.—(1) Notice of an appeal under section 22 against a decision must   6.108
be given to the Inland Revenue in the manner prescribed by regulations within the period of thirty days after the date on which notice of the decision was given.

(2) Notice of such an appeal must specify the grounds of appeal.

(3) An appeal under section 22 is to the General Commissioners but the appellant may elect (in accordance with section 46(1) of the Taxes

Management Act 1970 (c. 9)) to bring the appeal before the Special Commissioners instead.

(4) Subsections (2) to (7) of section 31D of the Taxes Management Act 1970 (which relate to an election to bring proceedings before the Special Commissioners) have effect in relation to an election under subsection (3) (as in relation to an election under subsection (1) of that section).

(5) On the hearing of an appeal under section 22 the Commissioners may allow the appellant to put forward grounds not specified in the notice, and take them into consideration if satisfied that the omission was not wilful or unreasonable.

(6) Part 5 of the Taxes Management Act 1970 (appeals to Commissioners) applies in relation to appeals under section 22 (as in relation to appeals under the Taxes Acts, within the meaning of that Act), but subject to such modifications as are prescribed by regulations.

(7) Any regulations under section 56B of the Taxes Management Act 1970 (c. 9) which are in force immediately before the commencement of subsection (6) apply, subject to any necessary modifications, for the purposes of appeals under section 22 (until amended or revoked).

DEFINTIONS

6.109   "General Commissioners": s.29.
          "Inland Revenue": s.29.
          "Special Commissioners": s.29.

GENERAL NOTE

6.110   This section provides that appeals are to be dealt with through the normal tax appeals machinery and subject to those procedures. Thus appeals must be lodged within 30 days (subs.(1)), stating grounds (subs.(2)); see further ss.23 and s.24 and General Note to s.21.

Temporary modifications

6.111   **24.**—(1) Until such day as may be appointed by order—
          (a) section 21 has effect subject to subsection (2),
          (b) section 23 has effect subject to subsection (3), and
          (c) section 182(2ZB) of the Finance Act 1989 (c. 26) has effect subject to subsection (4).
          (2) The references to—
          (a) the General Commissioners or Special Commissioners in subsection (9) of section 21, and
          (b) the Commissioners in subsection (10) of that section,
          are to the appeal tribunal; and an appeal from a decision of the appeal tribunal under subsection (9) of that section lies to a Social Security Commissioner rather than the High Court or the Court of Session (so that the reference to the court in subsection (10) of that section is to the Social Security Commissioner).
          (3) An appeal under section 22 is to an appeal tribunal (rather than to the General Commissioners or Special Commissioners) so that—
          (a) subsections (3), (4), (6) and (7) of section 23 do not apply, and

(b) the reference to the Commissioners in subsection (5) of that section is to the appeal tribunal.

(4) The reference to the General Commissioners or the Special Commissioners in section 182(2ZB) of the Finance Act 1989 is to an appeal tribunal.

(5) Regulations may apply any provision contained in—

(a) the Social Security Act 1998 (c. 14) (social security appeals: Great Britain),

(b) the Social Security (Northern Ireland) Order 1998 (S.I. 1998/1506 (N.I. 10)) (social security appeals: Northern Ireland), or

(c) section 54 of the Taxes Management Act 1970 (settling of appeals by agreement),

in relation to appeals which by virtue of this section are to an appeal tribunal, or lie to a Social Security Commissioner, but subject to such modifications as are prescribed by the regulations.

(6) "Appeal tribunal" means an appeal tribunal constituted—

(a) in Great Britain, under Chapter 1 of Part 1 of the Social Security Act 1998, or

(b) in Northern Ireland, under Chapter 1 of Part 2 of the Social Security (Northern Ireland) Order 1998.

(7) "Social Security Commissioner" means—

(a) in Great Britain, the Chief Social Security Commissioner or any other Social Security Commissioner appointed under the Social Security Act 1998 or a tribunal of three or more Commissioners constituted under section 16(7) of that Act, and

(b) in Northern Ireland, the Chief Social Security Commissioner or any other Social Security Commissioner appointed under the Social Security Administration (Northern Ireland) Act 1992 (c. 8) or a tribunal of two or more Commissioners constituted under Article 16(7) of the Social Security (Northern Ireland) Order 1998 (S.I. 1998/1506 (N.I. 10)).

DEFINTIONS

"appeal tribunal": subs.(6)   6.112
"General Commissioners": s.29.
"Social Security Commissioner": subs.(7).
"Special Commissioners": s.29.

GENERAL NOTE

Although s.23 provides for appeals to be routed through the tax appeals 6.113
machinery, this section provides that, for the time being at least, any appeals
relating to child trust fund matters will be heard by appeal tribunals constituted
under the SSA 1998, with a right of further appeal to the Social Security
Commissioner. This applies to appeals against penalty decisions under s.21
(subs.(2)) and other child trust fund decisions under s.22 (subs.(3)). The same
type of "temporary modification" has applied to tax credit appeals since their
introduction in April 2003 and shows no immediate sign of coming to an end
(see Tax Credits Act 2002, s.63).

Northern Ireland

6.114   25.—In Schedule 2 to the Northern Ireland Act 1998 (c. 47) (excepted matters), after paragraph 9 insert—

"**9A** Child Trust Funds."

GENERAL NOTE

6.115   The child trust fund scheme is added to the Schedule of excepted matters in the Northern Ireland Act 1998, so ensuring that the Fund is governed by legislation common to the whole of the UK (see also s.30).

6.116   **26.**—*[omitted]*
6.117   **27.**—*[omitted]*
6.118   **28.**—*[omitted]*
6.119   **29.**—*[omitted]*
6.120   **30.**—*[omitted]*
6.121   **31.**—*[omitted]*

The Fines (Deductions from Income Support)(Amendment) Regulations 2004 (SI 2004/2889)

6.122   These regulations, which entered into force on December 18, 2004, amend the Fines (Deductions from Income Support) Regulations 1992 (SI 1992/2182). Regulation 2 amends those regulations to allow the Court to require an offender to provide details as to his address, name, national insurance number and the name of the benefits to which the offender is in receipt, in order to process an application for benefit deductions. Section 24(2A) of the Criminal Justice Act 1991, inserted by s.96 of the Courts Act 2003, makes it an offence where an offender fails to provide this information. Regulation 2 also amends those Regulations to increase the maximum amount that may be deducted from benefits to £5 where this complies with the provisions relating to maximum deductions set out in those Regulations.

The Social Security, Child Support and Tax Credits (Decisions and Appeals) Amendment Regulations 2004 (SI 2004/3368)

6.123   These Regulations, which came into force on December 21, 2004, remove the power of tribunals to strike out misconceived appeals. They do this by revoking the definition of "misconceived appeal" in reg.1(3) of the Social Security and Child Support (Decisions and Appeals) Regulations 1999, together with regs 46(4), 47(2)(b) and 48 and they make consequential amendments to regs 36 and 47(2).

　　In addition, they substitute reg.39(1) to (4), providing for a form on which the parties must notify the clerk to the tribunal whether they want an oral hearing and requiring a tribunal to hold an oral hearing if one is requested, unless the appeal is struck out. Further provision is made, by amending regs 46 and 47, to allow a clerk to strike out an appeal for failure to notify him whether or not an oral hearing is desired and for reinstating an appeal if representations are subsequently made.

Finally, in para.5 of Sch.2, sub-paras (a) and (bb) are substituted and sub-paras (b), (c), (d) and (e) are revoked. This has the effect that there remains no appeal against a decision as to which of two partners should make a claim for income support, jobseeker's allowance or state pension credit but that, otherwise, appeals may be brought against any decisions under regs 4 to 6 of the Social Security (Claims and Payments) Regulations 1987. In particular, it is now possible to appeal against a decision disallowing a claim on the ground that it is defective.

Amendments, similar to those made to regs 39, 46 and 47 of the 1999 Regulations in relation to notifying the clerk whether an oral hearing is desired, are made to regs 12, 16 and 17 of the Tax Credits (Appeals) (No.2) Regulations 2002.

The Child Trust Funds Act 2004 (Commencement No.2) Order 2004 (SI 2004/3369)

This Order brings the main (and remaining) provisions of the Child Trust Funds Act 2004 into force on April 6, 2005 (which is the start date for child trust funds to operate). An earlier Commencement Order (the Child Trust Funds Act 2004 (Commencement No.1) Order 2004 (SI 2004/2422 (C.103)) brought transitional provisions into force on January 1, 2005. **6.124**

The Child Benefit and Guardian's Allowance (Decisions and Appeals) (Amendment) Regulations 2004 (SI 2004/3377)

These Regulations come into force on December 21, 2004. They insert the words "under regulation 5" after the words "following an application for revision" in reg.28(2)(c) of the Child Benefit and Guardian's Allowance (Decisions and Appeals) Regulations 2003, thereby deliberately introducing the anomaly revealed in *R(IS) 15/04* that, although there are a number of circumstances in which a claimant may ask for a revision of a decision some substantial time after it was made and revision will be permissible, it may in some cases be impossible to challenge a refusal to revise if the claimant applied for revision under any provision other than reg.5 (see the annotation to reg.31(2) of the Social Security and Child Support (Decisions and Appeals) Regulations 1999 on pp.610–611 of the main work). The argument in support of the change is that claimants have up to 13 months in which to challenge the original decision. Consistency with that argument might suggest that "official error", for **6.125** instance, might become a ground of supersession with limited back-dating. The anomaly at least has the advantage for claimants of unlimited backdating where the Secretary of State accepts that there are grounds for revision.

More positively, these Regulations revoke para.6(a) and (c) of Sch.2 to the 2003 Regulations so as to permit appeals against decisions that claims are defective.

The Social Security (Incapacity Benefit Work-focused Interviews) Amendment Regulations 2005 (SI 2005/3)

6.126 These Regulations amended, with effect from February 7, 2005, the Social Security (Incapacity Benefit Work-focused Interviews) Regulations 2003 (SI 2003/2439) (set out and annotated in paras 2.572–2.588 of Vol.III) to extend the numbers of persons that can be required to attend work-focused interviews as a condition of their continued entitlement to full benefit. These Regulations and the principal Regulations apply to certain persons who claim incapacity benefit, income support on the grounds of incapacity, income support whilst they are appealing against a decision which embodies a determination that they are not incapable of work or severe disablement allowance ("specified benefits").

The Schedule to these Regulations sets out the amendments to those 2003 Regulations. Paragraph 1 of the Schedule amends them so that they apply to an increased number of persons who reside in certain areas of the country ("new persons"). It amends the specified benefits so that they apply in respect of new persons. Paragraph 2 amends those provisions in the 2003 Regulations specifying who is required to take part in a work-focused interview. In particular, the amendments provide that a person who is entitled to more than one specified benefit but has not taken part in a work-focused interview is required to take part in interviews for only one benefit. It also provides for the Secretary of State to determine the date on which a new person's first interview is to take place. Paragraph 3 makes amendments so that new persons shall be required to take part in two rather than five further work-focused interviews. Paragraphs 3(e) and 4 make amendments that exempt a new person from the requirement to take part in any work-focused interviews if they are deemed to be exempt from undergoing a personal capability assessment (which assesses the nature of their incapacity) because they have a severe condition.

The Social Security (Claims and Payments and Payments on account, Overpayments and Recovery) Amendment Regulations 2005 (SI 2005/34)

6.127 These Regulations amend from May 2, 2005 the Social Security (Claims and Payments) Regulations 1987 and the Social Security (Payments on account, Overpayments and Recovery) Regulations 1988. Regulation 2(2) enables a person to make a claim for graduated retirement benefit and retirement pension by telephone unless the Secretary of State directs that the claim must be made in writing. Regulation 2(3) enables a person who has made such a claim to amend it by telephone. Regulation 2(4) provides for the date of a claim for graduated retirement benefit or retirement pension made by telephone. Regulation 3 enables the Secretary of State to give notice of the effect reg.11 of the Social Security (Payments on account, Overpayments and Recovery) Regulations 1988 would have, in the event of an overpayment, to a person who makes a claim for retirement pension and graduated retirement benefit by telephone, either orally or in writing.

The Social Security Pensions (Home Responsibilities) (Amendment) Regulations 2005 (SI 2005/48)

These Regulations, with effect from February 9, 2005, amended the **6.128** Social Security Pensions (Home Responsibilities) Regulations 1994 (SI 1994/704). Regulation 2(2) amends reg.1 of those 1994 Regulations by the insertion of a new definition of "the General Regulations". Regulation 2(3) amends reg.2 of those 1994 Regulations by the insertion of a new paragraph (para.(4B)) which applies to tax years from 2004–2005 onwards where child benefit entitlement is transferred to a person in respect of a child in the first three months of a tax year and child benefit would have been payable to that person for the part of that year falling before that transfer but for the provisions of reg.15(2)(b) of the Child Benefit (General) Regulations 2003 (SI 2003/493). Where it applies, new para.(4B) provides that such a person shall be treated as if he were entitled to child benefit and as if child benefit had been payable to him for that part of that year, in order to be treated for the purpose of the 1994 Regulations as precluded from regular employment in that year due to responsibilities at home.

The Tax Credits (Approval of Child Care Providers) Scheme 2005 (SI 2005/93)

This Scheme—which applies only to England—provides for the approval **6.129** of child care providers for the purposes of s.12(5) of the Tax Credits Act 2002. The Secretary of State is the "appropriate national authority" in relation to care provided in England. Qualifying child care (as defined) provided by a person approved in accordance with this Scheme constitutes care provided by a person of a prescribed description for the purposes of s.12(4) of the 2002 Act. Regulations made under s.12(1) of that Act prescribe the circumstances in which entitlement to working tax credit in respect of care provided by a person approved in accordance with this Scheme may arise. (See the Working Tax Credit (Entitlement and Maximum Rate) Regulations 2002 (SI 2002/2005)). Article 3 means that the approval body named in this Scheme is specified by the Secretary of State under s.12(7) of the 2002 Act. Under Art.7, applications for approval are determined by the approval body in accordance with criteria set out in this Scheme. The Scheme further provides: (a) in Art.8 for the approval body to operate a system for the determination of applications for approval; (b) in Art.9 for the approval body to provide information to the Commissioners of Inland Revenue in order to enable them to discharge their functions relating to working tax credit; (c) in Art.10 for the period of validity of an approval; (d) in Art.11 for the right to appeal against the refusal or withdrawal of approval), and (e) in Art.12 for the approval body to charge fees.

Article 13 revokes The Tax Credits (Approval of Home Child Care Providers) Scheme 2003 with savings for current approvals granted under that instrument.

NEW BENEFIT RATES FROM APRIL 2005

(Benefits covered in Volume I)

	April 2004 £ pw	April 2005 £ pw	6.130
Disability benefits			
Attendance allowance			
higher rate	58.80	60.60	
lower rate	39.35	40.55	
Disability living allowance			
care component			
highest rate	58.80	60.60	
middle rate	39.35	40.55	
lowest rate	15.55	16.05	
mobility component			
higher rate	41.05	42.30	
lower rate	15.55	16.05	
Carer's allowance	44.35	45.70	
Severe disablement allowance			
basic rate	44.80	46.20	
age related addition—higher rate	15.55	16.05	
age related addition—middle rate	10.00	10.30	
age related addition—lower rate	5.00	5.15	
Maternity benefits			
Maternity allowance			
standard rate	102.80	106.00	
Bereavement benefits and retirement pensions			
Widowed parent's allowance or widowed mother's allowance	79.60	82.05	
Bereavement allowance or widow's pension			
standard rate	79.60	82.05	
Retirement pension			
Category A	79.60	82.05	
Category B (higher)	79.60	82.05	

	April 2004 £ pw	April 2005 £ pw
Category B (lower)	47.65	49.15
Category C (higher)	47.65	49.15
Category C (lower)	28.50	29.40
Category D	47.65	49.15

Incapacity benefit

Long-term incapacity benefit

	April 2004	April 2005
basic rate	74.15	76.45
increase for age—higher rate	15.55	16.05
increase for age—lower rate	7.80	8.05
invalidity allowance—higher rate	15.55	16.05
invalidity allowance—middle rate	10.00	10.30
invalidity allowance—lower rate	5.00	5.15

Short-term incapacity benefit

	April 2004	April 2005
under pension age—higher rate	66.15	68.20
under pension age—lower rate	55.90	57.65
over pension age—higher rate	74.15	76.45
over pension age—lower rate	71.15	73.35

Dependency increases

Adult

	April 2004	April 2005
carer's allowance	26.50	27.30
severe disablement allowance	26.65	27.50
maternity allowance	34.60	35.65
retirement pension	47.65	43.95
long-term incapacity benefit	44.35	45.70
short-term incapacity benefit under pension age	34.60	35.65
short-term incapacity benefit over pension age	42.65	43.95
Child	11.35*	11.35*

Industrial injuries benefits

Disablement benefit

aged 18 and over or under 18 with dependants—

		April 2004	April 2005
	100%	120.10	123.80
	90%	108.09	111.42
	80%	96.08	99.04
	70%	84.07	86.66
	60%	72.06	74.28
	50%	60.05	61.90
	40%	48.04	49.52
	30%	36.03	37.14
	20%	24.02	24.76

		April 2004 £ pw	April 2005 £ pw
aged under 18 with no dependants—	100%	73.55	75.85
	90%	66.20	68.27
	80%	58.84	60.68
	70%	51.49	53.10
	60%	44.13	45.51
	50%	36.78	37.93
	40%	29.42	30.34
	30%	22.07	22.76
	20%	14.71	15.17

unemployability supplement
basic rate	74.15	76.45
increase for adult dependant	44.35	45.70
increase for child dependant	11.35★	11.35★
increase for early incapacity—higher rate	15.55	16.05
increase for early incapacity—middle rate	10.00	10.30
increase for early incapacity—lower rate	5.00	5.15

constant attendance allowance
exceptional rate	96.20	99.20
intermediate rate	72.15	74.40
normal maximum rate	48.10	49.60
part-time rate	24.05	24.80

exceptionally severe disablement allowance	48.10	49.60

Reduced earnings allowance
maximum rate	48.04	49.52

Death benefit
widow's pension
higher rate	79.60	82.05
lower rate	23.88	24.62
widower's pension	79.60	82.05

Benefits in respect of children

Child benefit
only, elder or eldest child (couple)	16.50	17.00
only, elder or eldest child (lone parent)	17.55	17.55
each subsequent child	11.05	11.40

Child's special allowance	11.35★	11.35★
Guardian's allowance	11.85★	12.20

★ These sums payable in respect of children are reduced if payable in respect of the only, elder or eldest child for whom child benefit is being paid (see reg.8 of the Social Security (Overlapping Benefits) Regulations 1979).

NEW BENEFIT RATES FROM APRIL 2005

(Benefits covered in Volume II)

6.131		April 2004 £ pw	April 2005 £ pw
Contribution-based jobseeker's allowance			
personal rates—*aged under 18*		33.50	33.85
aged 18 to 24		44.05	44.50
aged 25 or over		55.65	56.20
Income support and income-based jobseeker's allowance			
personal allowances			
single person— *aged under 18 (usual rate)*		33.50	33.85
aged under 18 (higher rate)		44.05	44.50
aged 18 to 24		44.05	44.50
aged 25 or over		55.65	56.20
lone parent— *aged under 18 (usual rate)*		33.50	33.85
aged under 18 (higher rate)		44.05	44.50
aged 18 or over		55.65	56.20
couple— *both aged under 18*		33.50	33.85
both aged under 18, one disabled		44.05	44.50
both aged under 18, with a child		66.50	67.15
one aged under 18, one aged 18 to 24		44.05	44.50
one aged under 18, one aged 25 or over		55.65	56.20
both aged 18 or over		87.30	88.15
child— *birth to September following 16th birthday*		42.27	43.88
September following 16th birthday to under 19		42.27	43.88
premiums			
family—*ordinary*		15.95	16.10
lone parent		15.95	16.10
bereavement		23.95	25.85
pensioner—*single person (JSA only)*		49.80	53.25
couple		73.65	78.90

	April 2004 £ pw	April 2005 £ pw
enhanced pensioner	73.65	78.90
higher pensioner—*single person (JSA only)*	49.80	53.25
couple	73.65	78.90
disability—*single person*	23.70	23.95
couple	33.85	34.20
enhanced disability—*single person*	11.60	11.70
couple	17.08	17.71
child	16.75	16.90
severe disability—*single person*	44.15	45.50
couple (one qualifies)	44.15	45.50
couple (both qualify)	88.30	91.00
disabled child	42.49	43.89
carer	25.55	25.80

Pension credit

Standard minimum guarantee		
single person	105.45	109.45
couple	160.95	167.05

Additional amount for severe disability		
single person	44.15	45.50
couple (one qualifies)	44.15	45.50
couple (both qualify)	85.90	91.00

Additional amount for carers	25.55	25.80

Savings credit threshold		
single person	79.60	82.05
couple	127.25	131.20

Maximum savings credit		
single person	15.51	16.44
couple	20.22	21.51

NEW TAX CREDIT AND EMPLOYER-PAID BENEFIT RATES 2005–06

(Benefits covered in Volume IV)

	2004–05 £pa	2005–06 £pa
Working tax credit		
Basic element	1,570	1,620
Couple and lone parent element	1,545	1,595
30 hour element	640	660
Disabled worker element	2,100	2,165
Severe disability element	890	920
50+ Return to work payment (under 30 hours)	1,075	1,110
50+ Return to work payment (30 or more hours)	1,610	1,660
Child tax credit		
Family element	545	545
Family element, baby addition	545	545
Child element	1,625	1,690
Disabled child element	2,215	2,285
Severely disabled child element	890	920
Tax credit income thresholds		
Income disregard	2,500	2,500
First threshold	5,060	5,220
First threshold for those entitled to child tax credit only	13,480	13,910
First withdrawal rate—37%		
Second threshold	50,000	50,000
Second withdrawal rate—6.67%		

Employer paid benefits	2004–05 £pw	2005–06 £pw
Standard rates		
Statutory sick pay	66.15	68.20
Statutory maternity pay	102.80	106.00
Statutory paternity pay	102.80	106.00
Statutory adoption pay	102.80	106.00
Income threshold	79.00	82.00